Suzy Gershman

. . . .

BORN TO SHOP

PARIS

. . . .

The Ultimate Guide for
Travelers Who Love to Shop

7th Edition

MACMILLAN • USA

For Mike and Judy and Richard and Ian:
We'll always have Paris.

MACMILLAN TRAVEL
A Simon & Schuster Macmillan Company
1633 Broadway
New York, NY 10019

Find us online at http://www.mgr.com/travel or on America Online at Keyword: **Frommer's.**

ISBN 0-02-860713-9
ISSN 1066-2790

Editors: Erica Spaberg and Ron Boudreau
Production Editor: Lori Cates
Design by George J. McKeon
Digital Cartography by Ortelius Design

CONTENTS

MAP LIST

WHAT THE SYMBOL MEANS

. . . .

🛍 SUZY'S FAVORITES
Stores, restaurants, and accommodations you
should not miss.

TO START WITH

This is a new edition of my Paris guide, not to be confused in any way with *Born to Shop France*, published for the first time last year. The beauty of this edition is that not only is it devoted almost solely to Paris, but that it's on a different publication cycle than *Born to Shop France*. Because the two guides are revised in alternate years, it gives me an opportunity to revisit my French sources for each guide, always ensuring that you get *le dernier cri*, or the last word, on shopping in France.

While it is true that I also reported the shopping chapters for *Frommer's Paris '97* and *Frommer's France '97*, I promise you won't find the same listings here. *Born to Shop Paris* is based on separate reporting trips and covers the shopping scene in more depth. This is the book that has the little shoemaker no one has heard of; this is the book that explains the background of a house or a designer or a creation, so you understand how to make the best buy. This is the book that even has a listing in it that was given to me years ago by Princess Grace (actually, it's that little shoemaker I just mentioned). This is the book for the reader who wants to know *everything*.

If you've been reading *Born to Shop* for years, you'll find that the organization of the guides has changed to fit more closely with the format of a Frommer's guide. In particular, there are more hotels and recommendations of places to eat while shopping. (Not that finding a place to eat in Paris is a chore!)

Brussels is still a part of the guide; the last chapter is devoted to it as a suggested weekend trip from Paris.

The work for this revision was done under difficult circumstances, including the famed *Greve*, or strike—which just about everyone has forgotten, except those of us who lived through it. My friends in Paris, and throughout France, got me through it as well as all the researching tasks. For that, *merci beaucoup aux toutes.*

I also owe a big round of thanks to the staff at the Hôtel de Crillon: General Manager Philippe LeBoeuf and especially the chief concierge, Christian Ferron, who helps me so much. At the Hilton, Laurent Voivenel is part of a new team set on making its area of Paris sing. And Patrick Arton has been great help with the new Westin-Demeure hotels in Paris.

Thanks also to my French family, Gérard and Marie-Jo Bizien; and to Walter and Patricia Wells and Alexander Lobrano, my best American friends in Paris. Pascale-Agnès Renaud, who has been the Paris correspondent for *Born to Shop* since we started the series in 1984, continues to drive me places, teach me things, check my translations for errors, and teach me French.

My new friend, retail king Philippe Houzé, helps me test restaurants, talks retail with me, and even sent me to Inno during the strike with his car and driver. (I promise you, I am the only shopper who's ever arrived at a French dime store with a car and driver!)

Oh yes, let's see, the cover was shot by my wonderful Ian Cook. He wasn't around for the snow, the rain, or the yucky weather part of the research, but he did manage to celebrate Paris. For the cover, he caught me at my favorite Paris kiosk at the Tuileries, where I buy all my magazines. And yes, he bought me that scarf at one of the tourist traps on the rue de Rivoli, because it was my birthday. After all, it was April in Paris.

Chapter One

. . . .

PARIS *VITE*

PARIS IS BEST

. . . .

Putting the best of Paris into one list is an impossible task; it seems that every store I walk into is the best store in Paris. Just to be in Paris, pressing your nose to the windows of the stores, is a best-of-show experience.

With that in mind, the selections presented here are really for people in an incredible hurry, who have no time to stroll and shop leisurely. If you have more time, you owe yourself the luxury of checking out the finds described elsewhere in this book. But if you must hit and run, flash dancing your credit cards as you beat a hasty exit, I hope these choices will be rewarding.

THE BEST SPECIALTY PERFUME SHOP

. . . .

SALONS SHISEIDO
*Jardins du Palais-Royal, 142 Galerie de Valois,
1er (Métro: Palais-Royal).*

This tiny shop with high ceilings and royal purple decor is the showcase of makeup genius Serge Lutens, who used to create makeup for Christian

THE BEST GIFTS FOR $10 OR LESS

- Hot chocolate mix from Angelina, the most famous tea shop in Paris. $5. Angelina, *226 rue de Rivoli, 1er (Métro: Tuileries)*.
- A box of Mère Poulard cookies. These indescribably good cookies are imported from Mont St-Michel, but are sold in any Parisian grocery store. $1.50.
- A bag of coffee. I buy Carte Noire at any grocery store, but there are other brands; Grand Mère has a cute package. $3.
- A jar of mustard. I buy Maille brand at any grocery store. $2.
- A mixed selection of 15-ml sample-size products from Sephora's house line of bath and beauty products. Sephora, *70 ave. des Champs-Elysées, 8e (Métro: F-D-Roosevelt)*.
- Potpourri or sachets from Rosemarie Schulz. Rosemarie Schulz, *30 rue Boissy d'Anglas, 8e (Métro: Madeleine)*.
- Anything from L'Occitane, the Provençal soap maker, including 13 F soaps. Available in all major department stores or in Occitane shops, like the one right off rue de Rivoli. Occitane, *1 rue 29 Juillet, 1er (Métro: Tuileries)*.
- A copy of *Elle* magazine (in French!) or for a teen, *Top Model* (also in French). 13 F apiece.

THE BEST STATUS GIFTS FOR UNDER $25

- Hermès soap, sold in the Saddle Shop. Hermès, *24 rue du Faubourg St-Honoré, 8e (Métro: Concorde)*.
- Christian Dior and Nina Ricci, both on the avenue Montaigne, have tables laden with affordable gift items that begin around $25. Christian Dior, *28–32 ave. Montaigne*; Nina Ricci, *39 ave. Montaigne, 8e (Métro: F-D-Roosevelt)*.

- Lanvin chocolates, sold in any grocery store!
- Dalí lipstick. It comes in a tube that was inspired by a Dalí painting; very French, very whimsical, very special—sold in most perfume shops.
- Champagne. There are plenty of good champagnes. In addition to the ones you've heard of, there are several good ones that aren't as well known in the United States. Check out any branch of the wine chain Nicolas or a grocery store. I usually buy it in grocery stores. Also note that France sells more sizes of champagne, by more makers, than you can imagine, so you can bring home several mini-bottles and still meet your liquor allowance.
- Anything from Boutique Crillon. Yes, there are choices in this price range.

THE BEST SHOPPER'S BREAK

. . . .

SALON DU THÉ BERNARDAUD
11 rue Royale, 8e (Métro: Concorde).

Pick your own dishes! That's right, if you have tea at this tea salon, they bring you a tray of gorgeous Bernardaud china, and you pick which style of china you would like everything served on. How's that for a great gimmick?

THE BEST GIFTS FOR KIDS

. . . .

- Manitoba Jeunesse publishes adorable French books for children—*Ma Maison, Ma Ferme,* and *Mon École*—that lie flat like any book but can be built into a house! 43 F each.
- Monoprix, a chain of "dime stores," is packed with items, ranging from a selection of books (Disney translations are nice) to Legos.
- Inno, a cross between a "dime store" and a grocery store, is another good bet for children's gifts. My favorite item is the miniature French shop-

ping cart for 60 F. Inno, *31–35 rue du Départ,
14e (Métro: Montparnasse/Bienvenue).*

THE BEST CHILDREN'S CLOTHING STORE
. . . .

CLAUDE VEIL
8 rue du Jour, 1er (Métro: Les Halles).

Expensive but sublime Euro-Asian waif heaven. It's
about $100 for a cotton dress, but oh my dear, this
is Paris.

THE BEST NEW WEARABLE DESIGNER FIND
. . . .

MARYSE CEPIÈRE AT
UN DIMANCHE DANS NOS CAMPAGNES
*59 rue Bonaparte, 6e (Métro: St-Germain-
des-Prés).*

I have no idea who Maryse Cepière is, or even how
to pronounce her name. I discovered her knits at
the perfect Left Bank store, Un Dimanche dans nos
Campagnes. The clothes are chic, while still being
oversized, comfortable, and yet proportioned to
height, so they don't overwhelm. They aren't cheap;
expect to pay $250 for a knit dress.

THE BEST NEW FANTASY DESIGNER FIND
. . . .

LEE YOUNG HEE
*109 rue du Bac, 7e (Métro: Bac or
Sèvres-Babylone).*

The Korean name should be a giveaway. These
French clothes are inspired by Korean traditional
garments and have an edge of whimsy to them that
doesn't make them too practical for my lifestyle.
If, however, I had to go to a ball or was getting
married, this is where I'd go. She also has a shop in
Seoul.

Chapter Two

. . . .

PARIS DETAILS

WELCOME TO PARIS

. . . .

I was looking through a French magazine the other day and stopped in mid-glance to gawk at an ad for a watch. It was a rather ordinary, if expensive-looking, chronographic watch, classical in its features; but its image filled an entire page of the magazine in order to show all the details.

What was extraordinary about the watch was the bright blue crocodile watch strap. I was mesmerized by the color, the grace, the moxie, the statement. As I gazed, dazzled by the watch, I realized that all of Paris was summed up in one visual statement.

Nowhere else in the world, except Paris, would they think to combine the classic and the outrageous in this way. To me, nothing better defines all that Paris is and all that Paris offers to the shopper. Even if you don't buy a watch like I saw advertised, in Paris you'll see such creative ideas there, you can't help but be inspired.

A while back I saw a feature on Karl Lagerfeld and Chanel accessories in another French magazine. Even though I could not read the text, the pictures not only made me drool to own a Chanel but also showed his genius unfolding in his work. Karl Lagerfeld introduced a fragrance called Sun Moon

Stars. A year later, bored with the knockoffs of his work, and to keep it new and fresh, he began to work suns, moons, and stars—along with interlocking CC's—into his accessory collection.

Even though Lagerfeld isn't actually French and creativity is a universal language, I look at the flowering of his originality as another example of what we go to France to see and to buy. We go to France for genius, for light.

So welcome to Paris, the City of Light, where Karl Lagerfeld and I both hope to give you the sun, the moon, and the stars. *Bienvenue* and welcome to Paris, the *new* Paris where tons of new stores have opened and entire new neighborhoods are being created and re-created as we speak.

After your first evening in town, you'll know why Paris has been dubbed the City of Light. In addition to all the glorious lights emanating from the buildings (even the I.M. Pei pyramid at the Musée du Louvre is lit from within), you're going to feel light—light-headed from the shopping opportunities you spied throughout the day, light-headed from just thinking about all the style yet to come. But you'll also feel light on your feet, especially if you've just waltzed through a fixed-price lunch at a Michelin two-starred restaurant. Ah, the incredible lightness of being in Paris.

Paris is one of the world's premier shopping cities. Even people who hate to go shopping enjoy it in Paris. What's not to like? The couture-influenced ready-to-wear? The street markets? The most extravagant kids' shops in the world? Jewelers nestled together in shimmering elegance? Fruits and vegetables piled in bins as if they, too, were jewels? Perfumes and cosmetics at a fraction of their U.S. cost? Antiques and collectibles that are literally the envy of kings? It's not hard to go wild with glee at your good luck and good sense for having chosen such a place to visit.

Paris

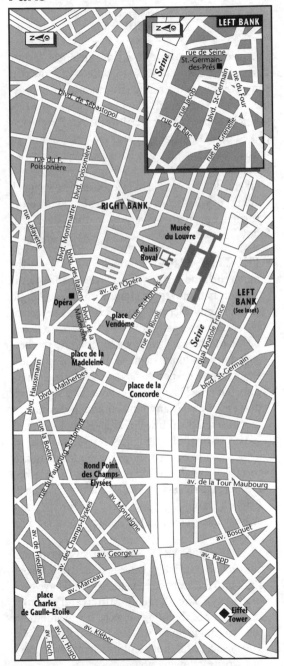

PARIS NEWS
. . . .

I've seen Paris move from a slow melancholy daze during the recession to a snappy fox trot, now that some portions of international economy are improving. While France still has plenty of its own economic problems (don't we all?), the retail scene has picked up dramatically. Few grand cities of Europe have changed as much as Paris has in the last two years.

If you don't get to Paris once a year, here's a quick checklist of what's new and what's hot; there's more information on these venues in the pages that follow.

- **THE LEFT BANK** I thought "there goes the neighborhood" when I discovered that **Louis Vuitton** had moved in along with **Etro, Giorgio Armani,** and **Hermès.** *Au contraire.* The neighborhood has actually gotten better. While a teensy bit of the funky flavor is easing away, the new stores offer a funky deluxe feel that's just divine. I've never been a personal fan of Vuitton merchandise, but now I beg you, don't miss this store. You don't have to buy anything (although there's now much to tempt you, see p. 191)—simply stare.

   Along with the big designers, several small names have recently opened shops on the Left Bank. A formerly abandoned old market has been turned into an American-style mall. Cult brands such as **Estéban** (famous among Parisians for its home scents) have chosen the district for their first stores.

- **VIADUC DES ARTS** This massive strip mall cum rehab job, built under defunct train tracks, right into the arches of a viaduct, could have been one of the late François Mitterrand's *grands travaux,* or big building projects. It's an ambitious rehab meant to house artisans and workshops. Not 100% successful (not all of its tenants are super), but worth following nonetheless.

- **LUCIEN PELLAT-FINET**   The new cult hero for the wickedly rich, Pellat-Finet makes cashmere sweaters for women with wit, style, and grand luxury. The sweaters sell for about $1,000 in the U.S. (at Barney's, of course), but if you're in the in crowd, you buy in Paris. If you prefer to spend less on your clothes, perhaps you want to visit **Le Shop,** near place des Victoires, which is considered the window where the next hot names in French fashion will pop up.

- *PARAPHARMACIES*   This is a new category of store; there are now a zillion of them in Paris, and a few to be found in other big cities across France. They specialize in French beauty treatments, diet, and bath/spa products. In olden days, French law required that beauty treatments from chemical companies be sold through pharmacies. Now the law has been modified so that if a store has a pharmacist, it can sell the goods.

   Thus even **Monoprix** stores have *parapharmacies,* and independents are popping up all over. Often there is a beautician on hand as well. I don't need to tell you how much the French woman believes in her beauty regime. These stores are packed with fun products; I'll let you find your favorites to test. I can't honestly tell you that I think any of this stuff really works, but God, it's fun. Note that most *parapharmacies* discount by 20% and also have a frequent-user card for more discounts, called a *fidelity* card.

KNOW BEFORE YOU GO

· ·

The French Government Tourist Office in the United States is an excellent source for visitor information and trip-planning advice. They have a 900 number that costs 50¢ per minute to call: France On Call. Everyone who answers the phone speaks English, and the average call takes five minutes. They will mail any booklets or brochures you request (some of them have coupons for discounts) and provide you with first-hand information. Call 900/990-0040. They do not make actual bookings but will guide you to a local travel agent, if you need one.

If you prefer, you can call one of their several offices in the U.S. In New York, ☎ 212/315-0888; in Chicago, ☎ 312/337-6301; in Dallas, ☎ 214/720-4010; or in Los Angeles, ☎ 310/271-6665.

The French Government Tourist Office has also initiated a special program called Club France, in order to provide information and discounts to American Francophiles. Membership is $75 a year (each additional family member is $35) and entitles you to a quarterly newsletter that describes current promotions, upgrade and/or discount coupons for hotels and car rentals, a Paris Museum Pass, and a few other perks. Write: Club France, c/o French Government Tourist Office, 444 Madison Ave., New York, New York 10022; or call 212/757-0229.

MORE INFORMATION, PLEASE

All you need is a copy of *Paris par Arrondissement*. This is your source for street maps, bus lines, and the *métro*. It fits in the palm of my hand and is so complete. I can look up an address in the front of the book, then check a chart to find the nearest *métro* stop for that destination.

If you want to learn more, try digesting local magazines. French magazines are my secret passion—I spend a lot of my time in Paris in my tub, on a park bench, or in bed simply browsing. I can't even read French very well. Never mind. The ads alone are fabulous; the pictures make universal sense. I also "read" *Le Figaro* every day because it has good fashion coverage and covers new stores that are opening.

Figaro publishes a weekly insert, called *Figaro-scope*, that tells you about everything that's going on in the city; this includes special flea markets and shopping events. It appears in the paper every Wednesday.

Also consider *Pariscope*, a small-format weekly publication. It has movie listings and information about upcoming cultural events. It also lists special events such as big flea markets. Not many tourists use this weekly because it's in French only. Buy it at any news kiosk.

Time Out, the weekly British cultural magazine, publishes a Paris edition in English, available at most kiosks. They also publish English-language guide-books and annual "what's hot" guides that are sold in the U.S., as well as in English-language bookstores in Paris.

I subscribe to several French publications. They are expensive, but essential to these pages. Prices vary enormously depending on a variety of factors, so get prices on several types of magazines before you decide you can't afford this luxury. I use a French Canadian service, which seems to have slightly bet-ter prices than direct subscriptions. Call **Express Magazines** at 800/363-1310 and ask for their bro-chure. They speak English.

The monthly magazines seem to be affordable; a year's subscription to *French Vogue* is a little over $100, as are *Côte Sud* and *Côte Ouest*, respectively. But you can get a price break on the latter if you subscribe to both (and you want both!). I pay an outrageous $350 a year for the weekly *Madame Figaro*, which happens to be almost the same price I would pay for the weekend edition of *Le Figaro* in which *Madame Figaro* appears, but I do get it within days of publication. Not only do these magazines keep me up-to-date, they're great for improving my French!

Electronically Yours

The Internet is a fabulous source for researching your upcoming trip to France. Hotels, airlines, and travel agents all have their own Web sites, which can give you a glimpse at properties . . . or more.

Here are a few Web site addresses you might want to check out:

http://web.culture.fr	The French Culture Ministry
http://www.paris.org	Pictures of Paris
http://www.info-france-usa.org	The French Embassy Press and Information Service in Washington, D.C.
http://www.minitel.fr	Minitel. You pay to subscribe, but it's fabulous! Yes, you can get train schedules.

GETTING THERE

. . . .

From the U.S.

While getting to Paris may seem easy enough—after all, most of the major carriers fly there—I've got a few secrets that might make getting there more fun . . . and less expensive.

The cheapest airfares are always in winter. Furthermore, winter airfares are often accompanied by promotional ticketing gimmicks, such as buy one ticket, get one half-price; buy one ticket, bring along a companion for a discounted price; or kids fly free. There are deals out there during the chilly months. Also during winter, frequent-flyer miles may go on sale.

We all know that every winter there are airfare price wars. Last winter when **Air France** announced a $269 weekend fare to Paris, I think half of New York tilted into the Atlantic in a mad rush for tickets. And, of course, all the other airlines flying to

France matched the fare. Meanwhile, a new niche was carved out—winter weekend European travel. Just about every country now has deals that allow for Thursday or Friday departures and Monday or Tuesday returns. The problem with these tickets is that you can't add the week in between; you are limited to *le weekend longue*.

If you happen to buy a ticket at price A, and then a price war ensues, making the same ticket you purchased available at price B, a better price than you paid, don't just sit there and stew. The airlines will allow you to pay a service charge and get your ticket rewritten. This charge is usually $50, but you may save another $50 to $150. Or more.

If you don't care that much about frequent-flyer miles, try ticket brokers or consolidators for deals (very few of the tickets they sell earn you miles). I often call **Moment's Notice** (☎ 212/750-9111), a firm specializing in selling trips that no one else has bought at discounted prices. Moment's Notice usually requires a membership fee, but they'll let you join up after you've found a deal you want. I sometimes call Moment's Notice just to listen to their tape.

Also check out consolidators who will unload unsold tickets on scheduled flights for discount prices (which vary with the season, as do regular prices). Again, no frequent-flyer miles. These tickets are great for last-minute travelers who do not qualify for the 21-day advance purchase prices. You need only about four business days notice.

I called **Unitravel** (☎ 800/325-2222) and was offered a round-trip flight from New York to Paris for $628 plus departure taxes on Northwest Airlines during the summer peak season. You pay by credit card on the phone; they FedEx the tickets to you at no extra charge. They did say that their online service was even cheaper and this made me really uncomfortable, implying that I was a chump for not surfing the net.

C.L. Thomson is another consolidator, but they must be contacted by your travel agent (☎ 800/833-4258).

Packages that include your airfare and hotel accommodations always give you good prices, especially if you can get those prices guaranteed in dollars, which is possible through many big wholesalers, airlines, and hotels. If the dollar is depressingly low, or merely unstable enough to make you nervous, look carefully at deals in which prices are frozen in U.S. dollars. Car rental agencies also have some of these offerings.

Finally, don't forget to check out Disneyland Paris packages that include airfare, hotel, and transfers. Disneyland Paris is trying to rebuild its image and has various good deals from the U.S. and Europe.

Call **Now Voyager** (☎ 212/431-1616) to volunteer to be a freelance courier; you'll get a round-trip ticket for approximately $200, although your luggage allowance will be severely restricted. You get to take only one carry-on bag, measuring about 9 × 14 × 22; and a freight company may have your baggage allowance. Most flights are international and leave from New York or Newark; some departures are from Miami and Houston. Trips usually last one week, but there are some two-week and a few open-ended tickets available. Bookings are for singles. If you are with another person, be prepared for your partner to go the day before or the day after you. Reservations can be made up to two months in advance and are nonrefundable. You pay a $50 registration fee; they take cash or credit cards (cash offers you a discount).

Air France is part owner of a domestic airline called **Air InterEurope.** For those of you who are not French residents and want to travel beyond Paris, Air France and Air InterEurope offer a variety of passes for travel within France. One, called Le France pass, allows seven days of unlimited travel within France within a one month period (your days of travel do not have to be consecutive). The ticket costs a flat fee ($339 at the time of this writing), and you must purchase it in the U.S. before you depart for France. Call Air France for details. For information about other passes that can help you save on air travel within France, see *Born to Shop France*. Note that several new French airlines have popped up in the last year or two, mostly for intra-French travel, so Air InterEurope (previously called Air Inter) is not the only regional carrier in France. Price wars are now normal, whereas they were unheard of two years ago.

British Airways has several deals on flights from the U.S. to Europe, aside from their tours. One is their European Air Pass system. You must buy three coupons, but the total cost of travel can come out cheaper. Depending on which U.K. airport you use for your connections, each leg of your journey costs $75 to $99. You can take in Britain and France and save money. Also note that transatlantic airfare from the U.S. to the U.K. is much lower than to France, so you may want to take the time and trouble to fly through Great Britain or layover in Manchester or London.

Now that my friend Richard Branson is part of the consortium that took over the running of the Eurotunnel, **Virgin** is offering transatlantic packages through Britain that connect you to Paris via Eurostar (the Chunnel train).

I've never flown **Tower Air,** but they offer deals that cannot be ignored: This charter airline was advertising business class seats to Paris at $349 each way. This translates to a round-trip of $698 plus taxes (about $25) on their regularly scheduled 747 flights; nonstop every weekend. They also have coach seats. My friend Ken once flew them coach and said it wasn't deluxe, but everything was fine. The food service wasn't wonderful, according to him, but the plane was newish, and the seats were relatively comfortable. They have their own terminal at JFK. His round-trip coach ticket was about $520, but that was in peak season. ☎ 800/34-TOWER.

Rates are lower if you book through French tour operators/wholesalers like **Nouvelles Frontiers**, a major chain of French travel agents that calls itself **New Frontiers** in the U.S. (☎ 800/366-6387).

From the U.K.

If you think you'll just make a quick little hop from London to Paris on a whim, you may be shocked to realize that the regular airfare between the two cities is outrageously high, depending on the day and time you fly. For a regular round-trip ticket, figure on paying $300 to $350 per person. If you buy your ticket 14 days in advance and stay over a Saturday night, the fare will drop slightly.

However, since the opening of the Chunnel, airfares have come down dramatically, and just about every form of transportation between the U.K. and France (train, plane, ferry) has promotional deals—most require advance purchase and cannot be changed. Call both **British Airways** (☎ 800/247-9297) and **Air France** (☎ 800/237-2747) to check for fare wars, promotions, etc.

You may also want to check out, separately, the rates offered by the two major competing British carriers (BA and Virgin) for transatlantic fares plus Paris add-ons, and then for locally priced add-ons, which could be on sale or promotion.

If you need one-way transportation between London and Paris and want to fly, a round-trip ticket bought in advance to include a Saturday night stay will be less expensive than a one-way ticket. Just throw away the unused portion. *C'est la vie.*

From Brussels

Don't look at me like that! Brussels happens to be just two hours from Paris, thanks to brand-new speedy train lines. You can easily fly into Brussels and out of Paris (or vice versa) or even go to Paris for the weekend from Belgium. Sometimes, when there are airfare deals and promotions, all seats in and out of Paris are sold. Try Brussels for one leg and you won't be sorry!

Brussels has a new terminal to make the airport even more efficient. Also, **Sabena** (☎ 800/955-2000) has so many fabulous promotions these days, you have to take both the airline and Brussels quite seriously. Please note that Delta and Sabena have gone into partnership on a code-sharing basis to offer a strong Brussels hub. There are two flights a day from New York alone.

Brussels is my Paris travel tip of the decade.

By Train

The Chunnel (Channel tunnel) now connects Britain and France and Belgium. You can arrive almost anywhere by Chunnel in approximately three hours. There is no shopping on the train itself. There's a duty-free shop in Folkestone, where you board **Le Shuttle,** the car service for passenger cars, but for assorted complicated and political reasons, there are no duty-free shops in any of the international Eurostar train stations or on the trains themselves.

Do not get confused and think that all trains now use the Chunnel. Old-fashioned train service between the two cities, where you are put on a ferry for the crossing, still exists. To ride a train through the Chunnel, you must specifically book through **Eurostar** (☎ 800/677-8585). You can also book through **RailEurope** (☎ 800/4-EURAIL). Then book for either London–Paris or London–Brussels.

BritRail USA has several packages that allow you to choose which method you'd like to use for getting from the U.K. to the continent; their Continental Capitals Circuit connects London with Paris, Brussels, and Amsterdam. The pass costs a flat fee (about $275 for second class and $350 for first class) and is good for a period of six months after the date of issue. It gives you unlimited stopovers in those four cities; call 212/575-2667 for more information.

There are other BritRail passes, geared to travel to specific countries (such as the BritFrance pass) that enable you to save money on train travel. If you buy some of these products, you get an automatic discount (about 30%!) off your Chunnel train ticket. Note that the Eurostar ticket is not a part of any pass currently available; it must be bought as an add-on.

RailEurope (☎ 800/4-EURAIL) not only has tons of train passes, but also books transatlantic air, hotels, car rentals—the works. One of the greatest things about their system is that there are different prices based on age (youth passes, seniors, etc.) as well as on the number of people traveling together. Not only do they believe the more the merrier, they also think the more, the cheaper. See *Born to Shop France* for more information about their specific France passes.

ARRIVING IN PARIS

This is a very important lesson that I learned the hard way: Every now and then you actually get to pick which airport you will use for arrival and/or departure into and out of Paris. There is no crisis here. Practice saying "Orly" at bedtime, so the word rolls off your tongue.

There is no reason to use Charles de Gaulle Airport if you can avoid it. Not that there's anything wrong with it, it's just bigger, more confusing, and farther away than Orly. Who needs it?

If you arrive at Orly you'll be welcomed by a small, efficient airport (with 18 duty-free shops—so don't worry) and a down-home feel. It's only when you depart that you will panic. There are two parts to Orly: Orly Nord (Orly North) and Orly Sud (Orly South), and your ticket probably does not say which you want. Fear not. If you are flying American or Delta, you want Orly Sud.

Orly is to the south of Paris, not as far away from town as CDG (the abbreviation for Charles de Gaulle International Airport). Expect a taxi to the 1er to cost you approximately $40, including tip.

All major car-rental agencies have offices in the airport, or you can take a bus or train into town. Orlyval trains get you to town in 20 minutes; Orlybus takes you directly to the RER station at Denfert-Rochereau on the edge of Paris, where you can get a taxi or connect to the *métro*. For English-language information on Orly transport, call 1/49-75-15-15.

Charles de Gaulle Airport is composed of two parts, Terminal 1 and 2. Terminal 1 has various satellites, Terminal 2 has pods designated A to D. I have been lost in those pods, and I want to tell you it was not pretty.

A taxi to the 1er from CDG will cost about $60. Take note that most French taxis are small; if you have a lot of luggage, hold out for a Mercedes taxi. If you have a lot of family, plus a lot of luggage, plan on using two taxis. Or you can send one person and all the luggage in a taxi and let the other members of the family take public transportation. Air France offers bus service from Etoile (take a taxi to your hotel from there); or you can take Roissy Rail, which lets you off at either the Gare du Nord or Châtelet, both in-town locations.

There are two lines of bus service, aside from Air France: One drops you at Nation; the other, at Gare de l'Est. For English-language information about transport at CDG, call 1/48-62-22-80.

You may buy individual tickets for public transportation. Use a *carnet* of six tickets (good for families) or show your *carte orange* (see below).

GETTING AROUND PARIS

Paris is laid out in a system of zones called *arrondissements,* which circle around from inside to outside. When France adopted the Zip code method for its mail, Parisians incorporated the arrondissement number into their Zip codes as the last two digits. Thus a Zip code of 75016 means the address is in the 16th arrondissement (16e).

Think about arrondissements when planning your shopping expeditions. Check the map frequently, however, since you may think that 1er and 16e are far apart, when in actuality, you can walk the distance and have a great time doing so. (Take the rue du Faubourg St-Honoré toward the Champs-Elysées, and you even get a tour of the 8e thrown in.)

If you see a number with a small *e* written after it, this number signifies the arrondissement. The first arrondissement, however, is written 1er. Knowing the proper arrondissement is essential to getting around rapidly in Paris. It is also a shorthand system for many people to sum up everything a place can or may become—simply by where it is located, or by how far it is from something that is acceptably chic.

With its wonderful transportation system, Paris is a pretty easy city to navigate. Tourists are usually urged to ride the *métro,* but buses are available and often a treat—you can see where you're going and get a free tour along the way. Your edition of *Paris par Arrondissement* usually has bus routes as well as a *métro* map. *Métro* maps are handed out free at your hotel and are printed in almost every guidebook. Keep one in your wallet at all times.

By *Métro*

There are many *métro* ticket plans for easiest access to the city. If you can speak a little bit of French and visit Paris often enough to take the time to do this,

Paris by Arrondissement

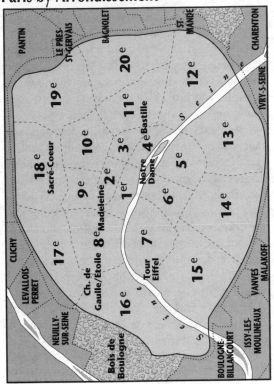

buy a *carte orange*. It is exactly what it sounds like: an orange card that bears a passport-type photo of yourself. (Bring a photo with you or use the photo booth in the Concorde station.)

The *carte orange* is good for unlimited travel on bus or *métro* for a one-week period, Monday to Monday. Once you have your permanent orange card, with your photo in place, you will then have to buy only a coupon for each week you want to travel—I've had the same orange card for about 15 years.

Now for the tricky part. A coupon is good for one week, beginning on a Monday. It is sold Monday through Wednesday. Depending on the amount of travel you plan, even if you arrive on a Wednesday, it may behoove you to buy a coupon, because it is indeed less expensive than the next type of weekly pass. A coupon costs about $10 (45 F); you may also buy a monthly version (about $40). The *carte orange* is about half the price of the weekly ticket pushed for tourists—called "Sesame." Bargain shopping begins at the *métro* station, *mes amis*.

Note: You probably cannot get your first *carte orange* unless you speak enough French to negotiate the purchase and can answer a few questions that will be asked. Touristy-type tourists will be guided toward other kinds of more expensive ticket arrangements, such as the above-mentioned Sesame. I ask the hotel concierge to write down everything I need and then I slide the paper under the window at the ticket booth at the Concorde *métro* station. Only a handful of *métro* stations do the first timers' *carte orange* and Concorde is one of them. Remember, you will need a passport photo. Also remember where you put the card when you return home (I keep mine with my passport) because once you have the actual card, you bring it back with you each subsequent trip.

If you just want individual tickets, please buy them by the *carnet*. The *carnet* is made up of 10 tickets, can be bought at any station, and can be used for the bus or the *métro*. An individual ticket to the *métro* costs about $1 a ride; with the *carnet*, the price drops significantly. Note that Paris has switched from a yellow ticket to a turquoise ticket; if you have old tickets from a trip many years ago, they will probably still work. If the electronic gate rejects your ticket, exchange it at the ticket booth.

"Paris Visite" is a transportation pass providing travel for three to five days (depending on what you buy); it costs up to $30 but includes rides to the airport, outlying suburbs, and even Versailles, and is an awfully good deal if you plan to use it. The pass comes in a black case in which you insert something that looks remarkably like the same coupon used in a *carte orange*. This pass is sold at RATP stations (big *métro* stations or RER stations—I look at the acronym and think "rapid transit"), SNCF stations (French national trains), and ADP (airports de Paris) booths—at either airport, Orly or Charles de Gaulle.

There are Travelcard passes, good for unlimited one-day travel that cost about $5, but remember, the *carte orange* costs about $10, and it's good for a whole week. You can't go to Versailles on the *carte orange*, but it costs only about $5 (round-trip) for a regular RER ticket to Versailles anyway.

By Bus

Paris buses take the same coupons as the *métro*, or real money. They are much slower than the underground, but you get to see the sights as you go by. For bus information for the airport, see page 21.

By Car

If you plan to visit the countryside or Disneyland Paris, you may want to rent a car. As long as you avoid driving around the place de la Concorde, you'll be fine. As an added convenience, most major car-rental agencies will allow you to drop the car at a hotel, saving you the time and trouble of returning it yourself. I once returned a car at the Inter-Continental on a Sunday, but then worried it wouldn't be picked up until Monday and I would be charged for an extra day. Many phone calls later, I discovered the clock stopped ticking the minute the concierge notified the agency (Hertz) that we were ready. I needn't have worried.

Should you be renting a car in Paris from **Kemwel,** ask them to fax you a map with the location of the pick-up point (Citer at Gare du Nord) marked, since you'll have to navigate a number of tricky one-way streets to get there. Confirm their hours of operation as well, as they may not be what you expect. Isn't travel fun?

If you intend to drive around Paris (silly you), be sure you know about parking regulations and how to work the meters that provide a ticket proving you've paid for curbside parking. (Display it prominently on your windshield.) Just because you don't see a meter like we have in the U.S. doesn't mean that parking is free.

If you prefer a car and driver, call **Carey France** at 1/42-65-54-20, or their American headquarters at 800/336-4646. Their fax number in France is 1/42-65-25-93. Or try **Euro Limo** (☎ 1/40-11-30-30; fax 1/40-11-25-84). You can request a limo, a sedan, or even a van. I've met two drivers in Paris who speak English and will pick you up at the airport or train station. **Shah Jimmy** (☎ 1/07-82-45-17) has a station wagon, and **Alain Hamel** (☎ 1/45-58-63-23), a big Mercedes.

PHONING HOME

Using a French pay phone is not particularly difficult, especially if you use a French Telecom *telecarte*. You can buy one at any newsstand. It'll also help you save money on phone calls to the U.S. Another way to save is to use a direct-dialing service through your long-distance carrier at home. For **AT&T,** call 00-800-00-11; for **MCI,** call 00-800-00-19; for **Sprint,** use 00-800-00-87.

Of course, the most expensive way to phone home is from your hotel room. Very few of Paris's fanciest hotels have in their lobbies pay phones that take phone cards, making it inconvenient to save a franc. One that does, however, is the **Paris Inter-Continental,** right in the heart of the best Right Bank shopping. In fact, it has two pay phones: one that accepts *telecartes* and another than accepts credit cards. Both charge France Telecom rates. I spoke to Cannes from the latter for two minutes for $2, billed directly to my Visa card. Not a big bargain, but a lot less than you might otherwise be charged.

POSTCARDS FROM THE EDGE

. . . .

Postcards in Paris are as original and arty as the city itelf—there are truly thousands of designs and styles to choose from, but watch out: Many of them cost between $1and $2 each! The enormously cute, large-sized Disney cards (sold in Paris, not Disneyland Paris) cost even more! The better the postcard design, the higher the price. Look before you leap.

You can buy postcards for a mere 1 F each if you shop the tourist traps carefully; you may even luck out and find 15 cards for 10 F; 12 cards for 10 F is more easily done. Walk along the rue de Rivoli, where the tourist traps are thick, checking prices as you go. The price per card drops the higher uptown you go (away from Concorde, toward the Musée du Louvre), and the bulk deals get better. Tourist traps near Notre-Dame also sell postcards for 1 F each and often offer bulk deals.

You can buy stamps at a PTT (post office), at a tobacco shop, or from your hotel concierge. Postage to the U.S. (even for a postcard) is rather pricey, but if you have friends in other European Union countries, it's a bargain.

SHOPPING HOURS

. . . .

Shopping hours in Paris are extremely irregular and independent. Welcome to France. Thankfully, they are big-city hours, so you needn't worry about a lot of down time, as in Italy or even the French provinces. There are plenty of shopping opportunities even on Sunday and Monday.

Monday can be a tad moody, but generally speaking, stores are open Monday, or part of Monday. Those stores that tend to be closed on Monday morning will open anytime from noon on, sometimes 1pm, 2pm, or even 3pm. For the most part, they are small stores, Mom-and-Pop operations that are open on Sundays. The department stores and branches of the major chains are open on Monday morning. About 50% of the stores on the Left Bank, in the prime shopping areas, are open.

During the rest of the week, most stores consider 10am to 7pm to be standard hours of operation, but there are so many variations to this rule, such as it is, that you can lose your mind. Some stores open every morning at 10am, then at 9:30am one day of the week. Some stores are open until 10pm on Thursday nights only. A few stores are open until 8pm or 9pm every weekday, especially in high-traffic areas. My favorite is Au Printemps, which opens not at 9:30am, but at 9:35am! It's impossible to know or keep track of every store's hours.

In summer, many stores close for lunch on Saturday, but stay open later in the evening. Some stores are open for lunch during the week, but close for lunch on Saturday and then reopen. (Hermès does this.)

France has about 15 bank holidays a year; stores may close on these holidays. Many are religious festivals and occur on Monday.

The entire month of August may be unusual. Most of France closes down on August 15 for Pentecost, but some stores close for the entire month of August, or just from August 14 to August 31. Bastille Day, July 14, is a holiday (stores are closed), but some Parisian retailers open up, if only for a few hours, to take advantage of the crowds in the streets.

Sunday in the Park with Georges

Although traditional Parisian retail is closed on Sunday, there is still an enormous amount of shopping going on. Aside from the flea market business, which has always been hot on Sunday, nowadays entire neighborhoods are jumping on Sunday. Check out **the Louvre** (with the adjoining mall Carrousel du

Louvre), **the Marais,** and **Virgin Megastore** on the Champs-Elysées.

Many stores that open on Sunday are closed on Monday.

While **The Drugstore** (Champs-Elysées) is open on Sunday—along with many other drugstore-type places and local stores—the best Sunday shopping is along the banks of the Seine. Slowly and carefully wander the fruit and vegetable markets and the flea market. Buy a crêpe from a stand, watch the people walking their dogs in the park, or savor a hot chocolate at Angelina. Here's my perfect Sunday:

Start at the flea market at Vanves (see p. 175) and the fruit, vegetable, and dry goods market one street over. Arrive early, 9am is just fine, and finish in time for lunch or even a picnic supplied by the street market.

Stroll along either side of the river (or both!) where the booksellers and their stalls are most dense. I like to take the *métro* to the Right Bank, hop out, and cross over to the riverbank. I then stroll the quai, walking all the way (not that far) to the Village St-Paul, where there are numerous antiques shops. This is a good after-lunch or midday project. The booksellers vary one from the next. Some sell antique books, others sell just postcards or prints. Some of these dealers come to Paris just for the weekend, returning to other cities and other jobs Sunday evening.

You'll find the **Village St-Paul** near the Bastille, at the edge of the river. Only open on Sunday afternoon, it has a building with dealers within and a bunch of antiques shops at street level—very French, and very un-touristy. It's also in an easy-to-reach location, especially if you're already out walking on the quai. If you want to *métro* there, get off at St-Paul and walk toward the river, behind the church (named after St. Paul, of course).

Antiquing on Sunday is a national hobby; don't forget to check the newspapers or ask your concierge about any special shows or events which might be planned for the weekend. From February through May, the weekends are dense with special events—many of which highlight shows for antiques and/or *brocante* (used items, not necessarily antique).

When the weather is good, shops in the main flow of tourist traffic may open on a Sunday just to catch the extra business. Every now and then a duty-free shop will open up; tourist traps near popular attractions are almost always open on Sunday afternoons. On a Sunday by 5pm, though, it's hard to find any place that's open.

If you are with a bored teenager, you may want to visit the Champs-Elysées on a Sunday afternoon. There, at the Virgin Megastore, Richard Branson has been defying local laws (he pays a huge fine) by opening his doors for business. It's great good fun. In fact, you don't have to be a bored teenager to enjoy it.

Note that the French government currently allows retailers to be open on five Sundays during a given year; these Sundays are usually in the fall.

SALE PERIODS

As Sunday shopping is changing, so are the traditional sale periods. Officially, the French government sets the dates of the sales, and there are only two sale periods: one in winter (January) and one in summer (June to July). Retailers, strapped for cash, offer assorted promotions and discounts these days. A few of them, like Hermès, have special events held outside the store. These events are advertised and listed in papers; check the page called *Le Carnet du Jour* in *Le Figaro* for sale ads.

PERSONAL NEEDS SHOPPING

Pharmacies are marked with a green neon cross; at least one in each neighborhood must be open on

Sunday. When a pharmacy is closed, the nearest open pharmacy is indicated on a sign in the window.

Condoms are sold from machines in all *métro* stations and at pharmacies. I had a hard time finding them in **Monoprix,** where only one brand was available. There is a national television campaign to teach kids the importance of using condoms, so condoms are often given away free (even in stores).

If you need a book in English, **Brentano's** is at 37 avenue de la Opéra; **W.H. Smith & Son,** 248 rue de Rivoli. Both sell American and British books and periodicals. Most luxury hotels sell the London newspapers or at least the Sunday editions. There's also a small cadre of Left Bank bookstores that sell books in English and serve as hangouts for expats.

Airport Shopping

Both Orly and CDG have more than their share of shopping opportunities for visitors—in fact, the shopping is so brisk in these airports that they have their own shopping bag. Stores at CDG are fancier than those at Orly, but you will have no trouble dropping a few, or a few hundred, francs. Prices at the airport duty-free shops may be slightly cheaper than at comparable retail stores in Paris, but not much. My best exception to this rule is Hermès, which I do find considerably cheaper at the airport duty-free shop or even on the airplane.

You should have already purchased your cosmetic and fragrance bargains in Paris at the duty-free shops that offer 20% to 40% savings; you will save only 13% at the airport. The selection at the airport may be better than the selection on your airplane, but the airline's prices can be better. It pays to take the duty-free price list from your plane when you arrive and save it for when you're shopping at the airport at the end of your trip if you need to shop at airports. I also keep a Saks Fifth Avenue price list in my wallet for each of the fragrances that I like. Saks prints them constantly in mailers, bill stuffers, ads, etc. You'd be surprised how often a duty-free price can be the same as the Saks Fifth Avenue price!

Aeroports de Paris is a real company; they have their own shopping bags and everything. All of the stores in Paris's two airports are affiliated with the company, whether they are duty-free shops or not. Aeroports de Paris publishes free booklets with coupons that can be used in their stores—the last booklets I picked up at the airport offered 50 F off on different types of purchases. About $10—not a bad discount.

Chapter Three

. . . .

MONEY MATTERS

UNIFICATION & YOU

Will the so-called unification of Europe affect your shopping habits? When (and if) the EU (European Union) goes to a single currency, it will make paying and refunding much easier. But right now, unification does not really affect you significantly. It has changed a few things, as well as created an area of muddy waters, where rules and regulations continue to be changed; but for those who are just visiting Paris, very few major changes have come about because of it. Since Europeans themselves can't agree on what unification is going to mean to them (and it could easily take the rest of this century for them to work it out), the changes that come down the Chunnel will be slow, indeed. Not to worry. Just make sure you understand how to get your *détaxe* refund.

THE FRENCH GOVERNMENT & YOU

Changes that the French government has instituted that do affect you, the visitor, are a higher value-added tax and a lower *détaxe*. This was done partly to keep up with continually changing EU regulations, but also to get the economic situation more

in line with what it should be in order to provide
for a single EU currency. The value-added tax, called
TVA in France, was recently raised to over 20%
(okay, so it's 20.6% to be precise), while the *détaxe*
(the refund you can get on the TVA) was lowered
from 2000 F to 1200 F. The price of gas continues
to go up, while the price of an international phone
call continues to go down. Train tickets and rail
passes are up. Expect more fluctuations: The dust
won't settle for years.

FRENCH BUSINESS & YOU

When the French government pressures the business community and private citizens in response
to economic problems, such as issues regarding
unification or the possibility of a unified currency,
the effects are passed on to us. If French business
needs to raise cash to pay higher taxes, prices are
raised.

Some of the changes are more cultural and possibly more xenophobic. There are some French businesses that want to remain very French and do not
want to go international. They are changing their
ways of doing business to make certain that they
get more French or don't fall under EU modifica-
tions. These same businesses are raising prices on
their goods, limiting distribution channels, and dis-
allowing discounts through regular stores. There are
other French businesses that want to go global, so
they present themselves to the French with one face,
but to the rest of the world with other prices and
other marketing formats.

They are making it harder for you to get goods
in France, in the hope it drives up their value.
The cost and availability of goods, especially status
and deluxe names, are changing as you read. Until
the dust settles, make sure you have priced French
items in the U.S. before you assume they cost less
in France.

French Deluxe

The concept of name brands was invented in France hundreds of years ago based on the very simple, and correct, assumption that people would pay anything for the very best quality. This notion remains the core of French marketing today.

Brands are fiercely marketed in order to keep their image. Sales are strictly regulated by the government (the French government allows only two legal sale periods during the year) and makers of fakes are hunted down and prosecuted. All of this is done not only to protect the image of a deluxe brand, but to protect the shopper who paid full price. Discounts are limited to duty-free stores.

Meanwhile, duty-free goods are set to be eliminated within the EU in 1999. To adapt, the multi-zillion-dollar duty-free business is busy reinventing itself as a fancy discount source. Most of the big names—only a portion of which are French—have been successfully wooed as suppliers and will sell or make for limited sale goods that can be discounted in duty-free shops. (Many goods already sold in duty-free stores at airports are created for sale there and are not part of a regular retail line.)

Because the deluxe philosophy is so innately French, French consumers believe it with all their hearts. They have been happily brainwashed. French men and women save their money and make their wish lists before Christmas and birthdays to include deluxe goods from French luxury houses. I have French friends who have a list of the items they "must" have; when an item on their wish list materializes, I think they are more relieved than grateful. It would be hard to face their friends without these items.

Americans may have trouble understanding the difference between the concepts of status and deluxe goods. Status items are bought because the labels impress either the owner or the owner's circle. Luxury goods are meaningful because of their beauty and quality of workmanship; they've been created to last forever.

Because these two kinds of goods are produced and sold with two different objectives in mind, don't be surprised by the protective French attitude you may encounter. Certain luxury or deluxe goods are actually considered national treasures. You may even consider French salespeople in such stores to be rude. They're not rude; you just don't know the system.

CURRENCY EXCHANGE

Exchanging currency in a foreign country can be downright depressing. I've taken to changing money at my hotel—and buying traveler's checks in French francs before I leave home—because the time and aggravation involved in exchanging money in Paris can drive you nuts.

The rate announced in the paper (it's in the *Herald Tribune* every day) is the official bank exchange rate and is not usually available to tourists. Even by trading your money at a bank, you will not get the same rate of exchange that's announced in the papers. And you will pay a fee for the bank's services. I've stood in lines at banks for 20 to 30 minutes to try to save $3 and realized it was a total waste of my time. I've also been to those Exchange booths that dot the rue de Rivoli and the Champs-Elysées and found that even if they advertise a great rate of exchange, there is usually a hidden hook— a $10 fee!

You may get a better rate of exchange for a traveler's check than for cash because there is less paperwork involved. But the rate of exchange you get anywhere is usually not negotiable with that establishment. While you can shop for the best rate available, you cannot haggle for a better rate from a certain source.

Hotels generally give the least favorable rate of exchange, but they do not charge a fee to guests. As far as I'm concerned, if there's no line and the people are pleasant, this is the best bet!

Shops may negotiate on the rate of exchange they'll give you. Say the item you buy costs the equivalent of $40, and you sign over a $50 U.S. traveler's check. The shopkeeper may ask you the rate of exchange, or say something like "Let's see. Today the dollar is trading at. . . ." Then, he (or you) will pull out a calculator and figure out how much change you will get. If you have bought a lot, you may ask for a more favorable rate of exchange on your change, or bargain a bit. But exclusive shops will be insulted at this maneuver. Use credit cards there, anyway.

Do not expect a bank to give you a better rate than your hotel. Remember, the bank usually charges a commission. If you exchange one traveler's check each day, expect to get a lousy rate and pay $5 per exchange.

The best rate is generally offered by American Express. Their main office is on rue Scribe, across the street from the Opéra and the Le Grand Hôtel Inter-Continental. This is a convenient place to visit (Galeries Lafayette is a block away!), and you can save money if you're a cardholder (they won't charge you a commission). Other financial services are provided as well.

If you are going to Brussels and want correct change, do not exchange money in France first (even at American Express), because you will be charged to change your U.S. dollars to French francs, and then your French francs to Belgian francs! The American Express office once gave me Belgian money that had been out of circulation for over three years and was totally worthless.

If you want to change money back to dollars when you leave a country, remember that you will pay a higher rate for them. You are now "buying" dollars rather than "selling" them. Therefore, never change more money than you think you will need, unless you plan to stockpile for another trip.

Have some foreign currency on hand for arrival. After a lengthy transatlantic flight, you will not want to stand in line at some airport booth just to get your cab fare. You'll pay a very high rate of exchange and be wasting your precious bathtub time. Your home bank or local currency exchange office can sell you small amounts of foreign currency. No matter how much of a premium you pay for this money, the convenience will be worth it. I get $100 worth of currency for each country I visit to have on me on arrival; I buy it at the airport before I depart. This pays for the taxi to the hotel, tips, and the immediate necessities until I decide where to change the rest of my money.

Keep track of what you pay for your currency. If you are going to several countries, or you must make several money-changing trips to the cashier, write down the sums. When you get home and wonder what you did with all the money you used to have, it'll be easier to trace your cash. When you are budgeting, adjust to the rate you paid for the money, not the rate you read in the newspaper.

Keep a rough estimate of the conversion rate in your mind. Know the conversion rate for $50 and $100 so that in an instant you can make a judgment about a purchase. If you're still interested in an item, slow down and figure out the accurate price.

HOW TO GET CASH OVERSEAS

Go to American Express for quick cash. Card members may draw on their cards for cash advances or may cash personal checks. Never travel without your checkbook.

It's all a relatively simple transaction—you write a personal check at a special desk and show your card; it is approved; you go to another desk and get the money in the currency you request. Allow about half an hour for the whole process, unless there are long lines. Usually you get the credit advance on your card at the same desk.

ATM MACHINES

. . . .

Sacré cash card!

This is the start of something big and will soon be the easiest and possibly best way for exchanging money—*le bank machine.*

Bank cash machines are being used in Europe, but don't count on finding them everywhere you go, and don't be surprised if they won't take your card. I tried a machine in Paris and was instructed, in French, mind you:

"Please introduce your card."

I inserted my card.

"Your card is not remembered."

The card was returned to me.

That's not to say that a bank machine won't work for you, you just have to find the right machine to match your card. For the location of the ATM nearest to where you plan to stay in Paris, call 800/424-7787 for the Cirrus network or 800/843-7587 for the Plus system before you leave home.

Also note: American Express machines will dispense cash if you are already set up for this service.

STRANGE CHANGE

. . . .

See page 61 for tips on spotting fake 10 F pieces.

TIPS ON TIPPING

. . . .

Tipping in Paris can be confusing, because a service charge is added to all restaurant and hotel bills. While you do not have to add a tip to a restaurant check, it's often done—simply round off the bill or plunk down a few extra francs. It's all the waiter will see of your real tip.

Figure 5 F per suitcase when tipping bellboys; and 2 F or 3 F to doormen who hail you a taxi.

Round off for taxi drivers or give 10% for longer rides (such as to the airport).

SEND MONEY

You can have money sent to you from home, a process that usually takes about two days. Money can be wired through Western Union (someone brings them cash or a certified check, and WU does the rest—this may take up to a week), or through an international money order, which is cleared by telex through the bank where you cash it. Money can be wired from bank to bank, but this works only when your American bank has branches in Europe or a relationship with a French bank. Banks usually charge a large fee for doing you this favor. Call Western Union at 800/325-6000 in the U.S.

In addition, American Express can arrange for a MoneyGram, a check up to $500 that can be sent to you by family or friends at home. You then cash it at the American Express office in Paris. Call 800/543-4080 in the U.S. for details.

PAYING UP

Whether you use cash, traveler's check, or a credit card, you are probably paying for your purchase in a currency that is not American dollars. Airports and airplanes often take dollars anywhere in the world, and you can tip a bellboy with a dollar bill, if need be, but in France you're going to need French francs.

I think you'll do best using a credit card. Plastic is the safest to use, provides you with a record of your purchases (for U.S. Customs as well as your books), and makes returns a lot easier. Credit-card companies, because they often are associated with banks, also give the best exchange rates. You may even "make money" by charging a purchase to a credit card, because the price your credit-card company gives you on an exchange ratio is almost always better than what you can get for cash in a foreign country.

One thing to note about credit-card charges: Your purchase is posted in dollars the day your credit slip clears the credit-card company (or bank) office, not the day of your purchase. If the dollar goes up in the two- or three-day lag between these two transactions, you make money; if the dollar loses strength, you pay. However, the difference is usually no more or no less than what you would suffer on the streets with a volatile exchange rate.

If you go to a shop that does not honor any of the cards you hold, but does have a display of cards in the window, ask them to pull out their credit forms to find the names (and pictures) of their reciprocal bank cards. Chances are you can make a match. Access, a common European credit card, happens to be the same as MasterCard—yet this is rarely advertised.

If you happen to be given a book of discount coupons by your hotel or tour guide, you will also notice that you get a 10% discount for cash, but only a 5% discount when you use credit cards. Storekeepers much prefer you to pay in cash. Remember this also when you are bargaining at flea markets. A credit-card transaction costs the retailer 2% to 5%. If you pay cash, you should be able to get that amount as a discount.

Traveler's checks are a must—for safety's sake. Shop around a bit, compare the various companies that issue checks, and make sure your checks are insured against theft or loss. I happen to use American Express traveler's checks, but they are not the only safe game in town; choose your type of check by what you can get without paying a fee. If you are a member of **AAA** (American Automobile Association), you can get American Express traveler's checks without paying a fee—this alone is worth AAA's membership dues.

I also use AAA to obtain traveler's checks in foreign currency. They don't come in every currency, but they are available in French francs. You may have to order ahead. If you don't travel to France frequently, you don't want more than you can use, but a few hundred dollars worth of francs will make changing money that much easier, since you are not converting currency. Do watch the rates for a few weeks while you contemplate this purchase; once you buy, you are locked into a rate.

American Express now offers a "Global Money-pac" that provides foreign cash and/or traveler's checks in the currencies you'll need for your trip. Call 800/414-6914 in the U.S. and pay with your American Express or Optima credit card. They'll charge a commission, and there's an extra fee if you need courier delivery. Currencies available are: French francs, Britsh pounds, Japanese yen, Swiss francs, Deutsche marks, and Canadian dollars. You're on your own for that trip to Italy.

Finally, when you are trying to figure out how much things cost, remember to divide by the rate you paid for your money, not the bank rate.

DÉTAXE

Détaxe is the refund you get on TVA, the value-added tax of 20.6% that is levied on all goods sold in France. It's similar to sales tax in the United States. The French pay it automatically. Tourists can get a refund on it, as can visitors from other EU countries when the tab is big enough. The amount of the tax credit varies with the type of item bought. The furniture tax is different from the luxury goods tax; and the luxury goods tax rate is falling due to pressure to realign taxes with other EU countries.

The basic *détaxe* system works pretty much like this:

You are shopping in a store with prices marked on the merchandise. This is the true price of the item that any tourist or any national must pay. If you are a French national, you pay the price without thinking twice. If you are a tourist who plans to leave the country within six months, you may qualify for a *détaxe* refund. But wait: There's a hitch. Each store establishes the amount of money you must spend to qualify for the refund on an individual basis. You must immediately ask a salesperson, "What is the minimum expenditure in this store for the export refund?" The rate varies from shop to shop, although the minimum is set by law. Currently the *détaxe* is refunded to a person who spends 1200 F or more in one store. Many stores let you save up receipts over a period of six months.

Once you know the minimum, you must decide if you will make a small purchase now and come back another time for a bigger haul, or if you will horde receipts. Only you know how much time your schedule will permit for shopping or what your bottom-line budget is. Spending to save doesn't always make sense. Keep the discount in perspective.

If you are going to another European country, consider the export tax credit policy there. The tax-free program in Italy is now working and it requires a lower expenditure to qualify. If you are going on to Italy from France, you may want to make your big purchases there. If you're planning to visit England next, you can get a VAT refund on most purchases there. Usually, you need to spend only £50 to qualify, but that, too, is flexible. (Harrods makes you spend £100 before you get a refund.)

Balance local good buys against foreign *détaxe* credits as well. In other words, perfume is not a good buy in England, so who cares if you get a 15% refund, when the markup is much higher than in France? France or the French West Indies are absolutely the best places in the world to buy French perfume—no discount plan or VAT refund plan should persuade you otherwise.

U.S. Customs & Duties Tips

To make your reentry into the United States as smooth as possible, follow these tips:

- Know the rules and stick to them!
- Don't try to smuggle anything.
- Be polite and cooperative (up until the point when they ask you to strip, anyway).

Remember:

- You are allowed to bring in $400 worth of duty-free merchandise per person. (Books are not included, as they are duty free.) Before you leave the United States, verify this amount with one of the U.S. Customs offices. Each member of the family is entitled to the deduction; this includes infants.
- Currently, you pay a flat 10% duty on the next $1,000 worth of merchandise.
- Duties thereafter are based on the type of product. They vary tremendously per item.
- The head of the family can make a joint declaration for all family members. The "head of the family" need not be male. Whoever is the head of the family, however, should take the responsibility for answering any questions the customs officers may ask. Answer questions honestly, firmly, and politely. Have receipts ready and make sure they match the information on the landing card. Don't be forced into a story that won't wash under questioning. If you tell a little lie, you'll be labeled as a fibber, and they'll tear your luggage apart.
- Have the customs registration slips for your personally owned goods in your wallet or easily available. If you wear a Cartier watch, be able to produce the registration slip. If you cannot prove that you took a foreign-made item out of the United States with you, you may be forced

continues

to pay duty on it. If you own such items but have no registration or sales slips, take photos or photographs of the goods and have them notarized in the U.S. before you depart. The notary seal and date will prove you had the goods in the U.S. before you left the country.

- The unsolicited gifts you mailed from abroad do not count in the $400-per-person rate. If the value of the gift is more than $50, you pay duty when the package comes into the country. Remember, it's only one unsolicited gift per person. Don't mail it to yourself.

- Do not attempt to bring in any illegal food items—dairy products, meats, fruits, or vegetables (coffee is okay). Generally speaking, if it's alive, it's *verboten.* Any creamy French cheese is illegal, but a hard or cured cheese is legal.

- Antiques must be 100 years old to be duty free. Provenance papers will help (so will permission to export the antiquity, since it could be an item of national cultural significance). Any bona fide work of art is duty free, whether it was painted 50 years ago or just yesterday; the artist need not be famous.

- Dress for success. People who look like "hippies" get stopped at customs more than average folks. Women who look like a million dollars, are dragging their fur coats, have first-class baggage tags on their luggage, and carry Gucci handbags, but declare they have bought nothing, are equally suspicious.

- Elephant ivory is illegal to import. Antique ivory pieces may be brought into the country if you have papers stating their provenance.

- The amount of customs allowance is expected to change. If you are a big shopper, check before you leave to see if there's any news.

If you go for the *détaxe* refund, budget your time to allow for the paperwork. It takes about 15 minutes to fill out each store's forms and may take 20 to 60 minutes for you to receive the forms especially if you are shopping in a big department store during the tourist season. I have zipped through the line in less than 5 minutes, however, so you never know. Allow more time than you need, just in case.

You will need your passport number (but not necessarily the passport itself) to fill out the paperwork—a carbonless multicopy. The space that asks for your address is asking for the name of your hotel. You do not need to provide its address. After the papers are filled out, they will be given to you along with an envelope (including a copy for your records). Sometimes the envelope has a stamp on it; sometimes it is blank (if the latter, you must affix a stamp to it before you leave the country). At other times, it has a special government frank that serves as a stamp. If you don't understand what's on your envelope, ask.

When you're at the airport, go to the customs official who processes the *détaxe* papers. Do this before you clear regular customs or send off your luggage. The customs officer has the right to ask you to show him (or her) the merchandise you bought and are taking out of the country. Whether the officer sees your purchases or not, he or she will stamp your papers, keeping a set (which will be processed) and giving you another set. Place this set in the envelope, and mail the envelope to the shop where you made your purchases. Usually the envelope is preprinted with the shop's name and address or has been hand-addressed by the shop for you. Sometimes, however, the customs officer keeps the specially franked envelopes. Don't worry, they'll be mailed.

Please note: Since unification in 1993, you now claim your *détaxe* when you leave your final destination to return to the U.S. If you are going on to Belgium from France, you claim everything as you exit Belgium and process your paperwork there. You'll get the French laws and the French discounts, but the paperwork itself is done at Belgian customs. Ditto for Britain, Italy, or elsewhere in the EU.

When the papers get back to the shop and the government has notified the shop that their set of papers has been registered, the store will then grant you the discount through a refund. This can be done on your credit card, of which they will have made a dual pressing, or through a personal check, which will come to you in the mail, usually three months later. (It will be in a foreign currency—your bank may charge you to change it into dollars.)

So that's how the system works. Now, here are the fine points: The way in which you get your discount is somewhat negotiable! At the time of purchase, discuss your options for the refund with the retailer. Depending on how much you have bought, how big a store it is, or how cute you are, you may get a more favorable situation. Here are two ways in which you can get the refund, in order of preference to the tourist:

- The retailer sells you the merchandise at the cheapest price possible, including the discount, taking a loss on income until the government reimburses him. For example: The bottle of fragrance you want costs $50. The discount is $7.50. The best possible deal you could ever get is for the retailer to charge you $42.50 flat, give you the *détaxe* papers, and explain to you that he will not get the rest of his money unless you process the papers properly. Being as honorable as you are, of course you process the papers.

- You pay for the purchase, at the regular retail price, with a major credit card. Your card is passed through a second time for a refund slip, marked for the amount of the *détaxe*. You sign both slips at the time of the purchase. When the papers come back to the retailer, the shop puts through the credit slip. The credit may appear on the same monthly statement as the original bill or on a subsequent bill. Just remember to check that the credit goes through.

With the most common method, you pay the regular retail price, with cash, traveler's check, or credit card. You're given the forms and go through the refund process as described above, get on your plane and go home. Several months later (usually about three) you get a check in the mail, made out for the refund. This check is in the currency of the country in which you made the purchase and will have to be converted to dollars and cents, a process for which your bank may charge you a percentage or a fee. Or you can go to a currency broker and get the money in the currency of origin to save for your next trip to that country. Either way, it's a pain in the neck.

A new system is sweeping EU countries—it's run by a private company, ETS (Europe Tax-free Shopping), that handles VAT refunds for all European tourists. It's more advanced and established in other countries but is just beginning to get up to speed in France. ETS opened a VAT refund service at Charles de Gaulle airport in the summer of 1996. You turn in your *détaxe* paperwork and get the refund in the cash of your choice while you wait! That's right: dollars, francs, or even yen. Look for the kiosk or ask for it—it's dressed in red, white, and blue like the French flag and says "Tax Free for Tourists."

Détaxe on Trains & Ferries

If you leave Paris by train—as I do frequently—you may be in a panic about your *détaxe* refund. Not to worry. As mentioned above, you now apply for the refund as you leave the EU. If your train is taking you to another EU country, you do not even have to think about filing for your French *détaxe* refund.

If your train (or ferry) is taking you to a non-EU country, you will need to do the paperwork on board the train. No problem. Shortly after you board the international train, the conductor for your car will poke his head into your cabin, introduce himself (he speaks many languages), ask for your passport, and give you the customs papers for the crossing of international borders. If you are on a sleeper, he handles the paperwork in the middle of the night while you sleep. If you have *détaxe* papers, provide them at this time. You can act nervous and fuss a bit, but this guy knows exactly what to do. It is customary to provide a small tip for him when you depart anyway; if he has secured your papers you may want to add to the depth of the tip.

ONE LAST CALCULATING THOUGHT

Unless you have a Ph.D. in mathematics from MIT, I suggest you keep a calculator in your purse. Furthermore, it should be the kind that uses batteries. Solar-run calculators are very cute, but your purse is dark inside, and many shops are, too. There's nothing worse than trying to do a hard bit of negotiating when your calculator won't calculate. If you use your calculator frequently, or if your children like to play with it as a toy, buy new batteries before you leave on the trip.

If you do not have a calculator with you but are contemplating a large purchase, ask the store to provide a calculator or to "run the numbers" for you. The difference between dividing by 5 and 5.3 can matter.

Chapter Four

. . . .

SHOPPING STRATEGIES

PARIS PLANS

. . . .

Unless you have scads of time on your hands, you'll find shopping in Paris involves making choices: You'll always be sorry you didn't get to one neighborhood or another; but you'll always have an excuse for returning to the City of Light. No matter how little time you have, you'll have no trouble spending your budget or finding something worth buying.

A map is called a *plan* in French, so start planning for your savings before you leave home—or as soon as you arrive at your hotel. By studying a map, you'll get a feel for the relationship between the sights you want to see, the places you want to eat, and the areas you want to shop. Make plans with your *plan* in hand or arrive with a schedule.

If you have a map at home, spend a little time doing what I do: make charts that outline each day and your goals for that day. I rarely get everything done (I go much slower than I think I will), but at least my time, my directions, my transportation, and my shopping priorities have been thought out and organized to maximize my Paris power.

Be sure to think about what kind of *métro* pass to buy, as well. Some of these are pegged to the day of the week, so pay attention before you arrive. That way, no matter how much jet lag clouds your brain on arrival, you're ready to start saving (see p. 22).

BARGAIN SMARTS
. . . .
Prices in Paris are not low, so to sniff out the bargains you're going to need some background information. The bargains go to the shopper who is ready to recognize them, and that means doing some homework.

If you have favorite designers or targets of acquisition for your trip, shop the major department stores and U.S.-based boutiques for comparison prices. Don't assume you will get a bargain on a Parisian purchase. Many international designers and retailers set prices that are virtually the same all around the world. Even so, within that structure, you can find a deal.

If you do not live in a city that has a lot of European merchandise, do some shopping through *Vogue* and *Harper's Bazaar.* In the ads for the designer boutiques, you'll find phone numbers. Call and ask about prices and sales. Don't be afraid to explain that you are contemplating a shopping trip to Europe and are doing some comparison pricing. If you live in a city that dresses conservatively, you'll find clothing in Paris to be much more vibrant and exciting. If you think creatively, you'll find a way to adapt it to your lifestyle.

Read French magazines to get familiar with the French look and the hottest shops. They can cost a fortune (sometimes $14 a magazine in the U.S.), but many libraries have these magazines. Many French magazines now have U.S. and U.K. editions that do not have the foreign advertising you want, but will keep you in touch with the look.

Understand the licensing process. Designers sell the rights to their names, and often their designs, to various makers around the world. Two men's suits may bear an identical label—of a well-known French designer—but will fit differently because they are manufactured differently.

French cosmetics and fragrances can be extraordinarily less expensive in France, or just marginally so. Know prices before you leave home. Also note that the marketing concept "gift with purchase" is pretty much an American thing. While you can find it in Europe on occasion, you won't get as good a gift. The value of the gift in the U.S. may indeed exceed the value of the discount when you buy it retail in France.

Don't be fooled into thinking that merchandise with foreign-sounding names is made in Europe, or is French, or offers a bargain. Because Americans are so taken with European names, many American-made products have foreign, especially French, names. Since the biggest rage in France these days is American-made products, don't be lured into buying something in France that could be bought at home for less.

BEST BUYS IN PARIS

· ·

Perfumes, Cosmetics & Hair Care Products   Perfume savings get to the heart-stopping level once you make the commitment to spend enough to qualify for the *détaxe* (1200 F). Beyond that, actual savings on discounted perfumes are getting hard to find, because of changing business practices in France and a united crackdown by the big-name fragrance and makeup makers to try to stop non-*détaxe*-related discounting. This is aimed mostly at French locals but may also impact you. Know your U.S. prices and understand that new laws have been passed within the last year, so that what you paid last trip, or how discounts were handled at that time, could be very different now.

I tend to buy fragrances that have just been introduced in Paris and are not yet available in the U.S. as gift items for my American friends because of their novelty value; therefore price isn't an issue.

If you find your beauty creams are no longer the bargain they once were, it may be time to visit a *parapharmacie*. These stores carry drugstore brands of beauty products—no Chanel or Yves Saint Laurent—at a 20% discount. This is the place to load up on fancy hair care products, skin creams, bath products, and possibly even face powder. Barney's New York has made Leclerc all the rage; now they have it everywhere in Paris.

Limoges Blame this one on Carolyn Bloodworth— she got the collecting bug from Princess Diana, no less. Carolyn now buys Limoges boxes in pretty shapes—fruits, vegetables, animals, and so on. Each box costs between $75 to $100 in Paris, but twice as much in the U.S.

Hermès Now that the *détaxe* requirement has been lowered, you can look like a genius if you shop at Hermès. The price of the famous scarf is 1300 F— just 100 F more than the *détaxe* requirement. I rest my case. Hermès Paris prices (with a *détaxe* refund) are definitely lower than in New York. In addition, you can frequently find Hermès bargains at various airport duty-free shops and in airline duty-free catalogs that are even better than Paris retail prices. London may also be less expensive than Paris!

Baccarat All French glassware can be dramatically less expensive in France, but the cost of shipping it abroad voids the savings. However, have you seen the Baccarat crystal medallions that hang from a silk cord? They are drop-dead chic and cost approximately $100 in the U.S. and in France. Get onto an airplane that has Baccarat in its duty-free catalog, and lo and behold, the same trinket sells for not much more than $50. This is a serious bargain. My birthday is in the middle of April. Thank you.

Candies, Foodstuffs & Chocolates These make great gifts, especially when wrapped in the distinctive packaging of one of Paris's premier food palaces. I buy Maille's tomato soup–colored "Provençale" mustard in grocery stores (no fancy wrap for me, thanks) and give it to foodies around the world—it's unique and special. I haven't found it in any U.S. specialty stores yet. Some Maille flavors are available in the U.S. (and U.K.), but not this particular one. Maille has just opened its own shop at place de la Madeleine.

I also stock up on carmelized almonds in beautiful tin boxes (under $10 [£6.50]), or create baskets containing a variety of fancy foodstuffs. Foods make fabulous gifts and souvenirs in the $2 to $10 price range.

Collectibles   It's pretty hard to give advice about the ever-changing collectibles market, but the things that catch my eye have all turned out to be bargains when I compared prices at American flea markets (why didn't I buy more?). I bought an empty postcard album—probably from the turn of the century—at the flea market in Vanves, in perfect condition, for $10. I saw a similar one in a dealers' show in Greenwich, Connecticut, for $150. I bought a funky straw hat from the 1950s for $40 and a country-style tablecloth for $5. I thought these were fair prices; I hope you'll agree.

Stockings   I have a hard time finding stockings (and tights) that are long enough for my frame in the U.S. and the U.K. Not so in France. I also like to wear a garter belt and stockings sometimes; fancy stockings (with lace border tops) are easy to find in Paris—far easier than in other countries. I can also count on the French for gorgeous garter belts; Victoria's Secret, please wake up.

Kitsch   I'll admit up front that I adore kitsch. I can't help but buy kitschy souvenirs for myself and my friends. My usual hangout for fun junk is the rue de Rivoli. Every visit I find another reason to buy a pencil with the Eiffel Tower attached by a slim gold chain, a bath sponge that looks like the French flag, a scarf with tacky illustrations of Paris's best sights, boxer shorts emblazoned with baguettes, or a T-shirt from the Sorbonne. These items are carefully priced with tourists in mind and never cost more than $10. While the more tasteful part of me wants to advise you not to load up on tacky gifts and instead save your money for something worthwhile, the truth is, I can't stop buying (and using) this junk.

LESS-THAN-STELLAR BUYS

Some things are simply not a bargain in any sense. Unless you are desperate, avoid buying:

American-made Goods   Whether they be designer items, such as a Ralph Lauren jacket or a pair of Joan & David shoes, or mass-market items like a Gap T-shirt or a pair of Levis, American-made goods are rarely good buys. Ditto for British goods (Aquascutum, Hilditch & Key, or Marks & Spencer), men's business attire, electrical goods (wrong voltage), and Coca-Cola purchased at bars, cafes, or hotels. Postcards priced at $1 or more are no bargain (see p. 27 for how you can do better), and neither are massive amounts of Disneyland Paris souvenirs. Unless they are on sale or you qualify for a *détaxe* refund (or you've just sold the movie rights to your life's story), big-name designer clothes are another less-than-good buy.

THE MOSCOW RULE OF SHOPPING

The Moscow Rule of Shopping is one of my most basic shopping rules and has nothing to do with shopping in Moscow, so please pay attention. Now: The average shopper, in her or his pursuit of the ideal bargain, does not buy an item she wants when she first sees it, because she's not convinced she won't find it elsewhere for less money. She wants to see everything available, then return for the purchase of choice. This is a rather normal thought process.

If you live in a former Iron Curtain country, however, you know that you must buy something the minute you see it, because if you hesitate—it will be gone. Hence the title of my international law: the Moscow Rule of Shopping.

Naturally you can't compare the selection in Paris to what's on hand in Moscow (Russians would swoon at the airport shopping alone) but the fundamental principle is still applicable.

When you are on a trip, you probably will not have the time to compare prices and then return to a certain shop; you will never be able to backtrack through cities, and even if you could, the item might be gone by the time you got back, anyway. What to do? The same thing they do in Moscow: Buy it when you see it, understanding that you may never see it again. But remember, since you are not shopping in Moscow and you may see the same item again, weigh these questions carefully before you go buy:

- Is this a touristy type of item that I am bound to find all over town?
- Is this an item I can't live without, even if I am overpaying?
- Is this a reputable shop, and can I trust what they tell me about the availability of such items?
- Is the quality of this particular item so spectacular that it is unlikely it could be matched at this price?

If you have good reason to buy it when you see it, do so. The Moscow Rule of Shopping breaks down if you are an antiques or bric-a-brac shopper, since you never know whether you can find another of an old or a used item, whether you can find it in the same condition, or whether the price will be higher or lower. It's very hard to price collectibles, so consider doing a lot of shopping for an item before you buy anything. This is easy in Paris, where there are a zillion markets that sell much the same type of merchandise in the collectibles area. At a certain

point you just have to buy what you love and be
satisfied that you love it.

THE INTERNATIONAL ICON RULE OF SHOPPING

And so it came to pass that I had to give a business
gift to a French businessman whom I do not know
very well. It had to be expensive (approximately
$100) and it had to be prestigious. Since I had never
had a personal conversation with him, I decided that
God had created ties for this very purpose.

I carefully shopped all the designer stores and
settled on a drop-dead chic Prada tie. It came elegantly wrapped up, complete with a card testifying
to its authenticity. However, much to my later re-
gret, I also bought a fake designer tie from a street
market for $10 and wrapped that in an Hermès box.

When it came time for the presentation of the
gifts, the businessman seized the Hermès box like a
particularly gleeful child at a birthday party and
said, "You bought me an Hermès tie. You shouldn't
have."

I quickly added that it wasn't an Hermès tie and
handed him the Prada box with great ceremony. He
smiled weakly at the Prada box, exclaimed that the
tie was very nice, and promptly forgot about it.

When I replayed the scene in my mind, I realized
that a Frenchman is interested only in French status
symbols, unlike Americans, who respond to status
items from many countries. Despite the EU and the
so-called unification of Europe, Europeans are still
regional people who want status and luxury goods
from the houses they know best. Despite the fact
that an Hermès tie and a Prada tie cost virtually
the same amount, the Prada tie was lost on a
Frenchman.

Then, it happened to me in reverse. I bought a
French tie for an American businessman who repre-
sents French hotels, figuring it was the perfect gift.
It was not, however, an Hermès tie. It was a famous

French brand, and any Frenchman would have known its status, but my American friend did not. He smiled weakly. Even as I explained to him what the tie meant and where it was from, I knew that for the same amount of money I would have looked like a genius if I'd simply bought him an Hermès tie.

So in the hope that you'll learn from my missteps, here are a few thoughts to bear in mind. First, if you have to give an international business-cum-status gift, make sure the person to whom you are presenting the gift recognizes the name you have chosen. If you must give an American gift to a European, make sure the European knows the American name. Second, the next time you complain about high prices in designer shops, think twice. Remember that these high retail prices cover the cost of international advertising and image-making, which in turn bestows importance on the gift you choose. Finally, never buy faux anything and try to pass it off as the real thing.

FRANC-LY MY DEAR

You can moan and groan about the good old days when one dollar was equal to 10 French francs, but I call that negative thinking. Instead, remember back to when the dollar was equal to four francs, which is where the equation stood for years and years. (If you are not old enough to remember, you'll just have to trust me here.)

Now that you've readjusted your thinking, things aren't looking so bad, are they? It's all a matter of perspective! The recession proved to even the French that the 1980s are over. The fanciest hotels in town (well, some of them) have lowered prices or begun to add value. Led by Claude Terrail of the famous Tour d'Argent restaurants—and I'm talking about famous tables with multistarred Michelin chefs—have added on fixed-price meals, so that just about anyone can afford to eat at the best tables in Paris.

There are tricks out there so that Paris can give you more bang for your franc than in past years. You can save on transportation, meals, and more. Combine your luxury hotel room with some down-and-dirty consumer facts and enjoy the best of both worlds. Here are just a few:

Buy Cokes and mineral water at the grocery store and keep them in your minibar. Every chic Frenchwoman in Europe carries a large tote bag with a plastic bottle of mineral water. If you really want to save money, avoid drinking Coke completely and tell your children to do the same—it's expensive everywhere in Europe. If you must splurge, enjoy one Coke in your room—after you've bought a six-pack at the market. A whole six-pack costs almost as much as one minibar Coke!

Buy food from fresh markets (one of Paris's most beautiful natural resources), supermarkets, and *traiteurs* who sell ready-cooked gourmet meals—hot or cold. You can eat a fabulous French meal for $5 to $10 per person this way. An entire rotisserie chicken, which feeds four, costs no more than $10 and can cost less (depending on the size and quality of the chicken). Pizza is another good buy.

Eat your fancy meals at starred Michelin restaurants that offer fixed-price meals. Lately, it's become trendy for hotels to acquire a one-star Michelin chef in order to attract guests and locals alike. These hotel restaurants are competing so fiercely with each other that they watch their prices carefully. You can eat a three-course gourmet meal at several one-star restaurants in Paris for the fixed price of 220 F to 250 F ($40 to $50), including tax and gratuity! Some of the most famous restaurants in Paris cost only slightly more. See page 82 for more on good deals on good eats.

Do your gift shopping either in duty-free stores (not at the airport, the Paris streets are crammed with them), *parapharmacies,* flea markets, or the *hypermarché;* don't scorn those tacky tourist traps for great $3 to $5 gift items. You can also find small gifts at Inno or Prisunic—even at *métro* stops.

ACCUMULATING RECEIPTS

Most stores, even Mom-and-Pop shops and little perfume shops, will allow you to accumulate your receipts over a six-month period until they total 1200 F, and you're able to apply for a *détaxe* refund. All department stores let you do this; most others will, too. Ask.

While few of you will be in Paris several times during a six-month period, this strategy can still work to your advantage. For example, you shop at a store on the first day of your visit, buying only a couple items. A few days later, you realize you could also use that gorgeous dress you tried on, as well as that fabulous handbag. You return to the store, with the receipt from your previous shopping spree in hand, and, if you spend enough the second time, you get your *détaxe* refund as an added bonus for good planning.

DEPARTMENT STORE DISCOUNTS & DEALS

The two major department stores in Paris, **Galeries Lafayette** and **Au Printemps,** both offer a flat 10% discount to all tourists. This has nothing to do with *détaxe* and applies to all goods in the store except in leased departments, which are usually luggage and fine jewelry. In order to get this discount, you need a coupon. These coupons are given away free in the stores, in most hotels, and even through U.S. travel agents.

COUPON BOOKS

A reader sent me a book of coupons called *Entertainment (dated), La Clé des Privilèges,* published in the U.S. by Entertainment Publications (☎ 313/ 637-8400). For $25, it offers a 25% discount at various restaurants and hotels. Tami, the reader, said that with one coupon she paid 1100 F for her room at the Hôtel Scribe instead of 2200 F, and she was thrilled. I've heard of only three or four of the restaurants that have coupons, and I think that 1100 F per night is about all you have to pay anywhere (you can even pay less at Hôtel Westminster, around the corner from the Hôtel Scribe), but Tami loved the program, so you may want to check it out.

FIDELITY CARDS

Fidelity cards are used all over the world, but seem to be particularly popular in France, especially in mid-range designer shops and *parapharmacies*. This is a small card, like a credit card, that is stamped or punched every time you make a purchase. Make a certain number of purchases or reach a total franc value and receive a discount or a gift.

SHOPPING SCAMS

Imagine my surprise one day when Pascale-Agnès grabbed the change out of my hand and began inspecting it very carefully. "We have to make sure it's not fake!" she announced.

Sure enough, there's been a flood of faux 10 F pieces; there are over eight million in circulation today. *Travel & Leisure* says the fakes are redder in color with a bad fit between the silver core and the brass edge. Pascale-Agnès says badly etched lines give away a fake, particularly the arm holding the torch, which has fuzzy edges on a counterfeit piece.

Meanwhile, many of my friends who live in Paris are complaining about being shortchanged—mostly by taxi drivers but also by vendors. Stand there and count your change. I don't think I've ever been outright cheated in a store in Paris, but I have fallen into a few shopping canyons where a smarter person might have worn a parachute.

At a perfume shop in Paris (not my regular one), I asked the price of the perfume of one of my favorite scents. The price I was given sounded fair; not a bargain, but fair. I decided to make the purchase. The entire time that I was doing this, I was assuming that we were talking about 1 ounce of perfume. I never said specifically, "What is the price for 1 ounce of Tocade?" When I got home, I discovered that I had bought a ¼-ounce bottle of Tocade in a very, very fancy, but very, very tiny atomizer.

Here's another size-count story. I priced a roll of French tricolor ribbon at the flea market at Vanves. It was a full roll; the asking price was 10 F. I had trouble arguing with that. I found a second full roll of ribbon and asked the price for two rolls. I was told 20 F. I said, "That's no bargain. I want a deal."

So the vendor offered me all of the tricolor he had in a box on the ground for 50 F. I was overwhelmed by my good fortune. I handed over the 50 F. Hours later, I took out all the rolls of ribbon and rewound them, so that each spool was filled with ribbon, just like the first two. I had four spools of ribbon, or 40 F worth!

Had I rewound the spools at the flea market, or even lined up all the spools and said to the guy, "Hey buddy, this isn't the equivalent of five spools, how about 40 F?," then I'm sure he would have gladly taken 40 F. But I was stupid.

GETTING TO KNOW YOU

Personal relationships are very important in France. People continue to do business with the same people, indeed the same salesperson, in the same stores and markets for years, even generations. This is cultural, but it also helps the customer make sure he or she is not cheated.

When you find stores you like, spend the time to develop a personal relationship. Reinforce the connection with faxes or little notes during the year, announcing when you will return to Paris. Go so far as to make an appointment, if you feel this is warranted. The more you are known, and this truly takes years of repeat business, the more chance you'll have of getting a discount or a family price, and extra perks.

DUTY-FREE SHOPPING STRATEGIES

Discount is a dirty word in France. In recent years, a few upstarts began to discount major names so that locals could get a fraction of the price breaks non-EU passport holders get through duty-free shops. These discount sources so threatened the big-name makers and department stores that makers now limit the amount of goods released to discounters and the amount of discount allowed.

Few shops use the word *discount* at all. The proper name to hide behind is "duty free." Paris is famous for its duty-free shops. It is one of the few cities in the world where there is a lot of duty-free–style shopping, not just at the airport but on city streets.

Most duty-free shops sell makeup, fragrances, and deluxe gift items—designer earrings, scarves, ties, and even pens. Some of accessories have been created specifically for the enormous duty-free business and are not sold through the designer boutiques. Duty-free stores like to tell you that they give a 40% discount. The truth is, the notion of a 40% discount is based on the days when the luxury tax on real perfume (not *eau de toilette*) was 18%. Then you were getting a 20% discount off the top and an additional 18% discount on the *détaxe*. Because France has lowered the luxury tax on perfume, the amount of the *détaxe* refund has also been lowered.

In reality, expect to get a 20% discount without too much trouble; a 25% discount, if you are lucky; and no further discount unless you qualify for a *détaxe* refund. If you do get a 25% discount and also qualify for a *détaxe* refund, your total savings will be 45%!

Duty-free shops are good places to buy fragrances and cosmetics, even though the prices on these items are controlled and may offer you little or no savings over U.S. prices, especially if you shop at discounters.

On American brands, savings are iffy.

On French brands, savings tend to vary enormously.

This is where homework pays off. Saving $1 on a Lancôme mascara is not my idea of anything to brag about. Sometimes the savings are related to the cost of the dollar. When the dollar was high, I saved $4 on a Lancôme mascara. Now the dollar is lower, and Lancôme prices are higher. Life goes on. But there are enormous savings to be made if you qualify for a *détaxe* refund and shop wisely.

Note that in the department stores, the export rebate is 13%.

SPECIAL-EVENT RETAILING

· ·

Paris is filled with special shopping events. Watch for the **Braderie de Paris,** held in December and June at the Porte de Versailles. It's rather like a church bazaar. An ability to speak French will help, but is not required. All the big designers donate items for sale; there are bargains by the ton. Ask your concierge for details and the exact dates, although the event is advertised in magazines and papers. (I know you read *Madame Figaro* when you are in town, so you probably know it all anyway.) There is easy access by *métro*.

Hermès has twice yearly sales that can only be described as world-class sporting events. Held in March and October, the exact dates of the sale are revealed only moments before in newspaper ads. The sales have become such an event that they are no longer held at the store. The average wait in line is four hours before admission; items are marked down to just about half price. Unfortunately, a code is worked into your purchase that tells the world your item was bought on sale. It is not obvious, but look for a teeny-tiny S in a scarf.

The event you really want to catch, however, is the **Biennale Internationale des Antiquaires,** the single biggest, most important antiques event in the world. It's held only every other year, usually in September, at the Grand Palais, which is roughly halfway between the place de la Concorde and the Rond Point. It's most easily reached by *métro.*

Check the design trades for the actual dates or ask your concierge. You need not be a designer to attend.

Annual antiques shows are held at the Grand Palais each year from late November through early December, and they, too, are wonderful. But if you ever make it to the big event, you will never forget it.

There are also a number of antiques shows that happen at the same time every year and become special events to plan trips around. April or May in Paris means only one thing: time for the **Brocante de Bastille.** Celebrated outside, in stalls planted around the canal at Bastille, it is truly a magical shopping affair to remember.

For information about any of the big shopping events, look in *Allo Paris* or *Figaroscope.* **The French Government Tourist Office** in New York (☎ 212/315-0888) can supply you with the dates of these special events as well.

RENTING COUTURE

In Paris for a special occasion, such as New Year's Eve or your 25th wedding anniversary? Why not rent a couture gown for that big night out? The

French do. The proper place to rent is **Sommier**, 3 Passage Brady, 10e. Since French women want only the finest quality, but are too practical to buy a couture gown for a once-in-a-lifetime formal event, they rent. If it's been your dream to wear a couture gown, you can have a very good choice for about $100 to $150.

MAKEUP & PERFUME SHOPPING TIPS

Perfume and makeup are possibly the absolute best buys in Paris. I'm talking French brands here. If you understand the ins and outs of the system and are willing to do some work, you can score gigantic savings. There will be a quiz next Friday.

Makeup in France is different from French makeup in the U.S. This is because makeup (even French brands) sold in the United States must be made according to FDA regulations, regardless of whether it's manufactured here or in France. When you get to France, the names of your favorite products may be the same or different, and even makeup with the same name may not be identical in shade. In addition, some products available in France are not sold in the U.S. at all. This can be because they haven't been launched yet or because the FDA has not approved them.

French perfume is also different in France than in the U.S., mainly because it is made with potato alcohol (yes, you can drink it—just like Scarlett O'Hara), while Anglo-Saxon countries use cereal alcohol. Potato alcohol increases the staying power of the fragrance, as well as the actual fragrance—to some small degree. If you've ever shopped for perfume in the Caribbean, you know that certain stores make a big brouhaha over the fact that they import directly from France. Now you know why that's important. The French version is considered the best or most authentic version.

Many American brands you see in France are made in France (or Europe) for the European market, such as Estée Lauder and Elizabeth Arden. You may save on these items when *détaxe* is credited to your purchase, but generally you do not save on American brands in Europe.

If you ship your beauty buys, you automatically get a 40% discount; you need not buy 1200 F worth of merchandise. But the cost of postage can be high on beauty products that are in heavy jars. The cost of shipping fragrance is surprisingly modest. Discuss shipping costs before you get into any mail-order deals.

French perfumes are always introduced in France before they come out internationally. This lead time may be as much as a year ahead. If you want to keep up with the newest fragrances, go to your favorite duty-free store and ask specifically for the newest. If you are stumped for a gift for the person who has everything, consider one of these new fragrances. The biggest spring launch comes in time for Mother's Day in France, which is usually a different day than in the U.S., but it is always in spring—May or early June.

The converse of this rule also applies. Some older scents are taken off the market in the U.S. and U.K. because the sales figures aren't strong enough to support them. These fragrances are still sold in France. I saw an American woman at Catherine doing a gang-busters business in Fidji, which she says is no longer sold in the U.S.

Finally, some scents are never brought to the U.S. at all. Guerlain is big on this.

The amount of the basic discount on perfume and cosmetics varies from one shop to the next, as does the system by which you gain your *détaxe* refund. Ask at several shops until you find a program that makes you comfortable, or simply go for a flat discount and avoid the fuss.

Chapter Five

. . . .

SLEEPING IN PARIS

ARE YOU SLEEPING?

. . . .

Some of the world's best hotels are in Paris, and it can be a positively dreamy place to stay. There's just one very frightening factor you ought to know about: You can stay in a fabulous hotel or you can stay in a terrible hotel for the exact same amount of money. The kind of trip you have is very much related to the hotel you book. Please take the time to research value and make sure you don't get burned. Also remember the importance of "The $50 Difference" (see p. 73) because sometimes you have to spend a little more to save a lot more.

When pricing hotels, especially during promotions, make sure to read the fine print and understand what you're getting. Most hotels require a minimum stay of two consecutive nights for you to qualify for a bargain price. Bear in mind as well that the price listed may be per person or per room. Also, several promotions may be offered simultaneously. Recently, Meridien was offering a promotional rate of $115 per person at the same time they were selling a double room (one room for two people) for $186.50. The $50 difference is breakfast.

Here are a few more of my hotel booking secrets:

- **Think winter.** The rack rate (the official room rate) at a luxury hotel in Paris is generally between $300 and $500 a night for a double room, or more. Don't flinch. It's rare that anyone has to pay rack rate. Paris is most attractive and most fully booked in May and June and September and October. Those are not good months to get a break on a fancy hotel room. Think December. Think January. Even February.

- **Visit in July and August.** Few Americans realize that July and August are considered dead times in Paris (locals all go to the beach), and therefore hotel rates—even at palace hotels—are ridiculously cheap. You can get a $400 room for $200 a night. Honest.

- **Work with hotel associations and chains.** Most hotels are members of associations or chains that have blanket promotions. Leading Hotels of the World offers a fabulous corporate rate at all their hotels. Most hotels have rates frozen in U.S. dollars for at least a portion of the year, especially when they are in a promotional period. These invariably have to be booked in the U.S., but usually offer incredible value.

- **Never assume that all hotels in a particular chain are equal.** Even if you are talking about big American hotel chains, such as Hilton or Sheraton, you will find hotels in every category of style and price within the same chain. Concorde Hotels, one of the most famous hotel chains in France, which has plenty of hotels in the moderate price range, also has the Crillon, one of the fanciest and most expensive hotels in Paris. By the same token, it's not unusual for a booking agent from any chain of hotels to try to trade you from one hotel in the chain to another, especially in a similar price bracket. Don't do it without knowing the properties.

Believe me, there are tons of fabulous hotels in Paris. Given the proper amount of advance notice, you should have no problem getting something great at the price you want. Once you know your favorite neighborhoods in Paris, spend some time developing your own network of nearby hotels that fit your needs and means. It is always acceptable to walk into a hotel, ask for a brochure or a tariff card, and request to see a room or two. You do not even need to tip the person who shows you around.

HOTEL CHAINS & ASSOCIATIONS

If you prefer to book all your reservations in one easy phone call, or don't want any surprises, almost every major hotel chain in the world has a property in Paris. I've found that the big American chains offer the same type of room you expect, while the smaller European chains can be very uneven in what they offer. I have listed only major chains or associations with properties in the most convenient neighborhoods for shopping.

U.S.-Based Hotel Chains

Inter-Continental: This could be the best Paris has to offer—two hotels that don't feel like members of a hotel chain, both in fabulous locations, and offering the best promotional rates in the business. You can even get frequent-flyer mileage points! While you can get a great hotel room in Paris for less than $200 per night, if you are willing to pay around $250 a night during one of their promotions (not offered year-round), you will never be sorry you went with Inter-Continental.

Both Inter-Continental hotels are great, but bear in mind that Le Grand Hôtel Inter-Continental caters to tour groups, has approximately 1,000 rooms, and can resemble Grand Central Terminal at 9am. A very stylish Grand Central Terminal, but you get the idea. The rooms are tiny. The location, especially for shoppers, is beyond sensational. The restaurants on the property are fabulous. The nearby transportation choices are the best in Paris. If you prefer a more elegant atmosphere, the Paris Inter-Continental is the right choice. ☎ 800/327-0200 in the U.S. for reservations.

Westin-Demeure: Demure little French Demeure ain't so shy anymore. This French hotel chain recently merged with Westin Hotels to offer French glamour with American reservation systems. There are five luxury properties in Paris, including my adored Hôtel Castille. Le Parc, nestled in the 16th arrondissement, is where Alain Ducasse has his new restaurant. There isn't a more chic address in town, especially for a foodie. Hotel guests do get preference for dinner reservations and can even order room service from the restaurant. The hotels are dotted across the 8th and 16th arrondissements. ☎ 800/228-3000 in the U.S. for reservations.

Marriott: In Paris, the Marriott is known as The Prince of Wales (Prince de Galles). Rather conveniently situated near the Champs-Elysées, this hotel is aptly named. Furthermore, they have frequent promotions and airline mileage packages. ☎ 800/228-9290 in the U.S. for reservations.

Sheraton: Sheraton has apparently decided to take over Paris. In their Sheraton Luxury Collection are a few former CIGA hotels, and they recently opened a spiffy new property at Charles de Gaulle airport that seems determined to kick derriere. ☎ 800/325-3535 in the U.S. for reservations.

European Hotel Chains & Associations

Relais & Châteaux: Nothing stands for luxury more than this organization representing small luxury properties all over the world. In Paris, their holdings include the Hôtel de Crillon. The phone situation is tricky, since the toll-free number works in only some states. If it doesn't in yours, call the New York number. ☎ 800/860-4930 or 212/856-0115 in the U.S. for reservations.

Forte & Meridien Hotels: Watch these hotels as the Grenada takeover is expected to influence them in the future. Grenada says they are keeping Meridien, but plan to sell some Forte hotels. Stay tuned. Hôtel Meridien Montparnasse was offering such a fabulous winter weekend promotional rate last year that they filled up and turned away guests. Definitely worth looking into. ☎ 800/225-5843 in the U.S. for reservations.

Warwick: Warwick is a very small international chain with a great deal of variety among its hotels. Hôtel Westminster in Paris is a winner as is The Royal Windsor in Brussels. ☎ 800/223-3652 in the U.S. for reservations.

Royal Monceau: A small chain with a variety of different hotels. They own the cozy Hôtel Vernet behind the Champs-Elysées as well as the rather grand Royal Monceau at the top of the Champs-Elysées. They have other properties dotted around France. Rates are guaranteed in U.S. dollars. Call Prima Hotels in the U.S., a luxury hotel booking service, for rates, reservations, and information (☎ 800/447-7462).

Sofitel: I've always been nervous about hotels represented by Sofitel because there are thousands of them, and they are very mixed. You must judge each one on an individual basis. I did, accidentally, bump into a few small, intimate three- and four-star Sofitels in prime shopping areas and thought they looked fine. Ask about Sofitel Pullman, not far from Etoile. ☎ 800/SOFITEL in the U.S. for reservations.

Concorde: Concorde is an unusual chain because it's really two different hotel chains in one: a set of drop-dead luxury hotels, which are among the fanciest in the world (Hôtel de Crillon, The Martinez, La Mamounia), and a set of perfectly fine but not as luxurious, four-star hotels. Some of these are in old buildings, in various states of repair and disrepair, and others are in brand-new, modern high-rises.

I almost always stay in Concorde hotels, but that's because I've gotten to know so many on an individual basis and can control the surprise factor. The group publishes its own guide with color pictures of each property that helps in choosing, but isn't fail-safe. You can't go wrong with the Hôtel du Louvre, one of my faves (see p. 77). The Hôtel Lutétia has a prime Left Bank location and plenty of rooms. The Hôtel Ambassador, with its split personality, half businessperson's hotel and half shopper's delight, is another one to consider. For business travelers, it's close to the Bourse, yet for shoppers, you're just one block from Galeries Lafayette. And best yet, the Ambassador has a one-star Michelin restaurant with a fixed-price dinner menu that's a good value. ☎ 800/888-4747 in the U.S. for reservations.

THE $50 DIFFERENCE

Many people book the hotel with the lowest rate, figuring it represents the best value. But frequently, a more expensive hotel—or a slightly higher package rate—turns out to be cheaper, if you add in the extras. Does the more expensive hotel have a better location that saves money on your transportation costs? Does their rate include breakfast, whereas the less expensive hotel's doesn't? The more people traveling with you (or sharing one room), the more vital this information is. Breakfast for a family of four can easily be $50. Hell, in a really good hotel, continental breakfast for two can be $50. Think also about what kind of breakfast is included. Is it a continental breakfast or a buffet? You'll notice a big difference between the two by the time lunch rolls around.

Make sure that tax and service are included in the price quoted to you as well, and then figure this into your comparison. Sometimes U.S. dollar promotions do not include tax and service. Finally,

remember that Paris has a 7 F per night room tax;
this is rarely included in any rate sheet and therefore should not be taken into consideration when
you're calculating your $50 difference.

THE GENERAL MANAGER'S SECRET
. . . .

The general manager (GM) of every hotel in the
world has only one bottom line: to sell hotel rooms.
He must book a 40% occupancy rate just to break
even. In order to fill rooms, a GM will do whatever
it takes. (Usually, there are a few palace hotels that
prefer to be empty rather than cut deals, but this is
rare.)

I am not saying that every GM will cut a deal
with you or that you should always call or fax the
general manager directly. I am saying that it pays to
go out of your way to meet the GM, especially if
you have decided to have a regular relationship with
a hotel. The GM has the ability to give you a better
rate; to upgrade you to a better room; to send you a
bottle of champagne or wine or a bowl of fruit; or
to do something else that adds an extra touch of
value to your choice. The GM has the ability to make
you feel like a valuable customer, which will always
enhance your stay.

Here's the best part: While the GM does not have
time to have breakfast with you and the kids, he
very much wants some type of relationship with you
so that you will feel a connection to the hotel and
will return. If he moves to another hotel (they
all move to another hotel), he'll want your name
and address so he can notify you, much like your
hairdresser.

If you have no time to meet the GM, write him a
follow-up letter after your visit, and wait for his re-
ply and business card. Networking pays, especially
in a competitive market like Paris. Once you have
his name and business card, the next time you want
a reservation, contact the GM directly by fax. If you

book with him and not a reservation service, the hotel saves a commission. You may turn that into a discount or an upgrade for yourself and your family.

Should you choose a hotel without knowing the name of the GM you want to approach, simply call the toll-free number of their U.S. reservations office and ask for the name (and correct spelling) of the general manager of your chosen hotel and his fax number. Hotels change general managers quite often, so verify the name if you already have one to make sure your GM is still there. If your own contact has moved on, but you want to return to the hotel anyway, write to the new GM and explain that you knew the former GM and tell what he did for you.

HOTELS IN THE 'HOOD

. . . .

I have made my own neighborhood in Paris. It's the portion of the city where the first and eighth arrondissements join, and I love it because it is the heart of the Right Bank shopping experience.

Because there are so many stores here, I usually stay at a hotel in either the 1er or the 8e. While my main squeeze has become the Hôtel de Crillon, I have, over the years, built up a list of other fabulous hotel finds in this shopping district.

When I stay here, I know my way around. I know where the local grocery store is, and I've learned all the shortcuts from the *métro* to my favorite haunts. I hate to lose valuable shopping time by learning a new neighborhood.

If my methods are too linear for you, not to worry. After spending a few days at the Hôtel Lutétia, the only grand dame hotel on the Left Bank, I was ready to give it all up and become a Left Bank person. If you are devoted to the Left Bank and don't share my enthusiasm for the Right, *pas de problem*, just see page 80.

HÔTEL DE CRILLON
10 place de la Concorde, 8e (Métro: Concorde).

Instead of raving on about how gorgeous this converted palace is, or how much fun it is to sit at the base of the Champs-Elysées and be a block from the rue du Faubourg St-Honoré, let me tell you a story that I think sums up the essence of why the Crillon is considered one of the best hotels in the world.

I arrived in Paris for a stay at the hotel and received a package from my girlfriend Jill, who lives in St-Paul-de-Vence in the South of France. I wanted to thank her, but realized I had brought the wrong telephone book with me and did not have her number. Furthermore, I knew that she uses a professional name, which is not her legal name, so she was unlikely to be listed.

Christian, the head concierge, first checked Minitel by the address (which I did know by heart), but found St-Paul too small to be cross-referenced by address. He checked under her professional name, but as I suspected, Jill had no phone listing in Minitel under that name.

Next, Christian called the concierge of the Relais & Châteaux hotel in St-Paul and sent him to Jill's home. He asked Jill for her phone number, then called back the Crillon and gave it to Christian. *Voilà!*

You tell me where you can find another concierge like that!

If you are pinching pennies, the Crillon is not for you. If you are on business or are a get-it-done person who demands the best, look no further.

How much will it cost you? At the rack rate, rooms technically begin around $400 a night, but $500 is more common. However, there are a number of packages and promotions with dollar rates. In addition, there are weekend and honeymoon specials, including one that includes dinner, which breaks down to be good value. The restaurant in the Crillon is one of the most famous in Paris; the chef, Christian Constant, is one of the most famous in the world, so it's safe to say that a stay that includes dinner is a memory in the making.

Member, Leading Hotels of the World (☎ 800/223-6800); Relais & Châteaux (☎ 212/856-0115). For reservations, call 800/888-4747 in the U.S. In France call 1/44-71-15-00; fax 1/44-71-15-02.

PARIS INTER-CONTINENTAL
2 rue du Castiglione, 1er (Métro: Concorde).

Only two blocks from Hôtel de Crillon, the Inter-Continental is an alternative, a chance to combine luxury and location, but not spend as much. Deep in the heart of the best Paris shopping, this hotel can have the best rates in town for a deluxe room if you hit it right.

The hotel has a nice old-fashioned feel that makes it comfortable without being as fancy as the Crillon. They have a million shops in the hotel and a good newsstand that I rely on, no matter which hotel I'm staying at. When they have their $279 price breaks, I can give up other faves in order to save. ☎ 800/327-0200 in the U.S. for reservations. In France call 1/44-77-11-11; fax 1/44-77-14-60.

HÔTEL DU LOUVRE
place André Malraux, 1er (Métro: Palais-Royal).

A friend recently asked me to suggest a hotel in Paris on the Right Bank that captures the core of what Paris feels like. Money was not an object, but she didn't want drop-dead fancy. She wanted funky/fancy with a great shopping location.

I sent her to the Louvre. Not the museum, the hotel.

This is a smallish, old-fashioned hotel that's a member of the Concorde group. This means you have the owners of the Crillon as your landlord and the benefit of a fabulous discount program used throughout the Concorde chain. Yes, you can get a room at the Louvre for under $200 per night.

The hotel overlooks the Garnier Opéra and is situated directly across the street from the Musée du Louvre. Its modern rooms are decorated in Laura Ashley–inspired French style. My favorite room has a gabled roof, blue-and-white *toile de Jouy* everywhere, and a gigantic bathroom with glass doors that overlook the Opéra. Another room, sort of a suite dream, had a tiny room for my son Aaron on the left, and a master bedroom for my husband, Mike, and me, but was laid out more like a mini-apartment than a hotel suite and was beautifully decorated. Both of these fifth-floor rooms are great places for those traveling with kids.

The only drawback is that tour groups have discovered it. But the location, the price, and the charm more than make up for the bother of sharing it with others. ☎ 800/888-4747 in the U.S. for reservations. In France call 1/44-58-38-38; fax: 1/44-58-38-01.

SMALL FINDS

. . . .

There are hotels that offer value outside of my regular neighborhood; below are my favorite choices. Please note that the price of a room at these hotels includes tax and service; breakfast may or may not be included. Always check (remember The $50 Difference?).

Right Bank Hotels

HÔTEL WESTMINSTER
13 rue de la Paix, 2e (Métro: Opéra).

I am a little reluctant to tell you about this hotel because it's already hard to get a room here in May, and I don't want to ruin it. Honesty insists that I shout: "Have I got a deal for you!" This hotel could be the cheapest luxury hotel in Paris. When you add in its great location (a block from the place Vendôme, a block from the Garnier Opéra), and its Michelin one-star chef, Emmanuel Hodencq, who offers an affordable fixed-price three-course gourmet meal, the deal just gets better.

Here are just a few details, so you can laugh all the way to your fax machine: The hotel is in the same building as Cartier (this beats breakfast at Tiffany's by a long shot); the rooms have just been redecorated; and the building was built in the early 1800s, with high ceilings, crystal chandeliers, wonderful moldings, wide corridors, and window boxes filled with geraniums. The lobby may not be much to look at, and some of the rooms up in the roof are tiny, but this is a find.

As at all Paris hotels, the rate varies with the season, but you can usually get a promotional rate, frozen in dollars, for $165 to $200 per night. Because this hotel is a member of the Warwick chain, it always offers *Born to Shop* readers the best rate possible. You may fax the hotel's general manager directly and request a *Born to Shop* rate. ☎ 800/ 223-3652 in the U.S. for reservations. In France call 1/42-61-57-46; fax: 1/42-60-30-66.

ASTOR HOTEL
11 rue d'Astorg, 8e (Métro: Madeleine).

My latest find is this former dump, now turned Cinderella—and what a prince! Joël Robuchon, the famed three-star chef, has left Le Parc, and now "consults" at this hotel's restaurant!

The property has 135 rooms and has been restored in resplendent 1930s style, with lots of oak and marble and a library for tea. All this splendor doesn't come cheap—the rack rate is a little over $400 a night—but this is the secret shopper's find of the moment, perfectly situated between Madeleine, place de la Concorde, and the Champs-Elysées. A Westin-Demeure Hotel. ☎ 800/228-3000 in the U.S. for reservations. In France call 1/53-05-05-05; fax: 1/53-05-05-30.

LE CASTILLE

37 rue Cambon, 1er (Métro: Tuileries or Concorde).

This is a relatively new hotel. The rooms are relatively small, but they are fresh and gorgeous, with chintz and trim and fancy bathrooms. The difference between a standard room and a deluxe room is negligible. The breakfast room is adorable. Rates vary enormously with the season, but you can sometimes make a week-long deal; expect to pay about $300 per night. ☎ 800/949-7562 in the U.S. for reservations. In France call 1/44-58-44-58; fax: 1/44-58-44-00.

HÔTEL MONTAIGNE

6 ave. Montaigne, 8e (Métro: Alma-Marceau).

Located on the toniest shopping street in all of Paris, this hotel is directly across from the five-star Plaza Athénée, yet offers elegance on a smaller scale. The rooms feel like a friendly Hilton, but since they are about $200 a night, you cannot complain. Everything is new and modern. Only 29 rooms. ☎ 1/47-20-30-50.

Left Bank Hotels

Many will tell you that you haven't been to the true Paris if you haven't stayed on the Left Bank. I have stayed on the Left Bank and generally find the hotels smaller, and the rooms smaller still. I'm personally happier on the Right Bank, with the possible exception of the Hôtel Lutétia.

HÔTEL LUTÉTIA

45 blvd. Raspail, 6e (Métro: Sèvres-Babylone).

I'm a fool for grand hotels. I adore them. I especially adore fancy old hotels. Take back your chrome and glass and steel, give me a grande dame with plaster and let me stare at the splendor. The Lutétia is the only grande dame hotel on the Left Bank, and it is right in the middle of all the best Left Bank shopping. It's also convenient to virtually everything else in Paris. If I could live anywhere in Paris, it would be right here.

The rooms are large, and some have views of the Eiffel Tower. Many have been refurbished by no less than Sonia Rykiel. As big a fan of hers as I am, I prefer the parts of the hotel that haven't been refurbished—the art deco-y older stuff.

There are two restaurants, one of which has a Michelin-starred chef and is quite famous. With Concorde's dollar rates (under $200 a night!), prices are excellent. There are also shopping and weekend packages. ☎ 800/888-4747 in the U.S. for reservations. In France call 1/49-54-46-46; fax: 1/49-54-46-00.

HÔTEL MONTALEMBERT
3 rue de Montalembert, 7e (Métro: rue du Bac).

If you want a charming but very chic hotel, in a great shopping location—search no further. There are only 50 rooms; each is decorated to the nines. While the rack rate is over $300 a night, there are packages for several nights that make it more affordable. Member, Prima Hotels. ☎ 800/447-7462 in the U.S. for reservations. In France call 1/45-48-68-11; fax: 1/42-22-58-19.

HÔTEL DE SEINE
52 rue de Seine, 6e (Métro: St-Germain-des-Prés).

Since the rue du Buci is one of my favorite streets in Paris, it's no surprise I love this small hotel nestled in the heart of the Left Bank, just half a block from the rue du Buci. They don't take credit cards, but a double room was 800 F when I last poked in; just have a few extra traveler's checks on hand. The feel is country French, but there are color TVs and all the amenities you need—even hair dryers. Left Bank hotels are always tiny, so don't expect Texas proportions. ☎ 1/46-34-22-80.

Chapter Six

. . . .

DINING IN PARIS

PARIS ON A ROLL

It's hard to get a really bad meal in Paris. The trick is to find a good meal that's not too expensive. You can count on me to have a nosh at every crêpe stand I pass; I've even been to McDonald's and am not ashamed to tell. I stand by that old tourist standby, **Café de Flore.** While it may cost $13 for coffee and croissants for two, it beats the $50 I'd have to pay for the exact same breakfast at my fancy hotel. And there's nothing better than the early morning air, a French newspaper, and a seat in one of the world's greatest theaters to start your day.

I eat a lot of pizza; pizza places are easy to find in every neighborhood. One of my favorite chains is **Pizza Express,** with two outlets in the 1e, 10 rue Cambon and 259 rue St-Honoré. They open at 7:30am, so you can easily get a fresh croissant or a low-cost breakfast, in addition to a quick pizza lunch. I also eat at **Venus Pizzeria,** 326 rue St-Honoré, which is not as deep into the big-name shopping district as Pizza Express but is convenient to the Louvre.

I eat a lot of picnics bought from grocery stores I pass by as I wander; you can shop the grocery stores of the rue du Buci or the rue Cler any day of the week.

I've also tested the offerings in the food court at Le Carrousel du Louvre, which is an American-style shopping mall attached to the Louvre. It's on a mezzanine level above the stores, and the food is great. My favorite is **Hector, le Poulet.** On a recent visit, Ian and I had a superb lunch there. We purchased a bottle of wine (from the wine-and-cheese vendor— wine is not sold at Hector's), two bottles of mineral water, and two chicken meals for $20.

I cover additional simple, fast, and affordable lunch and dinner choices below. Of course, I also love to eat at Michelin-starred restaurants, particularly when my schedule's more leisurely and I can order off a fixed-price menu and save. So you'll find my favorite formal dining choices listed below as well. In these listings, if both a fax and phone number are provided, you may want to fax ahead for a reservation. These restaurants are in greater demand than others.

SNACK & SHOP

If you are out alone or merely want a quick, easy lunch so that you can continue your explorations of Paris (and your shopping), perhaps you want to stop by any of these addresses.

Please note that I pick a "Snack & Shop" location based on a combination of factors: location in relation to good shopping, degree of visual stimulation, price, and quality of food. If you want to eat every meal in a Michelin one-star restaurant, or if you plan your day around where you'll have lunch, these suggestions may not be for you.

Right Bank

SALON DE THÉ BERNARDAUD
11 rue Royale, 8e (Métro: Concorde).

If you follow no other tip from me in your life, you owe it to both of us to please visit this restaurant, preferably for tea. But you can also have breakfast, lunch, or dinner.

What's so special about tea here is how it's served. You are brought a silver tray laden with tea cups. Pick the pattern you like best and your tea—and snack or meal—will be served in this pattern. Isn't that just the best gimmick ever? Especially since Bernardaud is one of the finest makers of French porcelain in history.

You can get here one of two ways. Step directly behind the Crillon (for the back approach), or walk through the small Galerie Royale mall. If you arrive via the mall, you'll see just a few seats. You can take your tea here or move to the dining area inside with celadon-colored ragged walls. Don't forget to buy an ashtray for 50 F when you leave. Open Monday through Saturday, 8:30am to 7pm.

ANGELINA
228 rue de Rivoli, 1er (Métro: Concorde or Tuileries).

If you've ever heard of Rumpelmayer's, the famed New York ice-cream parlor, then you'll understand the idea behind Angelina—a Parisian tea room opened by René Rumpelmayer in 1903. Famous for its hot chocolate, the restaurant also happens to be a great place for breakfast, lunch, or dinner. Salads and easy snacks are a breeze; pastries and desserts are simply the house specialty.

Prices are low to moderate; there is a fixed-price full meal, but I usually order a salad or light fare, so I can go for a dessert. They open for breakfast at 9:30am and are located in the first arrondissement, a great place to shop that's convenient to the rue de Rivoli and the Louvre. Since this is one of the most famous places in Paris, you may want to make a reservation. ☎ 1/42-96-35-60.

CAFÉ MARLY
Palais du Louvre, 1er (Métro: Musée-du-Louvre or Tuileries).

Once before you die, you have to eat, or have coffee, at the Café Marly overlooking the I.M. Pei pyramid in the courtyard of the Louvre. You may sit outside, weather permitting, or in any of the small salons filled with smoke and well-heeled locals. Despite its nature, this cafe serves locals as well as visiting firemen. Off-hours are less crowded; yes, you can sit with a coffee for hours, and pay only for the coffee. Light lunch is easy to do, be it a hamburger or a salmon platter. Open daily, 8am to 2am.

LA CHOPE DES VOSGES
22 place des Vosges, 3e (Métro: St-Paul).

If you're shopping the Marais, this is the place for you. Located right on the place des Vosges—in the heart of the Marais—this visually charming restaurant offers lunch and dinner, or simply tea, which is served from 3 to 7pm. With its old-fashioned front, stone interior, and wood beams, this is a cozy multilevel space. Lunch is about $22. You don't really need reservations for lunch. ☎ 1/42-72-64-04.

CHEZ CLÉMENT
123 ave. des Champs-Elysées, 8e (Métro: F-D-Roosevelt).

This is more for the family or a large group; it's a lively, silly place decorated with forks and knives and terrific Provençal fabrics. It serves bistro-style food—any dish can be ordered on an all-you-can-eat basis. I love the ambience and the food; I don't love every branch, so stick to this one. ☎ 1/47-01-13.

Left Bank

LA COUR ST-GERMAIN
156 blvd. St-Germain, 6e (Métro: St-Germain-des-Prés).

This is a regular spot for lunch or dinner on the Left Bank, although there are branches elsewhere in town. This is that adorable French restaurant you planned to enjoy, and it's not expensive! Part of a chain, they serve a fixed-price meal, which I consider French fun for the common man. It suits me just fine. The Left Bank address is a bit touristy and can get crowded; lunch is about $15 to $20 per person. You can choose from eight different menus. Dessert is extra. At prices like this, with such cute decor, I can handle some tourists. Call for reservations. ☎ 1/43-26-85-49.

DESIGNER & RETAIL DINING

For the last few years, the fanciest designer boutiques in Paris have been adding cafes or small restaurants for shoppers, right on the premises— often in the midst of the shopping experience. The trend was started by Lanvin, but has been picked up by several other designers and is spreading to regular retail.

Check out: Lanvin's **Café Bleu,** 15 rue du Faubourg St-Honoré, in the men's shop, lower level. On a recent visit, I went for the brunch, while Pascale-Agnès had terrific ravioli. Courrèges has **Café Blanc,** 40 rue Françoise, open Monday through Friday from 7:30am to 7pm. On the tony avenue Montaigne, there's **Joseph,** at no. 14.

Teens and 'tweens may prefer **Virgin Café,** 156 ave. des Champs-Elysées, although a serious lunch for two can run $40 per person.

DEPARTMENT STORE DINING

The major department stores, which make a true effort to bring in tourists of all nationalities, have restaurants geared to a quick meal or a well-earned coffee break.

Au Printemps
64 blvd. Haussmann, 9e (Métro: Chausée d'Antin).

Café Flo, on the 6th floor, is actually a chain of restaurants and food shops with an excellent reputation; it has taken over the space directly beneath the cupola at Printemps to offer easy meals. You can indicate your choice by pointing to a photo. Lunch starts at 59 F; there is also an 89 F menu that includes wine.

GALERIES LAFAYETTE
40 blvd. Haussmann, 9e (Métro: Chausée d'Antin).

There are several restaurants in the store. In summer, you can eat on the seventh-floor terrace. On the sixth floor is Le Grill, a sit-down restaurant, as well as a self-service cafeteria, Le Relais des Galeries. There's a branch of the famous Angelina on the third floor, as well as the very chic Lina's Sandwiches on the first floor. If you'd rather surf than shop, try the Internet Café on the first floor of the men's store. You can also grab a bite at the grocery store Lafayette Gourmet, right next door.

SAMARITANE
2 quai du Louvre, 1er (Métro: Musée-du-Louvre or Hôtel-de-Ville).

At Toupary, this very French department store's restaurant, only dinner is served. You'll understand why as soon as you enter: The lights and view are spectacular. Designed by the American designer Hilton McConnico, who is the rage of Paris design, this is a special place. Reservations are essential. ☎ 1/40-41-29-29. Closed Sunday.

FAMOUS FOOD HALLS

· ·

While it's easy to take home a picnic from any of the famous food halls, most of them permit you to dine in as well.

HÉDIARD
21 place de la Madeleine, 8e (Métro: Madeleine).

This gastronomical house of wonders was redone a
few years ago in a series of small dens and salons.
Now the displays of everything from fresh and
dried fruit and wine to spices are as tantalizing as
ever. Upstairs is a very chic restaurant. The spicy
entries (and there are plenty) are marked, as this is,
after all, a spice house. Reservations are advised.
☎ 1/43-12-88-99. Closed Sunday.

FAUCHON
26-28-30 place de la Madeleine, 8e
(Métro: Madeleine).

In its several storefronts, Fauchon has plenty of
places where you can buy lunch or foodstuffs to go.
Upstairs at no. 30, there's a lovely restaurant called
Le 30; call to reserve a table (☎ 1/47-45-60-11). In
the basement, there's a small cafe. Closed Sunday.

LENÔTRE
48 ave. Victor Hugo, 16e (Métro: Victor-Hugo).

Although famous for its chocolate, Lenôtre has a
salon for everything—chocolates, gourmet foods for
dinner parties, cocktail nibbles, coffee, and more.
You can have a meal or a snack.

MUSEUM DINING
· ·

Now almost all Parisian museums have gift shops;
many have cafes. Most Paris museums are open on
Sunday, but closed one day a week. French national
museums all have the same closing day, Tuesday.

   Check out: **Le Grand Louvre,** in the Louvre.
Closed Tuesday, but otherwise open from noon
to 3pm and 7 to 10pm. **Café Marly,** on the
Louvre property, see above. **Café Beaubourg,** 100

rue St-Martin, right across from the Centre Pompidou—an alternative to the top-floor cafe within the museum itself. **Musée d'Orsay Restaurant,** 1 rue de Bellechasse, closed on Tuesday, but otherwise open from 9am to 6:45pm.

And don't miss **Les Monuments,** in the Palais de Chaillot, which houses three museums (but no madwoman). My buddy Christian Constant, from Les Ambassadeurs in the Hôtel de Crillon, has taken over the food situation there.

GROCERY STORES

. . . .

There are grocery stores situated in neighborhoods frequented by tourists, so unless you're staying in one of the outlying arrondissements, you won't have to go out of your way to get to one. All the best shopping neighborhoods also have their share of grocery stores, so you can easily buy a picnic or do some of your souvenir shopping in one. The markets listed below are big modern supermarkets chosen for their location; you will be near one or all of them as you explore Paris. And don't neglect any Monoprix or Prisunic you come across.

Left Bank

INNO
*31 rue du Départ, 14e (Métro: Montparnasse/
Bienvenue).*

They have a running joke with me at the Crillon: I am the only guest at this super-posh hotel who also shops at Inno, a combination dime store/grocery on the Left Bank. I love it for its full basement grocery department with prepared foods, its excellent wine and champagne area, and the bakery upstairs. Check out the automated track for the shopping carts. It's something you'll see elsewhere in Europe, but not in the U.S.

MONOPRIX GOURMET
50 rue de Rennes, 6e (Métro: St-Germain-des-Prés).

This recently became a more upscale branch of Monoprix to befit the rising stature of the street address and the fact that Giorgio Armani has moved in next door. Don't be fooled by the small street-level space; downstairs is an entire world of food shopping. Open Monday through Saturday, 9am to 9pm.

LE GRAND EPICERIE
Le Bon Marché, 38 rue de Sèvres, 7e (Métro: Sèvres-Babylone).

This grocery store is actually part of Le Bon Marché, although it is housed in a separate building from the mother store. (There's a flea market upstairs!) In the street-level grocery, you'll find everything imaginable, including Fauchon and regional food-stuffs from all over France and the EU. There's a good wine and champagne department, a bakery, and prepared foods. Don't mind the other American tourists.

Right Bank

LAFAYETTE GOURMET
52 blvd. Haussmann, 9e (Métro: Chausée-d'Antin).

This store has its entrance above Monoprix. Go through the glass doors and upstairs. You can do your gourmet grocery shopping here, as well as have lunch; there are various serving areas in a circle surrounding a kiosk. Despite its location near the fancy food temples along the place du Madeleine, this store is just as fancy, but not nearly as expensive as Fauchon or Hédiard. Don't miss it for the world. Open Monday, Tuesday, Wednesday, Friday, Saturday, and Sunday, 9am to 8pm; Thursday, 9am to 9pm.

PRISUNIC CHAMPS-ELYSÉES
109 rue de la Boetie, 8e (Métro: F-D-Roosevelt).

Prisunic grocery stores are not as fancy as Gourmet Lafayette, the chain of grocery stores owned by Galeries Lafayette, but they are usually in handy places and can supply basic needs. This branch is open late, usually until midnight in summer and 10pm in winter. You'll also find Prisunic grocery stores in both of their retail stores: Prisunic St-Augustin, place St-Augustin (*Métro:* St-Augustin); and Prisunic Printemps, right behind the Printemps store on blvd. Haussmann (*Métro:* Chausée-d'Antin).

THE DISCIPLES
· ·

If you keep up with the latest chefs, then you are probably into the group of young chefs I call The Disciples. They trained with the most famous chefs in France and are now out on their own. A meal with them costs less than at one of the restaurants at a palace hotel and will put you on the cutting edge of table talk.

LES BOOKINISTES
53 quai des Grands-Augustins, 6e
(Métro: St-Germain-des-Prés or Odéon).

Alec took me here; I've been spreading the word ever since. The chef trained with Guy Savoy, and this restaurant is one of several in the Savoy Group. A fixed-price two-course lunch costs just over $25 per person (without wine), whereas a three-course lunch is about $35. Reservations are imperative. ☎ 1/43-25-45-94. It's closed for lunch on Saturday and Sunday.

LES ELYSÉES DU VERNET
Hôtel Vernet, 25 rue Vernet, 8e
(Métro: F-D-Roosevelt).

This restaurant is small, intimate, and formal, with a ceiling designed by Gustav Eiffel (yes, that Eiffel). The chef was trained by none other than Alain Ducasse; he has two Michelin stars. A complete lunch is about $65 per person; a dinner, about $70. It's located right behind the Champs-Elysées, so don't let the address throw you. In fact, you can get there easily if you cut through **Chez Clément** (123 ave. des Champs-Elysées), another restaurant favorite of mine. Fax ahead for reservations with as much notice as possible. ☎ 1/44-31-85-69.

LE JARDIN
Hôtel Royal Monceau, 37 ave. Hoche, 8e (Métro: Étoile–Charles-de-Gaulle).

Located on the far side of l'Étoile, the restaurant is in a garden, as the name implies. In winter, it's sort of like a gazebo inside a rocket ship; in summer, the doors open to reveal the garden setting. This chef also trained with Alain Ducasse; he has one Michelin star. Lunch is about $56 per person; dinner, $67. Book by fax, 1/42-99-89-92.

Chapter Seven

. . . .

RIGHT BANK SHOPPING NEIGHBORHOODS

THE BASTILLE IS UP

. . . .

Paris is a city of neighborhoods. Thanks to the Seine, there are Right Bank neighborhoods and Left Bank neighborhoods, and then all those arrondissements. But don't make the mistake of assuming the word *arrondissement* is synonymous with "neighborhood." Single arrondissements can hold several distinctly different neighborhoods, and there are neighborhoods that straddle portions of two or more arrondissements.

This chapter covers the best shopping neighborhoods on the Right Bank; the following chapter features the best shopping neighborhoods on the Left Bank. Since I tend to be a Right Bank person, this chapter comes first. But as the Left Bank may be the most exciting news on the Paris shopping scene, you won't want to miss it, even if, like me, you've always considered yourself a Right Bank type.

Now that we've got that straight, a few words about orientation. I tend to categorize sections of arrondissements into separate neighborhoods by their landmarks and stores. The Bronx may not be up and the Battery may not be down in this town, but the way I look at it, the Bastille is uptown and the Arc de Triomphe is downtown.

As a tourist, you'll probably stick to a dozen or so neighborhoods that are must-see, must-return-to areas. Some you visit just for their shopping, but most you wander for everything they offer—sights, shopping, dining, and more. There are streets that fulfill all your fantasies of what Paris should be. While the city limits of Paris may sprawl all the way to the highway loop Périphérique (and beyond), my parts of town are compact and easy to manage. See chapter 11 for shopping tours; in this chapter and the next, I give you an overview of the best of Paris.

RIGHT BANK ARRONDISSEMENTS

The First (1er)

The 1er is a prime shopping area, with several high-rent neighborhoods and four main districts: Louvre, Halles, Palais-Royal, and Vendôme (Tuileries).

You'll find the city's fanciest designer boutiques on the **rue du Faubourg St-Honoré** (which actually crosses into the 8e), and some wonderful boutiques on the **rue St-Honoré**. But it's also where you'll find tourist trap heaven (the **rue de Rivoli**) and some of the city's best museum shops, including the mall of the **Louvre**. Not to mention a big antiques center (right across the street from the mall) and the **Palais-Royal**. The most amazing thing about the 1er is its diversity of shopping opportunities.

The Second (2e)

The 2e is called Bourse and consists of four areas: Gaillon, Vivienne, Mail, and Bonne-Nouvelle. It is mostly a business district—basically the Wall Street of Paris—with some border areas for shoppers.

You may not find yourself in the 2e unless you are doing business or have the heart of a *garmento* and want to visit the **Sentier,** or garment center. There are tons of little wholesale-only shops in the Sentier, where if you have nerve you can ask if they'll sell to you. (Many will.) Glamorous, however, it is not.

The **Galerie Vivienne** is in the 2e; this is one of the most famous *passages* in Paris and is at the edge of place des Victoires. There are also a few hidden upscale treasures in and around here. Victoires is on the border of the 1er and 2e, and it is one of the highlights of Paris because of its designer and avant-garde shops. Kitchen supply houses (see p. 236) are here as well. You'll find them near the mall **Forum des Halles,** but also near rue Étienne Marcel, which is chockablock with designer stores. Many of the big-name jewelers on the far side of place Vendôme (**Cartier** and so on) are in the 2e, even though the 1er is across the street. All in all, the 2e has a good bit to offer.

The Third (3e)

Nicknamed either Temple or Marais, the 3e has become popular with the renaissance of the **Marais** and the **place des Vosges** (on the border of the 3e and 4e). This is a must-do experience. To most visitors, the 3e *is* the place des Vosges, not just the square itself, but the tiny, curvy little streets, arcades, shops, and offbeat finds all around it. It's everything you've dreamed Paris would be.

There's also a big covered market called the **Carreau du Temple,** where you can find old clothes (*fripes*) and some nice handcrafted items. It's open every day except Monday. When you're here, don't get confused between rue du Temple and boulevard du Temple. Boulevard du Temple, and the part of the neighborhood that backs up to place de la République, is a middle-class neighborhood with a good number of discounters and rather shabby outlets that probably aren't worth investigating, especially if you are a rue du Faubourg St-Honoré kind of customer.

The Fourth (4e)

This neighborhood backs up on the Marais and the place des Vosges and is a very grand and wonderful place to live. Not far away there is a famous and very colorful old Jewish neighborhood.

The **Village St-Paul** is here (antiques galore), and you are a stone's throw from the Bastille and the new opera house. Once you cross the boulevard Bourdon at the canal, you are in the 12e, but never mind, you are now in an area of town considered very *branché* (with it). The 4e also includes the **Île St-Louis,** whose local church is the **Cathédrale de Notre-Dame.** There is some very pleasant tourist shopping near the church.

The Eighth (8e)

The 8e, which is nestled between the 1er and the 16e, connects the rue du Faubourg St-Honoré with the **Champs-Elysées,** thus stretching right across some of the best shopping in the world. To me, the real soul of the 8e lies directly behind the Hôtel de Crillon, where you have not only the rue du Faubourg St-Honoré, but also the boulevard de la Madeleine, and the tiny rue Boissy d'Anglas, which is now packed with great stores stretching from the Crillon all the way to the place de la Madeleine.

The Ninth (9e)

The 9e sits on the far side of the 2e and is famous to most of the world as the location of the Opéra. But if you like to shop, it should be famous to you as the home of the big department stores, including the two French icons **Au Printemps** and **Galeries Lafayette.** There's also a giant **Marks & Spencer,** the Dutch owned **C&A,** and branches of the dime stores **Monoprix** and **Prisunic.** Does anyone need more?

Originally, the 9th owed its fame to the St-Lazare train station, which brought shoppers to the big department stores on boulevard Haussmann. Meanwhile, a new train connection and a new mall (**Passage du Havre**) are opening by the end of 1997 to make this area even more fun for shopping.

The Tenth (10e)

Wholesale, did you say you like wholesale? Well, the 10e is one of the many wholesale neighborhoods in Paris. It's known for its fur, glass, china, and coiffure suppliers, but also for its hookers, hoods, and dealers, particularly around St-Denis. It has a strong ethnic mix as well.

Not one of your must-see, must-write-home-about areas. Both the **Gare du Nord** and the **Gare de l'Est** are in the 10e, as is the **rue de Paradis**—a street filled with shops selling glass and china and crystal and, yes, those little Limoges boxes.

The Eleventh (11e)

République is a middle-class neighborhood. There are some discounters, but mostly this is not a neighborhood you would go out of your way to shop in, simply because there is little that is special here. The furniture business stretches along the **rue St-Antoine,** but it's not the kind of furniture you're looking for.

The Twelfth (12e)

This is the arrondissement of the moment—gathering no moss as it rolls across Paris from the far side of Bastille toward Gare de Lyon. The biggest news here is the **Le Viaduc des Arts,** a very long stretch of street under an elevated train track that has been turned into boutiques and artisan's workshops. Not far away is the **place d'Aligre,** with a great food market and a small flea market. You can walk from the Le Viaduc des Arts to place d'Aligre.

Tons of American artists live around here; the area is quite hip. But this is a very large arrondissement with a lot of different neighborhoods. What you get around the place de la Bastille is very different from what you get down the street at Ledru-Rollin (Jean-Louis Scherrer outlet store) and dramatically different from other parts.

Primarily, it is design, art gallery, and furniture territory. For bargain hunters, a not-so-touristy but terrific place to shop is the place d'Aligre. An open market, **Beauvau St-Antoine,** fills the streets every day except Monday until 1pm. It backs up to a covered market of the same name. At the open market, vendors sell fruit and vegetables, flowers, and *fripes.* Meat, fish, and fowl are sold in the covered market. It's a very "real people" neighborhood, not at all glamorous or quaint, but intensely French. The entire area is wide open on Sunday until 1pm. This is also where you'll find **Betty** (see p. 171).

The Sixteenth (16e)

To many Parisians, there's only one arrondissement in Paris, and its number is 16. The districts are Auteuil, Passy, Chaillot, Muette, and Porte Dauphine. What more could a yuppie want?

Rue de Passy is a terrific find for someone who wants to shop and see the real Paris, as experienced by the BCBG (*bon chic, bon genre*) crowd who hangs out in this district. The well-heeled residents of the 16e have their own park, the Bois, and it's very chic to live close to the park. More important, the 16e has lots of resale shops. The 8th and the 16th bump heads over couture shopping—*ooh la la.*

The Seventeenth (17e)

Another fashionable district, or at least parts of it. The acceptable neighborhoods for the BCBG set are Péreire, Ternes, and Monceau.

The Eighteenth (18e)

You've heard of the 18e because it includes **Montmartre.** Other districts are Clignancourt, Pigalle, Chapelle, and Goutte-d'Or. This is a very scenic part of Paris, a part that tourists like to visit in order to confirm their fantasies of Paris, and also the site of some of the fabric markets that design students haunt. (All students of shopping also know that Clignancourt means flea market in French.)

While the 18e was once charming and famous (*Irma la Douce* was shot here), now it is a less-than-charming place. The **place du Tertre,** near Sacré-Coeur, is crammed with tourists and con men. **Tati,** the famous French discounter, was so unchic for years that now it's chic. The fabric markets of St-Pierre near Sacré-Coeur (and Tati) are wonderful, but very funky. In fact, the 18th is funkiness personified.

The Nineteenth (19e)

This is really getting out of the swing of things, especially when you get to Villette, the part of this arrondissement that's at the edge of the highway that encompasses Paris. There's no shopping reason to visit.

The Twentieth (20e)

Maurice Chevalier made this area famous when he sang about Ménilmontant, but other than that historical fact, there isn't too much going on in this residential neighborhood, inhabited by people who can't afford high rents in other parts of town.

The famous Père-Lachaise cemetery is here; the only piece of retailing advice I have regarding the cemetery is to make sure you buy a map of the gravestones; otherwise, you will never find Jim Morrison's.

SHOPPING NEIGHBORHOODS
· ·

Luckily for the visitor, the prime shopping areas in the sprawling city of Paris are concentrated in a few neighborhoods. Despite the fact that many new stores come on board each year, the really good ones are smart enough to open in existing high-traffic areas.

The neighborhoods below are listed in rough geographic order, starting with the eighth arrondissement and fanning outward along the Right Bank. I've deferred a bit to tourist timetables. Let's face it: Everyone wants to go to Notre-Dame. You may as well know how to shop your way there.

Because there is so much to see and do in Paris, the best way to tackle the city is by neighborhood. Decide which museums and monuments you care about, and what kind of shopping experiences are important to you personally. Then use a map to see how the pieces all fit together to maximize your day.

I consider lunch, and tea, an essential part of the shopping experience, and you'll find recommendations in each neighborhood description. For more information on these picks and others, see chapter 6.

When it comes to shopping in Paris, you must decide if you are just looking or if you actually want to buy something. Do you want a fantasy experience or a real-people French experience? Do you mind crowds of tourists, or would you prefer to be surrounded by the people whose home you have invaded? Is your time so limited that you just want the one address that will give you the most value? Please answer these questions for yourself as you read up on my favorite shopping districts and browsing treats.

Allons.

Champs-Elysées, 8e

Métro: F-D-Roosevelt.

Shopping Scene: Teenage heaven.

Where to Have Lunch: Chez Clément, 123 ave. des Champs-Elysées, ☎ 1/47-20-01-13.

Where to Have Tea or Coffee: Virgin Café, Virgin Megastore, 156 ave. des Champs-Elysées.

I will tell you right up front in my all-too-American way: If you skip the Champs-Elysées, it's okay with me. The charm is mostly (but not completely) gone. I mean, when Richard Branson brought his Virgin Megastore to the Champs, it actually did a lot to liven things up. Now that Disney has moved in, I have to shrug and say, "There goes the neighborhood." Of course, I've been saying this all over Paris.

The neighborhood isn't gone; it's just different. It's become very teen-oriented; even Yves Saint Laurent moved out. The sidewalk has been widened to allow for more strolling, and everything is kept clean and neat. I just don't think it's the real Paris.

Should you decide to tackle the Champs-Elysées despite my opinions to the contrary, start at Rond Point. If you are standing at the Rond Point and looking straight ahead to the Arc de Triomphe, the good side of the street for shopping is on your right. You can begin at a shopping gallery called **Galerie-Elysées Rond Point,** which is a rather modern shopping mall not unlike one in your home city, except that it has only 16 shops.

Along the way you'll see numerous car showrooms, perfume showrooms, drugstores, airline offices, cafes, and change booths. A few big-name designers have stores here; **Galerie du Claridge**—another mini-mall—has two levels (go downstairs, too) and has the best selection among the kind of shops you want to see, most of them are big-name designers.

In two big blocks you'll be at **Prisunic.** If you travel with your children, don't miss this location for cheap clothes, cheap toys, and the grocery store on the downstairs level. Even if you don't travel with children, don't miss this store for cheap fun makeup, plastic shopping totes, grocery giftables, and fun novelties. Note that this store is open until 10pm in winter and until midnight in spring and summer.

If time is precious, you might want to make sure you've paid homage at **Prisunic** (109 rue La Boétie), pressed your nose (and toes) to the glass at **Charles Jourdan** (68 ave. des Champs-Elysées), and made a hearty tour of **Light** (93 ave. des Champs-Elysées). Light is one of those stores that, on first glance, you're ready to pass over, but on second glance, you realize you've misjudged. Its young, kicky (often cheaply made) clothes are trendsetters. This is affordable street fashion from the best street. The store is a known resource for buyers and designers from around the world.

If you want to walk from the ridiculous to the sublime, just cross to the other side of the Champs-Elysées and cut over two blocks to avenue Montaigne, the single most prestigious address a store can have in Paris. This is an easy walk, unless you have already done your grocery shopping at Prisunic or have two dozen jars of Maille mustard in your handbag.

Avenue Montaigne, 8e

Métro: F-D-Roosevelt or Alma-Marceau.

Shopping Scene: The rich, the chic, and the insatiably curious.

Where to Have Lunch: Joseph Café (fun, quick, inexpensive), 14 ave. Montaigne, ☎ 1/47-20-39-80; **Maison Blanche** (expensive, chic, great view), 15 ave. Montaigne, ☎ 1/47-23-55-99, fax 1/47-20-09-56; **Fermette Marbeuf** (Disney French), 5 rue Marbeuf, ☎ 1/47-23-31-31.

Where to Have Tea or Coffee: Joseph Café, see above.

You want the Paris that dreams are made of? You want stores that are drop-dead fancy, where the women who patronize them wear couture and carry little doggies under their arms? Little doggies with couture hair ribbons, right? You want architecture and trees with little lights in them, and even a view of the Eiffel Tower? *Ici.*

The avenue Montaigne has become a monument to itself. **Dior** and **Ricci** have always been here. For years, the **Chanel** boutique was a secret jealously guarded by those in the know. Then **Louis Vuitton** built its glitzy flagship store here, and Montaigne became the mega-address it is now. **Escada** has moved in, as has **Inès de la Fressange**, with her Henri Bendel look-alike salon. **Krizia** recently moved here. The shopping pace continues to quicken.

One stroll down the two blocks of retail in this short street will give you a look at these famous names, as well as **Harel** (for gorgeous shoes), **Loewe, Thierry Mugler, Ungaro, Porthault, Céline, Christian Lacroix**, and **Valentino**. Some of the other stores are old-fashioned French shops that deserve a visit just to soak up atmosphere; try **Au Duc de Praslin** (a candy and nuts store) and **Parfums Caron** with its giant glass bottles filled with perfumes.

Rue du Faubourg St-Honoré, 8e

Métro: Concorde.

Shopping Scene: Tourists with their noses pressed to the glass; rich regulars from out of town.

Where to Have Lunch: Café Bleu, Lanvin Homme, 15 rue du Faubourg St-Honoré, ☎ 1/44-71-32-32.

Where to Have Tea or Coffee: Bernardaud, 11 rue Royale, ☎ 1/42-66-22-55.

During the recession, when rents were low and storefronts stood begging, some new faces moved into this otherwise pricey real estate, so the feel to the street has changed. The Gap hasn't opened here, but it's more commercial than it used to be.

Façonnable has moved in, but so have **La Perla** (jazzy lingerie and bathing suits), **Diego della Valle** (JP tods), and even **Lolita Lempicka. Didier Lavilla,** the darling of the affordable-yet-chic-nylon-handbag set, has taken space here as well, yet **Hermès** remains the single most important address.

Are you actually going to buy anything on the Faubourg? That's up to you and your budget; surely during a sale period, you've got a good shot at it. And yes, I've found affordable items at Hermès. If you've never been before, you simply have to go, if only once.

Now then, one tiny grammatical point from someone who doesn't speak French. The word *faubourg,* a noun, means small street. There are thousands of addresses in Paris that carry the word *faubourg.* Because of the fame of this particular faubourg, it is often referred to merely as "the Faubourg."

Rue St-Honoré, 1er

Métro: Concorde or Tuileries.

Shopping Scene: Locals and smart shoppers who love to poke around and enjoy.

Where to Have Lunch: Ladurée (an old-fashioned French tea room), 16 rue Royale, ☎ 1/43-29-40-99; or **Pizzeria Venus** (a neighborhood pizza joint), 326 rue St-Honoré.

Where to Have Tea: Ladurée, see above; or **Angelina** (an icon tea salon), 226 rue de Rivoli, ☎ 1/42-60-82-00.

This is not your typical neighborhood. In fact, you may not have realized it exists, or you might think it's part of the Faubourg, even though it's not. This is my secret Paris. From the Hôtel du Louvre, where it is funky and neighborhoody, to the rue de Castiglione, where it begins to get hoity-toity, to the rue Royale, where it becomes super-fancy and eventually turns into the rue du Faubourg St-Honoré, this is the real Paris. It's authentic and untouristed, especially the totally hidden place du Marché St-Honoré.

Plenty of designer shops are located on the rue St-Honoré (**Laura Ashley, MCM, Lacoste**), but the area also offers quite a few Mom-and-Pop retailers. The farther you get from the rue Royale, the more casual the neighborhood gets. Be sure to wander onto the tiny place du Marché St-Honoré with some designer and would-be designer shops, as well as several food shops and groceries.

Get a look at places like **Biberon & Fils** (334 rue St-Honoré), which is actually an office supply store. Stand far enough back in the street to get a look at the entire storefront. It is preserved just as it was in 1836 and is often featured on postcards and in movies.

If you're out on a stroll, take the rue St-Honoré to the Comédie Française. Here you can hang a right and go to the Louvre; or take a left and shop in the arcades at the Palais-Royal, moving right along to Victoires and the 2e. Or you can hit the rue de Rivoli and circle back toward Concorde while you visit all the tourist traps and stop by Angelina's for tea. The arcade of the Palais-Royal is the essence of all Paris retail to me. You can have your Faubourg. I'll play the Palais.

Victoires, 2e

Métro: Palais-Royal.

Shopping Scene: Chic trendsetters.

Where to Have Lunch: Le Grand Véfour (weekdays only; expensively divine and famous), 17 rue Beaujolais, ☎ 1/42-96-56-27; fax 1/42-86-80-71.

Where to Have Tea or Coffee: A Priori Thé (cute and perfect), Galerie Vivienne, ☎ 1/42-97-48-75.

If you want to have a wonderful shopping experience that's very French, very uptown, and quite special, this is it. But it's not easy to reach, and you'll need to walk quite a bit. For example, the *métro* station I've given above, Palais-Royal, is a ways from where this neighborhood starts at the place des Victoires. That said, this neighborhood between neighborhoods is a sensational stroll.

You'll find the place des Victoires nestled behind the Palais-Royal, where the 1er and the 2e connect. Facing the place is a circle of hôtels; the ground floor of each has been converted to retail space. The spokes of streets shooting out of the place represent various retail streets as well, and they are filled with more wonderful shops.

Rue Étienne Marcel is the major drag, and it has long housed some of the big *créateurs* (designers). You can save this area for last, and depart the neighborhood by browsing this street before heading toward the Forum des Halles or the Beaubourg. Or you can start your stroll from the Étienne-Marcel *métro* stop and work backwards.

Between place des Victoires and the Palais-Royal (a distance of only a few blocks), you've got the rue des Petits-Champs, which has a lot of show-rooms and charming shops on it, as well as the Galerie Vivienne, one of Paris's famed *passages,* the covered alleys of stores that were the first mini-malls.

As for the place des Victoires itself, there's **Kenzo** and **Cacharel** and **Thierry Mugler,** but you will enjoy simply going from door to door around the circle and then branching out into the small streets. **Victoire** is one of the most famous names in France for ladies who want a pulled-together chic look that's just right. Don't miss **Henry Cottons,** an Italian, Ralph Lauren, weekend-chic sort of place with great architecture. Although the address is written as place des Victoires, the entrance is on the rue Étienne Marcel.

Don't forget to check your trusty map before you leave Victoires; because the location is so superb, you can continue in any number of directions. You can easily walk to the Forum des Halles or Opéra, or to the boulevard Haussmann and the big department stores, or simply to the rue de Rivoli and the Louvre. The world starts at Victoires, and it's a magnificent world.

Sentier, 2e

Métro: Bourse.

Shopping Scene: *Garmento.*

Some people have printer's ink in their veins; I've got garment center in my blood. If you do, too, you may want to go from Victoires into the Sentier—the wholesale garment district in Paris.

From place des Victoires, follow rue d'Aboukir, which leads you from the 1er into the 2e. Be forewarned: The Sentier may not be your kind of place; it sure ain't fancy here. This area is very much like New York's Seventh Avenue—men with pushcarts piled high with fabric, little showrooms that may or may not let you buy from them, hookers in certain doorways, junk in bins, metal racks and forklifts, and mannequins without arms.

There are few big-name designer names here, and there are no guarantees that you will find what you want. Any time you want to buy something in the Sentier, simply play dumb American: Ask the price and see what happens. For the most part, the area is closed tight on weekends. A few shops are open on Saturday, but Saturday is not the day to tour the neighborhood and see it all. Sunday is totally dead.

If you're not sure about exploring this neighborhood in depth, you may want to walk from place des Victoires on the rue Étienne Marcel. It'll give you a chance to take in designer shops, some wholesale places, and land you right at the rue Montmartre, for more *garmento* shopping before you move on to the mall Forum des Halles and the Beaubourg.

You'll also get the wholesale kitchen stores on this route (see p. 236), as well as **Mendès,** which is worth looking at if you've ever dreamed of owning anything with those little YSL initials. Also note that Mendès now makes Christian Lacroix and Claude Montana, so there should be quite a selection.

Rue de Rivoli, Part One, 8e–1er

Métro: Concorde, Tuileries, or Musée-du-Louvre.

Shopping Scene: International tourists.

Where to Have Lunch: Angelina (salads and pastries), 226 rue de Rivoli, ☎ 1/42-60-82-00; Food Court, Le Carrousel du Louvre (an American-style food court, but great), 109 rue de Rivoli.

Where to Have Tea: Café Marly (once, before you die), **Louvre**, 93 rue de Rivoli, ☎ 1/49-26-06-60.

The rue de Rivoli is the main drag that runs along the back side of the Louvre. Since the Louvre was once a fortress, you will understand why it seems to go on forever. They just don't build them like that anymore. Exit the *métro* at Concorde and face away from the Eiffel Tower. You are ready to walk. I call this part of the street "Part One" because it is the main tourist area. The rue de Rivoli continues after the Louvre, but has an entirely different character. Part One has a few chic shops on it toward the Hôtel de Crillon end, but soon becomes a good street for bookstores, such as **W. H. Smith & Son.** As you get closer to the Louvre, the stores get more and more touristy. Yep, there's tons of tourist traps here, all in a row.

Rue de Rivoli, Part Two, 1er–4e

Métro: Musée-du-Louvre or Hôtel-de-Ville.

Shopping Scene: Real.

Where to Have Lunch: Le Carrousel du Louvre (see above).

Where to Have Tea or Coffee: See the Marais, page 116.

The touristy stuff ends at **Le Louvre des Antiquaires,** but the street itself—rue de Rivoli—continues forever and has many stores on it. By the time you get up near the Hôtel de Ville, there's the giant department store **BHV,** which has a basement filled with wonderful hardware and gadgets for the home. Then there's another giant department store, this one with four parts, **La Samaritaine.** Check out the Inès de la Fressange home decor department, Magasin 2, on the fifth floor, and the brand-new street-level perfume department. Keep strolling along the rue de Rivoli, and you'll find one of my faves, **à l'Olivier,** at no. 23.

The rue de Rivoli will change names to become the rue St-Antoine, leading directly to the Bastille. Along the way there's some junk shops and discounters, as well as the path to the place des Vosges and/ or the Village St-Paul.

Jean-Paul Gaultier has just opened a shop on rue St-Antoine (no. 30); this is **Galerie Gaultier,** a new concept that has all sorts of designs (clothing and products for the home) in one space; there are similar stores in London and Tokyo. It's a long hike all the way from BHV to the Bastille, but it can be very rewarding. See page 115 for the Bastille neighborhood, which connects directly to this one, if you're strong enough to keep on walking.

Place Vendôme, 1er

Métro: Tuileries.

If you're looking for a neighborhood that says "Paris" and reminds you with every breath that they don't make 'em like this anymore, get yourself over to the place Vendôme, conveniently located between Opéra and rue de Rivoli. It's a subneighborhood of rue de Faubourg St-Honoré and rue St-Honoré, so you'll be eating elsewhere but dreaming here.

Formerly one of the finest residential areas in Paris, the place Vendôme is surrounded by old hôtels that now house either jewelry shops, banks, insurance companies, or all three. There's also a hôtel of the type you spend the night in—the Ritz. Besides the big jewelry firms, like **Van Cleef & Arpels** and **Cartier,** some ready-to-wear kings have moved in— like **Giorgio Armani, Natori,** and even Armani's **Emporio.** Natori is a little hard-to-find, but it's on the rear side of the Chanel jewelry store. (You do know, *cherie,* that Chanel now makes the real thing as well as costume, don't you? And that it, too, has a jewelry store in this 18-karat neighborhood.)

The far side of the place Vendôme is the rue de la Paix, which dead-ends two blocks later into Opéra. There are more jewelers here (and even a Burma, if you like to buy copies of what you have just seen) and a few other retailers. Don't confuse **Charvet** (a men's store) with **Chaumet,** a jeweler. It just so happens that there are several tony men's haberdashers on this street—everyone from **Alain** (Figaret) to **Zegna.** Figaret is not quite as famous as others in the neighborhood but is a local hero nonetheless.

The **American Express** office is on rue Scribe, right beside Opéra. How convenient.

Department Store Heaven, 9e

Métro: Chausée-d'Antin.

Shopping Scene: In summer, a zoo. At other times of the year, middle- to upper-middle-class French from the suburbs and out of town.

Where to Have Lunch: Lafayette Gourmet or **Au Printemps;** see pages 86–87.

Where to Have Tea or Coffee: Lafayette Gourmet or **Café Flo,** see above. There's also a branch of Angelina, the famous tea shop known for its hot chocolate, at **Galeries Lafayette.**

On the other side of the Garnier Opéra, and on the other side of the world from place Vendôme, is the boulevard Haussmann, where several department stores have their headquarters. This three-block-long and two-block-deep jumble of merchandise, push-carts, strollers, and shoppers is a central trading area. I frequently call it "the Zoo." If you insist on seeing it, go early in the morning (10am), when you are strong. Winter is far less zoolike than summer.

Check out **Lafayette Gourmet,** the grocery store attached to Galeries Lafayette—it's fabulous and located above **Monoprix.** The other department stores, lined up in a row here, are **Marks & Spencer** and **Au Printemps,** which sits opposite. Then you've got **Monoprix** and four buildings housing various parts of Galeries Lafayette.

Boulevard Haussmann hits the rue Tronchet a block after the string of department stores. Take a left and walk two blocks to the place de la Madeleine, where **Fauchon** and many other food landmarks are located. After you have finished up here, put the Madeleine at your back and turn right at Gucci for the Faubourg, or walk straight ahead for place de la Concorde and the Crillon.

Place de la Madeleine and the rue Royale are lined with big-name stores, including **Polo/Ralph Lauren** and the showrooms for the glass and porcelain shops. A new mini-mall is just blossoming due, no doubt, to the success of the American-style mall **Les Trois Quartiers.** Now this area is a big mall destination; there's branches of **Kenzo, Weill, Chacok, Body Shop, Marina Rinaldi, Burma, Dorothée Bis, Agatha, Mondi, Georges Rech, Rodier Homme, Stéphane Kelian,** and a huge perfume shop called **Silver Moon. Le Cedre Rouge,** sort of the French version of Pottery Barn, anchors the newer mall space across the street from **Les Trois Quartiers.** If you continue along the rue Royale, it brings you to the place de la Concorde. You haven't done it at all if you don't stop into **Bernardaud** for tea. If you're not too tired, please make time for **Hidden Madeleine** (see p. 112).

Several areas overlay each other near here, and can be considered one big neighborhood.

Madeleine, 8e

Métro: Madeleine.

Shopping Scene: Upscale international.

Where to Have Lunch: Hédiard, 21 place de la Madeleine.

Where to Have Tea or Coffee: Fauchon Bar, 30 place de la Madeleine.

Believe it or not, the shopping opportunities that surround the place de la Madeleine are so rich, it can be considered a separate neighborhood. Although there are a few designer shops here, the heart of this area is the famous food shops that stand almost in a row—**Hédiard, Fauchon, Nicolas** (the wine shop), **Maison de la Truffe,** and more. Almost all of these stores have many opportunities for you to eat; you can come back for lunch every day and try a new place. Fauchon has several places to eat, including a charming restaurant, one flight upstairs, and a coffee shop on the lower level (SS). Most of these food stores sell take-out food as well.

Hidden Madeleine, Parts One and Two, 8e

Métro: Madeleine or Concorde.

Shopping Scene: Secret chic.

Where to Have Lunch: See "Madeleine," immediately above.

Where to Have Tea: Bernardaud, 11 rue Royale, ☎ 1/42-66-22-55.

Part One: The **rue Boissy d'Anglas** is the street that runs behind the Hôtel de Crillon, from the place de la Concorde right past **Hermès,** down to the place de la Madeleine. It's kind of narrow and doesn't see that many tourists. What it does see are a lot of chic fashion editors and in-the-know types who pop in and out of their favorite stores, secure in the thought that the tourists are on the Faubourg and haven't caught on.

If you cut through the Passage de la Madeleine, just off the place de la Madeleine, which begins with a very good duty-free perfume shop (see p. 205), it leads you right to the chic part of the rue Boissy d'Anglas. Walk toward Concorde, to your left. Don't stop till you get to the Passage Royale, which will lead you to tea at Bernardaud.

Part Two: I've nicknamed **rue Vignon** "Honey Street," because it is the home of the **Maison de Miel,** one of the leading specialists in French honey. This street runs on the other side of **Fauchon,** just as the rue Boissy d'Anglas runs behind Hédiard. Vignon has a few other smaller clothing shops on it as well as other places I like to explore. It's chic without being touristy.

Victor Hugo, 16e

Métro: Victor-Hugo.

Shopping Scene: Chic, French, and rich . . . with dogs.

Where to Have Lunch: Maison Prunier (decadently chic and expensive), 16 ave. Victor-Hugo, ☎ 1/44-17-35-85, closed Monday.

Where to Have Tea or Coffee: Lenôtre (famed chocolate and pastry house), 48 ave. Victor-Hugo, ☎ 1/45-02-21-21.

When Jacqueline Kennedy Onassis lived in Paris, she lived on the avenue Foch, supposedly the fanciest residential street in Paris. It stands one spoke over from Victor-Hugo, one of the fanciest shopping streets in an uptown residential neighborhood. Years ago, many big-name international designers had shops here. Most of them have moved, giving the neighborhood an intimate feel. Most of the shoppers here today appear to be regulars who live nearby. This isn't the kind of street you visit to actually shop; you come here to get a feel for a certain part of Paris, with a lifestyle that is totally unknown in America.

Passy, 16e

Métro: Passy or La Muette.

Shopping Scene: Rich casual, with a black velvet headband and pearls.

Where to Have Lunch: Le Toit de Passy, 94 ave. Paul-Doumer, ☎ 1/45-24-55-37.

Passy is the main commercial street of one of the nicest districts of one of the nicest arrondissements in Paris. It has a little of everything and is convenient to other neighborhoods. You can visit Passy on your way to the Eiffel Tower, to Trocadéro, or to the resale shops of the 16e, or you can catch the *métro* and be anywhere else in minutes. If possible, do Passy on a Saturday morning because then you will really be French.

The street has been booming ever since **Passy Plaza,** an American-style mall with that number-one American tenant, The Gap, opened. Go to Passy Plaza for a lesson in French yuppie sociology. Shop the supermarket in the lower level, shop the various branches of American and British big names, and go to the French candy store. Check out **Franck et Fils,** a swanky department store, and **Sephora,** a cosmetics supermarket that will make you swoon if you've never been to one before. **Sephora** (no. 50) isn't a duty-free store, but it has an immense selection of brands. **Prisunic** also has a branch on Passy. There are numerous big-name boutiques that range from **Descamps** to **Max Mara.** This is a fun, let's-pretend neighborhood: You can stroll the street and pretend you are part of the French upper middle class.

Shopper's tip: When you get to the end of Passy (where the Max Mara shop is located), you'll find a back street called rue Paul-Doumer. If you love home furnishings, tabletop, and good design, you'll find a few winners along this tiny street (there's a branch of **Souleiado**). Forget about shopping this neighborhood on Monday until at least the afternoon.

Bastille, 4e–12e

Métro: St-Paul or Bastille.

Shopping Scene: Hip.

Where to Have Lunch: Bofinger (legendary Paris bistro), 6 rue de la Bastille, ☎ 1/42-72-05-23.

Don't look now, but Bastille is getting to be chic. Dare I say it? People are losing their heads over this up-and-coming neighborhood! A tad too far uptown for general retail, Bastille is benefiting from the rebirth of the Marais, one arrondissement over, and the ugly, but renowned, new opera house. The artists have moved in; so have the Americans (to live, not to set up shop). Long known for its home furnishings stores, the district is now taking on some galleries and interior design shops of note.

To see it all, take the *métro* to either St-Paul or Bastille. You can walk along the rue St-Antoine toward the column in the center of the place de la Bastille. This gives you the real-people view. If you want a more glamorous view, walk along the Seine, then cut in toward the Opéra along the residential boulevard Bourdon.

Once you've gotten to the opera house, you want to walk uptown along the rue Daumensil toward Gare Lyon, because that's where the real story is— **Le Viaduc des Arts,** an enormous restoration project. Here, the arches under a train viaduct have been filled in with boutiques, showrooms, and artisans' shops. You can also take the Ledru-Rollin *métro* here, which puts you conveniently near the **Jean-Louis Scherrer** discount shop. If you continue uptown, following the viaduct all the way, you will be deep into the 12e and can then walk to **place d'Aligre.**

Alternatively, you can head in the other direction from the far side of the place de la Bastille, past Bofinger. Continue on to the rue St-Antoine, where there are some discount houses. You can follow the signs to the **place des Vosges** from here, or you can visit the antiques market around St-Paul (**Village St-Paul**), or you can walk straight to the **Hôtel de Ville** and BHV.

Marais/Place des Vosges, 3e–4e

Métro: St-Paul.

Shopping Scene: Fabulous, funky fun.

Where to Have Lunch: Le Loir dans la Théière (cute and charming, serves a light lunch), 3 rue des Rosiers, ☎ 1/42-72-90-61.

Where to Have Tea or Coffee: Mariage Frères (seriously cute and famous), 30 rue du Bourg-Tibourg, ☎ 1/42-72-28-11.

The rebirth of the Marais is no longer news, but new shops continue to open here, making it a pleasurable area to explore every time you visit Paris. Take the *métro* to St-Paul and follow the signs toward place des Vosges. Or taxi to the **Musée Picasso** and wander until you end up at the place des Vosges.

The area between the church of St. Paul and the Seine hosts the **Village St-Paul** for antiques. The Marais lies nestled behind the other side of the rue St-Antoine and is hidden from view as you emerge from the *métro.* You may be disoriented when you come above ground. I've gotten lost a number of times. That's why taking a taxi here is a good idea. There's also no hint of charm until you reach the Marais.

While the heart of the neighborhood is the place des Vosges, this is a pretty big neighborhood with lots of tiny meandering streets that you can simply wander. Take in designer shops like **Popy Moreni** and **Issey Miyake** in an arcade that surrounds the place. The side streets are dense with opportunities:

from the chic charm of **Romeo Gigli** to the American country looks of **Chevignon.** In between there's a bunch of funky little shops selling everything from high-end hats to vintage clothing. Check out antiques at **Les Deux Orphelines** (21 place des Vosges) and modern, contemporary housewares and style at **Villa Marais,** 40 des Francs Bourgeois. Many stores are open on Sunday afternoon, but the entire area is dead on Monday.

Montmartre, 18e

Métro: Anvers.

Shopping Scene: Uphill, it's touristy; down by the *métro,* it's discount heaven, but very declassé.

Where to Have Lunch: There are many touristy cafes around the place du Tertre; I'd leave the neighborhood for lunch.

Mon Dieu, what a schlep! Ian and I investigated the famous place du Tertre in Montmartre, where the artists supposedly hang out, and were royally ripped off. On the other hand, Pascale-Agnès and I went to **Tati** and the various stock shops and fabric markets of St-Pierre and had the time of our lives. It's all possible in this shopping neighborhood and, if you leave out the touristy part, you don't have to climb too many stairs.

I'm not certain which facet of the adventure came closer to giving me a heart attack—the number of stairs we climbed to get to the church, or the fact that the portrait artists run price scams. Ian and I were told "150," which we assumed was French francs ($30), but our portrait artists were quoting U.S. dollars. After handing over our caricatures, they demanded $150 for each! It was a very unpleasant (and expensive) scene.

You'll be far happier if you skip the portraits and touristy parts and head for the soul of Paris: Tati and the down-and-dirty discount shops that rarely see the face of a tourist. Take the *métro* to Anvers.

Chapter Eight
· · · · · · · ·

LEFT BANK SHOPPING NEIGHBORHOODS

RIVE GAUCHE
· ·

To many, the essence of Paris is the Left Bank. I see it as several different villages—all with different personalities—nestled together. If you're the type who just likes to wander, go to the 6e and spend the day, or even the week. If your time is precious, perhaps you'd like to use my method of coping. After all, Gaul may be divided into three parts, but I've divided the Left Bank, an area of one or two arrondissements, into several.

In other words, there's more to the Left Bank that just the 6e. I don't happen to like the 5e that much—it's too full of students and funk for my taste—but I adore the 7e. My part of the 7e can easily connect to the 6e, so I have listed it below as if it were a subdivision of the 6e. Purists, forgive me.

LEFT BANK ARRONDISSEMENTS
· ·
The Fifth (5e)

This is the famous **Latin Quarter,** or student quarter, which is also called Panthéon. It's filled with little cafes and restaurants; it's paradise for book-hunters. There are shops selling *fripes* and jeans, as

that seems to be all that people around here wear.
This is the funkiest part of the Left Bank, just above
the chic part of the boulevard St-Germain.

The Sixth (6e)

With the enormous changes in retail that have taken
place in the 6e, you'd think I'd say "There goes the
neighborhood." Instead, one of Paris's best shopping districts has simply become better. This is one
of the most Parisian arrondissements for tourists and
shoppers. It's often called Luxembourg, because
the Jardin du Luxembourg is here, or St-Germain-
des-Prés, because of the church and boulevard of
the same name. Let's just call it heaven and be done
with it.

The district has everything. On the **rue de Buci,**
there's a street market piled high with fruit, vegetables, and flowers that's great for picking up
picnic supplies. Prices tend to be higher than at other
street markets in Paris because of the number of
tourists who shop here, but it's so luscious, who
cares? The antiques business is also clustered here,
and there are a number of one-of-a-kind boutiques.
But the area is no longer small and funky. Led by
Sonia Rykiel, who came in years ago, a herd of
major designers—**Louis Vuitton, Hermès, Christian
Dior**—has moved into this prime real estate. Their
shops are tasteful (and then some!) and respect-
ful to the soul of the neighborhood. Even the
American-style mall at the **Marché St-Germain** is
an addition to the neighborhood. And, of course,
many of Hemingway's favorite cafes and haunts are
here. This is a prime place for sitting at a sidewalk
cafe, watching all of Paris walk by, and having the
time of your life.

The Seventh (7e)

Difficult to get around because of its lack of *métro*
connections, the 7e is a mostly wealthy residential
area, with just a handful of shopping addresses.

The real story here is the **rue Cler,** which reigns as the street for serious food. Foodies from all over the world work this two-block street, take notes, taste everything, and discuss their finds for years. The main shopping streets are the **rue de Grenelle** (which is also partially in the 6e) and the **rue St-Dominique.** There are many small shops for rich ladies who just can't go so far as the crass rue du Faubourg St-Honoré or the crasser still avenue des Champs-Elysées.

The portion of the 7e that lies next to the 6e forms an invisible barrier much like that between the 1er and the 8e on the Right Bank; it is impossible to know where one begins and the other ends. The closer you get to the 6e, while still being in the 7e, the more you are in an enclave of hidden good taste. My favorite part is the **rue du Bac,** which lies partly in the 7e and partly in the 6e. It is crammed with wonderful shops for the neighborhood's rich residents—there's everything from fancy pastry shops and linen shops to fashion boutiques and tabletop temples. Chicer still is the **rue du Pré-aux-Clercs,** which took me years to discover. Along one block, some of the best talent in the world is lined up on both sides of the street. Shhh, don't tell the tourists.

The Thirteenth (13e)

One of the largest arrondissements in Paris, the 13e is mostly residential and of little interest to tourists. Its districts are Italie, Gobelins, and Austerlitz. Part of it is is known as the French Chinatown. You can pass.

The Fourteenth (14e)

Looking for a Sonia Rykiel outlet store? Step this way. The 14e is home to the rue d'Alésia, a street of several bargain shops, including the Sonia Rykiel outlet store. There's also a great flea market nearby (place de Vanves). Montparnasse—in all its high-rise glory—is here if it interests you. I use the tall skyscraper of Montparnasse as a beacon to guide me to **Inno** (see p. 172).

The 14e is large and has many districts—some are nice, others are not. The stock shops and the flea market should be your primary reasons to visit the 14e; although parts of the 6e do back right up to the 14e, so you can easily branch off to the Latin Quarter from here.

The Fifteenth (15e)

A piece of the 15e touches the back side of the Eiffel Tower, near the Paris Hilton. Rue de la Convention is a main drag. The Porte de Versailles is just beyond, and there are tons of commercial streets all around this portion of the neighborhood. See page 129 for some neighborhood shopping tips to this special part of town.

THE NEIGHBORHOODS

. . . .

The Left Bank is not very large; there is much overlap between its neighborhoods, and only the sophisticated eye will catch the nuances between some of them. You can use the St-Germain-des-Prés *métro* stop for all of these areas and select a lunch or tea stop from any of the choices I give below. You will find, however, that it's a pretty long schlep from one end to the other; I certainly cannot do it in a day, and I would not want to pick a lunch spot that was two miles from my afternoon shopping choices.

If you have no particular plan, at least look at a map, pinpoint the suitable *métro* stops, and decide where you want to be around noon. Not to sound like a major princess, but I most frequently stay on the Right Bank with the Concorde *métro* stop as my home base. I often arrange my patterns of exploration so that I end up going out of the Left Bank at the end of the day either through the Sèvres-Babylone *métro* stop or the rue du Bac *métro* stop, because then I don't have to change trains to reach Concorde. At the end of a hard day's shopping, especially if you are laden with packages, you might want to forego a long, complicated journey on the *métro*.

If you prefer a taxi, it can be difficult to flag one down in this area. Go either to the **Hôtel Lutétia** or to the taxi rank in front of **Emporio Armani** on boulevard St-Germain. Note that the traffic on the boulevard St-Germain moves one way, uptown.

Many of the restaurants I recommend for lunch are places first introduced to me by fellow journalist Alexander Lobrano, who lives on the Left Bank and keeps up with the latest chefs and their newest dishes.

St-Germain-des-Prés, 6e

Métro: St-Germain-des-Prés.

Shopping Scene: Young, hip, and busy, but somewhat touristy.

Where to Have Lunch: La Cour St-Germain, 156 blvd. St-Germain, ☎ 1/43-26-85-49.

Where to Have Tea or Coffee: Les Deux Magots (if it was good enough for Hemingway . . .), 170 blvd. St-Germain, ☎ 1/45-48-55-25; **Café de Flore** (ditto), 172 blvd. St-Germain, ☎ 1/45-48-55-96.

The main drag of the left bank is the boulevard St-Germain; the center of the universe of this neighborhood is the church St-Germain-des-Prés. Have a taxi drop you at the church (or take the *métro*, no sweat), and you'll have arrived at the center of all the action.

You can begin the day with breakfast coffee and croissants at any number of famous bistros, like **Les**

Deux Magots or **Café de Flore.** Sure, a cup of coffee costs $5 and continental breakfast is $15, but you can sit for hours and watch the passing parade. Nothing is more French.

Those who can afford the rent on the boulevard have their stores clustered around here. In addition to Etro, Armani Emporio, and other big names, there's **Sonia Rykiel** at no. 175 and **Shu Uemura,** a fabulous Japanese cosmetics firm, at no. 176. More than anything, the big names have revitalized the area and made it even more important for you to know what's happening here. **Inès de la Fressange** may have closed shop in this part of town, but everyone else is moving in. Also, there are several bookstores, artsy postcard and poster shops, a number of cafes, even a small but packed *parapharmacie.* You'll certainly have no trouble finding a cafe for coffee or a meal. If you are headed for the most famous places, try to eat at early or odd hours, especially if you want a seat with a view.

Behind the Church, 6e

Métro: Odéon or St-Germain-des-Prés.

Shopping Scene: Busy locals; less touristy than the main areas.

Where to Have Lunch: Allard (a local bistro, with few tourists), 41 rue St-André-des-Arts, ☎ 1/43-26-48-23.

Where to Have Tea: À la Cour de Rohan, cour du commerce St-André, 59–61 rue St-André-des-Arts, ☎ 1/43-25-79-67.

My favorite part of the 6th is located behind the church of St-Germain-des-Prés. Behind the church you'll find place de Furstemberg, rue de Buci, rue Jacob, rue Bonaparte, rue de Seine, rue du Bac, and Quai Voltaire. Many of these streets house antiques and decorating shops; and, of course, the rue de Buci offers a street market (open Sundays!), where flowers and food are sold in profusion. This is a must-do Paris stop; let those who appreciate a visual scene come feast their eyes.

These streets are mostly filled with boutiques, bakeries, eateries, markets, and—the fame of the neighborhood—antiques and design showrooms. It is very quaint back here, and the stores feel different from the ones in the other parts of the Left Bank. This is one of the most charming areas in all of Paris.

Rennes Central, 6e–14e

Métro: St-Germain-des-Prés, St-Sulpice, or Montparnasse/Bienvenue.

Shopping Scene: Real-people Montparnasse (14e) leads to touristy Left Bank.

At one of the major intersections of the Left Bank, two streets converge in a "V"—the rue de Rennes and the rue Bonaparte. Bonaparte runs behind the church as well; rue de Rennes does not. Rue de Rennes is the central drag of this trading area. It's a pretty big street with a lot of retail; the farther away it reaches from St-Germain, the less fancy the stores become. When you get to the branch store of **Tati,** you're more or less at the end of the glamour. Rue Bonaparte, a very nice street for strolling, is sort of smaller and runs off at an angle. See page 125 for a description of this area, which feels neighborhoody and very different from rue de Rennes.

Rue de Rennes has a big-city feel, so it isn't exactly the charming Left Bank kind of place you were expecting. Closer to boulevard St-Germain, but on rue de Rennes, there are many big-name designer shops, from **Céline** to **Conran's Habitat,** as well as **Guy Laroche, Stefanel, Courrèges, Kenzo,** and **Burberrys.** A number of hot-shot boutiques, such as **Loft,** and new trendsetters like **Estéban** (for homestyle) at no. 49, are also here.

As you move away from the boulevard St-Germain, there's still plenty to enjoy, but fewer designer stores. Teens can have **Morgan,** while I'll take **Geneviève Lethu** (no. 95) for tabletop and fresh fabric ideas. If you stay on rue de Rennes a mere block past St-Placide, you'll be at **Tati.** This is a branch store of Tati, not nearly the experience of the mother ship (see p. 140), but I can only tell you that no real shopper in the world would miss a trip to this discount hell on earth. If Tati turns you off, that's okay. There are plenty of days I just don't feel up to it either.

Whatever you do, don't bail out until you've shopped at **Inno,** a place that always makes my heart sing—it's a dime store/grocery store.

Little Dragons, 6e

Métro: Sèvres-Babylone or St-Germain-des-Prés.

Shopping Scene: Trendy.

Where to Have Lunch: Le Bamboche, see page 127; or **La Cour St-Germain,** see page 122.

Where to Have Tea: Bon Marché or Hôtel Lutétia.

To the right of Rennes Central (if your back is to the church) are several very small, narrow streets crammed with good things to eat and to wear. They are epitomized by the rue du Dragon, which is why I call this neighborhood Little Dragons. But you'll also want to check out rue de Grenelle and rue des Sts-Pères. This whole warren of tiny streets is crammed with great shops, many belonging to designers of fame and fortune (**Ferragamo, Sonia Rykiel Enfant, Philippe Model**).

This area is sandwiched between the Sèvres-Babylone *métro* stop and the neighborhood I call Rennes Central. To one side is **Le Bon Marché,** one of Paris's biggest and most famous department stores. You can also easily walk to St-Placide from here.

St-Sulpice, 6e

Métro: Mabillon or St-Sulpice.

Shopping Scene: Chic.

Where to Have Lunch: La Cour St-Germain, see page 122.

Where to Have Tea: Gérard Mulot, pâtisserie, 76 rue de Seine, ☎ 1/43-26-85-77.

The core of this area is between rue Bonaparte and the place St-Sulpice. It comes complete with a gorgeous church, a park, several designer shops (**Christian Lacroix, Castelbajac**) and some picture-postcard places. But it stretches over to the rue Tournon and the rue de Seine, and even includes the newish American-style mall, **Marché St-Germain.** The side streets are full of small designer shops, some with names you've heard of—like **Souleiado** and **Les Olivades**—but many more with names that are largely unknown to Americans and exciting to discover.

Although I hated the mall when it first opened, I've now gotten used to it and even pop in there every now and then. There are several branch stores of English multiples, such as **Monsoon** and **The Body Shop;** there's **The Gap** and a few French chain stores including **Koba,** which sells nice underwear. There's a rather well-stocked *parfumerie* as well, but on my last visit, they were having trouble under-standing the changes in the *détaxe* law, so you might want to make sure they are up to par before you buy anything.

Along the rue St-Sulpice, before you get to the park, you'll find all the kinds of shops you came to Paris to visit, including a store run by the magazine *Elle* (no. 30), which features items they also sell by mail-order from the U.S., and **Maison de Famille** (no. 29), which is adorable inside but does sell many items imported from the U.S. Both stores have upstairs levels to them, so don't miss any of the nooks or crannies.

Rue du Bac, 7e

Métro: Sèvres-Babylone or rue du Bac.

Shopping Scene: French Left Bank snob.

Where to Have Lunch: Le Bamboche, 15 rue de Babylone, ☎ 1/45-49-14-40.

Where to Have Tea or Coffee: There's a coffee shop of no particular charm, but much convenience above the grocery store (**Grand Epicure**) at **Le Bon Marché.** Take the escalator up to the first floor.

As a residential neighborhood, you can't beat the 7e—not even in the 16e. As a shopping neighborhood, you can't beat the rue du Bac, especially if you like looking at the lifestyles of the rich and Parisienne.

You can get here two ways: the easy method or the longer, more complicated, but more fun method. For the former, take the *métro* to rue du Bac and walk away from the river on rue du Bac. (See, easy.) For the latter, begin on the Right Bank, cross the bridge at the Louvre (see that bright golden statue of Jeanne d'Arc?), and hit the quai at rue du Bac. Walk toward the *métro* stop rue du Bac and away from the river. You get three or four more blocks of shopping this way. While it's not the best part of the rue du Bac, it's great good fun. The street twists a bit, but just wonder and wander, following the street signs. You will quit rue du Bac only when you get to **Le Bon Marché,** so *bon marche* to you.

You'll note that I've stopped you off for tea or coffee in the department store. One of the things I often do is get a pastry from **Hédiard** and sit in the tiny residential park for a quick break. If you prefer chocolate to stimulate you through the late afternoon, **Christian Constant**'s store is at no. 26.

Secret Seven, 7e

Métro: Rue du Bac.

Shopping Scene: Privately chic. You came with the car and driver, didn't you?

I don't suggest places to stop for lunch or tea in this neighborhood, because you will reenter the real world for these things; this is just a two-block stroll in another world, a world inhabited by very rich and chic women. Every boutique on both sides of the street sells cutting-edge chic clothing from either a French big-name, such as **Michel Klein,** or a hip-and-hot young designer, such as the Belgian **Anvers. Irié** is another local hero for those who wear tight skirts and body-hugging fashions.

You are going to walk along the rue du Pré-aux-Clercs, which is only a block or two in length. It lies between boulevard St-Germain and the river. If you come by taxi, just give the address of Michel Klein, 6 rue du Pré-aux-Clercs, and you will be whisked here.

Quai to Heaven, 6e

Métro: St-Michel.

Shopping Scene: Insiderish, quiet, and private.

Where to Have Lunch: Les Bookinistes, 53 quai des Grands-Augustins, ☎ 1/43-25-45-94.

Where to Have Tea: À la Cour de Rohan, see page 123.

Most of the serious antiques dealers on the Left Bank are nestled into the real estate between the river and the boulevard St-Germain. Many line the quai Voltaire. If you continue along the river and just shop the quais, you will pass the stalls that sell old books, ephemera, and junk. This is a tourist scene, which is fun to do once or twice as you get to know Paris. The real antiques scene is much more hidden. It's best to make appointments in advance, even.

While some browsing occurs, this is generally done by locals who continually visit the dealers, know them by name, poke around, chat, pat the dog, and then peek in the back room. Read *Life of the Party*, Chris Ogden's book on Pamela Harriman, to see how it's done.

Paris Hilton, 15e

Métro: Champs-de-Mars.

Shopping Scene: Hidden, French, residential, upper middle class.

Where to Have Lunch or Brunch: Paris Hilton or **Jules Verne.**

Where to Have Tea: Eiffel Tower.

For years I would have scoffed if you even mentioned the Paris Hilton to me. Sure, it's next door to the Eiffel Tower, but there's not much else for a shopper to do. My Hilton friend, Laurent Voivent, is now the number two of this hotel and has won me.

Aside from the obvious **Eiffel Tower** business (very little shopping, even in terms of souvenirs), none of the rest of the shopping here is immediately obvious. We come with the car; there really isn't that much of a *métro* connection. But the highlights are infectious: The **Quai Branly** sometimes has an exhibition, be it an art show or an antiques show; the **Village Suisse**—a village of antiques shops— is two blocks from the Hilton. And two blocks from there is a very nice Sunday street market, underneath the elevated rail track. I promise you, there are very few tourists here. It's on the rue Grenelle under the elevated railroad tracks of La Motte Picquet station. This market is held on Wednesday and Sunday only, from 8:30am until 1pm. Although it's mostly a food market, there are other vendors selling Provençal fabrics, olive oil, and the like.

Best of all, though, is the Sunday morning market on the **rue Cler,** where two blocks of the street celebrate French food. Yes, all the stores, even the ones that don't sell food, are open. Go early; everyone's gone by 1pm. Then have brunch at the **Hilton** or fast food at the **Eiffel Tower.** Or, if you've saved up for it and reserved ahead, have lunch at the Michelin-starred **Jules Verne** restaurant in the Eiffel Tower.

Discount Neighborhoods

ALÉSIA, 14E

Métro: Alésia.

Pronounced "Aleeeza" by some and "heaven" by others, this is one of the major discount districts in Paris. Prices in some of these shops may not be the lowest possible, but there are a good half-dozen shops to choose from. Not every store in this area is a discount house, so ask if you are confused. Don't make any false assumptions! Most of the discount houses have the word *stock* in their name, which means they sell overruns.

Some of the shops have a designer's name plus the word *stock* in their name; others have store names, without alluding to what is inside, such as **Stock 2,** a spacious space at no. 92, that sells men's, women's, and kids' designer clothes at discount prices. Most of it is from **Daniel Hechter,** but there are other brands.

Don't miss **Cacharel Stock** (no. 114), with fabulous baby and kids' clothes as well as some men's and women's things, although I've never found anything worthwhile here that wasn't for children. **Fabrice Karel,** no. 105, makes terrific knits similar to those of Rodier and is just across from Cacharel.

Diapositive is a big hip line in Paris; their stock shop is at no. 74. But the highlight of the block is undoubtedly **SR** (no. 64), which stands for, shout it out folks, **Sonia Rykiel.** The clothes here are old, but they are true blue Sonia.

When you shop this area, keep store hours in mind. Stores are generally closed Monday morning, but open at 2pm; many are closed the entire month of August.

St-Placide, 7e

Métro: Sèvres-Babylone.

This is not particularly near Alésia (although you can walk from one area to the other), but mentally the two areas are sisters—homes of the discount shop, the stock shop, the great bargain. St-Placide is a side street that is right alongside **Le Bon Marché,** the department store on the Left Bank. Take the *métro* to St-Placide and walk toward Le Bon Marché and the rue des Sèvres. Pass Le Bon Marché then turn left onto rue St-Placide.

There are maybe 10 stock shops in this one block, but they never do much for me. Every time I visit, which is about once a year, I come away empty-handed. The best of the bunch is a group of shops owned by **Le Mouton à 5 Pattes.** There's a children's shop, a designer shop, as well as a real-people shop. There were plenty of big names, like Gaultier and Ferre, in bins, the last time I visited.

St-Placide feels a bit seedy and isn't as attractive as Alésia, but there's nothing wrong with the neighborhood, and it is safe. Walk along the street, choosing what interests you, until you come to the rue de Sèvres, a main street of the neighborhood. Because Le Bon Marché is right here, many other retailers have come along with branch stores to catch the overflow department-store traffic. There's a **Guerlain,** a **Rodier,** and a **Dorothée Bis,** in addition to a lot of other nice stores. It is not fancy here, but it is quite serviceable. The Hôtel Lutétia is across the street, and there's a *métro* station in the square (Sèvres-Babylone). You can come and go from here, or take the rue de Sèvres for one block, and hit the really exciting, fancy, expensive stores of the Little Dragons neighborhood (see p. 125).

Chapter Nine
· · · · · · ·

BASIC PARIS RESOURCES
FROM A TO Z

ANTIQUES
· ·

Paris is one of the world's capitals for antiques. One
of the pleasures of shopping here is browsing its wide
variety of antiques shops. Whether you're buying
real antiques or just some "old stuff," remember
that U.S. Customs defines an antique as something
that is at least 100 years old. If a piece you purchase
does not come with provenance papers, you must
have a receipt or a bill of lading from the dealer that
says what the piece is and its origin and age. The
French are getting more and more stringent about
what can be taken out of the country; they are even
trying to keep *fripes* (used clothes) in the country
now.

Expensive museum-quality antiques are generally
sold in the tony shops along the rue du Faubourg
St-Honoré, although many of these shops moved
out during the recession. Mid-priced antiques are
predominantly found in antiques shops on the Left
Bank, in the *villages,* and at the markets of St-Ouen.
But you'll come across antiques shops everywhere
in the city.

If you just want to browse and get the feel of the
antiques scene, get over to the Left Bank. There's a
congregation of very important dealers between the
river and the boulevard St-Germain. They may be a
tad more expensive than the others in town, but they

are the real guys with the real reputations who do not even look up from their newspapers when you walk in.

There are also some funky antiques and collectibles shops as well as vintage clothing stores in the Marais not far from the **Village St-Paul.** I happen to adore **Max Spira,** 21 place des Vosges, which reminds me of a flea market in Santa Fe, New Mexico. Just look for the junk heaped on the arcade walkway of the place des Vosges. If nothing else, it makes a great photo op. Inside the store, you'll find lots of reproductions, but the charm of it all is devastating.

On the far side of the place des Vosges is **La Marotte,** 16 rue de Birague, which sells some nice vintage clothing in a charming atmosphere.

Antiques *Villages*

A *village* in Paris is not a subdivision of an arrondissement, but a place for good antiques. Villages are buildings that house many antiques dealers under one roof. If you need a rainy-day-in-Paris occupation, a trip to any village probably will do it; some are even open on Sunday.

VILLAGE ST-PAUL
rue St-Paul, 4e (Métro: St-Paul).

This, a village that's also accompanied by a block or more of street stalls selling antiques, can be a little hard to find if you aren't patient. It's hidden in a medieval warren of streets between the Seine and the church of St. Paul, very close to the Marais and the Bastille. The village itself is between the rue St-Paul, the rue Charles V, the rue des Jardins St-Paul, and the rue Ave-Maria.

Get off the *métro* at St-Paul and walk toward the river. Or walk along the quai going toward the Bastille and take a left when you spy your first antiques shop on the corner of the rue St-Paul. Hours are generally Thursday to Monday, 11am to 7pm.

There are many shops to visit. Prices can be steep, but the variety of the merchandise, combined with the charm of the neighborhood, makes this a delightful way to pass the time. A good stop to piggyback with your visit to the Marais; yes, there's life on Sunday afternoons.

Le Louvre des Antiquaires
2 place du Palais-Royal, 1er
(Métro: Palais-Royal).

This is a virtual antiques department store of some 250 dealers. You may have more fun here than at the museum! At least you can shop here. Many mavens claim this is the single best one-stop source in Paris because quality is high and the dealers have reputations to protect. You can even bargain a little. There are enough affordable small pieces that you're bound to find something you like, without having to pound the pavement going from shop to shop. Indoors is a restaurant and a shipping agent. Closed on Sunday in August; otherwise the Sunday scene is from a movie. Clean bathrooms.

Le Village Suisse
54 ave. de la Motte-Picquet, 15e
(Métro: La Motte).

You won't find any gnomes making watches here, just a lot of dealers in the mid- to high-priced range, with some very respectable offerings. There are 150 shops in an area one block long and two blocks wide—it's sort of like a mall that rambles from building to building.

The Village Suisse is near the Eiffel Tower and l'École Militaire; it is within walking distance of the Paris Hilton. Prices are not outrageous, but they aren't low, either; most stores offer shipping. There are no cute or funky stores here, but several shops are theme-oriented, selling nautical items or antique jewelry, for example. Sunday is a big day here.

LE BON MARCHÉ
38 rue de Sèvres, 6e (Métro: Sèvres-Babylone).

Le Bon Marché is indeed a department store, but it's really two stores in one. One portion is the full department store, the other, a grocery store with a flea market upstairs.

I can't tell you this is a must-do experience, but it can be fun. It's especially good if you are in the neighborhood or want a taste of a flea market without going to the trouble of getting to one. There's a place for coffee; closed on Sunday.

Auction Houses

For years, the big name in Paris's auction world was the Hôtel Drouot. But ever since Sotheby's gave up its Monaco offices and moved to Paris, the scene's become much more competitive.

In addition, preparations for the unification of Europe have forced France—especially Paris—to change its auction techniques in order to compete with the rest of Europe. Under the old system, an estate was auctioned off in its entirety, so that everything would come up for sale. Nowadays, you still have complete estates sold at the Hôtel Drouot, but you also have the categorical auctions that are popular in Britain and the U.S. When an entire estate is auctioned off today, there is usually nothing "important" (as the dealers tend to say) for sale. Important works are being saved for major auctions. Such big-time auctions are held in the relatively new Hôtel Drouot. (The house took over an existing theater on the avenue Montaigne.)

When you read auction catalogs in Paris, note that Hôtel Drouot listings with an "R" after them (for Richelieu) refer to the old location, and an "M" refers to the avenue Montaigne location.

HÔTEL DROUOT
9 rue Drouot, 9e (Métro: Le Peletier); 15 ave. Montaigne, 8e (Métro: Alma-Marceau).

If you prefer your used furniture to come by way of an auction house, Marie Jo swears this is the place for a serious deal. For years, the Hôtel Drouot tightly controlled the auction business in Paris. Now that the house must compete with Sotheby's, its influence may wane.

Some 90 auctioneers are in the main house, with several auctions going on simultaneously. The auctioneers are all shareholders—equal partners, in fact—in the business, and, as a result, it runs much like a law firm. Speaking of lawyers, there are lawyers in France who specialize in auctions, because this is a very, very different business from the one you know and love in the U.S. and the U.K.

Drouot is a weird and fascinating place. At the entrance, an information counter has catalogs and notices of future sales. Three TV sets on the ground floor show different parts of the building, and there is an appraiser who—free of charge—will tell you if an item you bring in is worthy of auction, and will appraise it for you on the spot. The estimate is done in a small private room. If you agree with the estimate, you can set a date for your auction. The seller pays an 8% to 10% commission to the house.

Auctions are held every day, except in summer, when they are not held on weekends. They always begin at 2pm and go until concluded, usually about 6:30pm. Previews are held on Wednesday until 11am. You can buy their magazine on newsstands and get an instant look at the auction of the month.

The auction rooms are various sizes; some can be divided or opened according to need. All the rooms are carpeted; art and/or tapestries are on the walls. The clients sit on chairs to watch the bidding; paddles are not used. Most of the clients are dealers; we have never noticed a very jazzy crowd here, even when we went to a Goya auction. All business is in French. If you are not fluent, please bring your own translator or expert, or book a translator ahead of time (☎ 01/42-46-17-11 to arrange for a translator).

You needn't register to bid; anyone can walk in, sit down, and bid. All auctions have catalogs, and the lots are numbered and defined in the catalog. You do not need a catalog to enter a preview or an auction, as you do in New York. The conditions of the sale are plainly printed inside the first page of the catalog (in French). You can pay in cash up to 10,000 F. French people may write local checks; Americans cannot write checks. If you have only American dollars on hand, there is an exchange bureau in the house. If you pay in cash, you can walk out with your item. Shills are occasionally used by some dealers to drive up the price. Auctioneers are familiar with all the dealers and could possibly choose to throw a piece their way. Dealers may even pool in on items.

You are responsible for shipping; there is no shipping office in the auction house. You start paying storage charges after 24 hours.

Brocante Shows

Sadema is an organization that hosts *brocante* shows. *Brocante* is a French term for items that aren't old enough to be antiques. *Brocante* shows are annual events, most frequently held at the same time and place each year. They are announced in the papers, or you can call, write, or fax for their schedule: Sadema, Tolbiac-Messena, 25 Quai de la Gare, Ce 18, Paris 75644; ☎ 1/45-85-01-85; fax 1/45-85-22-66. Some shows are weekend events; others last up to two weeks. Sadema charges admission, usually about 25 F per person.

Sadema is not the only game in town; there are other organizations that sponsor shows. Some are fancier and charge 40–50 F admission. In fact, the admission charge is a direct indication of how tony the dealers are; the higher the gate fee, the more expensive are the dealers and their wares.

There is an exhibition venue almost directly across the street from the Paris Hilton, on the **Quai** de Branly, 7e, which is a tented space where they hold the **Salon des Antiquaires**. This event is organized by Topexpo, ☎ 1/43-31-54-00; fax 1/43-37-19-08. I attended this event only once and found it way too fancy for me. Below I've listed the shows I adore.

- **Ferraille de Paris:** Held in the Parc Floral de Paris (Bois de Vincennes), this fair always occurs toward the end of February every year. This is a good-sized indoor fair, with a lot of affordable merchandise and approachable merchants. Everything from empty perfume bottles to the kitchen sink. The French country kitchen sink. *(Métro: Porte Dorée.)*
- **Brocante de Printemps:** A March event that usually lasts 10 days; heralds the coming of spring, of course. *(Métro: Porte Edgar-Quintet.)*
- **Brocante à la Bastille:** An annual event that you can tell, from its title, does not take itself or its merchants too seriously. This fair is usually held on both sides of the canal; pay near the place de la Bastille; there are bridges to the other side. Usually held for 10 days in April or May, this is particularly fabulous in fine weather. *(Métro: Bastille.)*
- **Brocante de Paris:** This huge event is the talk of the town for those who hope to get a designer bargain. Held for 10 days in May. *(Métro: Porte Brochant.)*

AMERICAN BIG NAMES

The second American liberation of Paris began quietly enough when Ralph Lauren opened a shop on the place de la Madeleine. Now the American look is the latest thing in town, and even French designers are copying it. You can see this merchandise at home and pay less for it, but here you may find your favorite items in shades you can't get at home.

CRABTREE & EVELYN
*177 blvd. St-Germain, 7e (Métro: rue du Bac);
Passy Plaza, 53 rue de Passy, 16e (Métro: La
Muette).*

ESPRIT
9 place des Victoires, 2e (Métro: Bourse).

THE GAP
*Passy Plaza, 53 rue de Passy, 16e (Métro: La
Muette); Marché St-Germain, rue Lobineau, 6e
(Métro: St-Germain-des-Prés).*

JOAN & DAVID
*6 rue du Faubourg-St-Honoré, 8e
(Métro: Concorde).*

JOSIE NATORI
7 place Vendôme, 1er (Métro: Tuileries).

OSHKOSH B'GOSH
32 rue de Passy, 16e (Métro: La Muette).

RALPH LAUREN/POLO
2 place de la Madeleine, 8e (Métro: Madeleine).

BARGAIN BASEMENTS

. . . .

The French are finally admitting that they've been
far too snobby about paying full retail, and factory
outlet malls are starting to pop up outside of Paris.
Most are in Troyes (see *Born to Shop France* for
details), but a few are in Paris proper. **Tati,** Paris's
most notorious bargain haven, has almost become
hip, with even a few Rothschilds confessing to shopping there. Because the pickings are hit-or-miss, you
won't want to devote an entire trip to these sources,
but there are more choices than ever before.

See page 214 for resale shops, which can offer
bargains on pre-owned designer clothing, and the
discount neighborhoods section of chapter 7, which
lists two different streets in Paris where you can go
from shop to shop in search of a bargain.

TATI

4 blvd. de Rochechouart, 18e (Métro: Anvers);
140 rue de Rennes, 6e (Métro: Rennes).

Tati is a discounter that sells clothing out of bins. It is not fancy; it is not smart. Because Tati sometimes sells designer or, at least, good-quality clothing, it has become famous. Or infamous. Although most of the shoppers include the great unwashed, celebrities, models, grand dames, and royalty have also been spotted here.

Over the years, Tati has grown like Topsy, buying up adjacent storefronts and conquering entire city blocks. There is the basic "Big Tati," in the 18th arrondissement, and then there is a smaller Tati on the Left Bank. The Left Bank store really gives only a glimpse at what the real thing is like. Closed Sundays, open 10am to 6pm.

🛍 ANNA LOWE

35 ave. Matignon, 8e (Métro: F-D-Roosevelt).

Disregard the discreet sign that reads HAUTE COUTURE. Disregard the beige marble and the fine windows. Anna Lowe's prices are good for designs by major names. (Yes, Chanel.) Nothing is cheap, but these aren't cheap clothes. Some are models' samples; if you're a size 6 or 8, you will do very well here. They will cost at least 25% less than in other Paris shops. This is the kind of shop Mother would call "a good find." They take plastic and speak English. Don't mind the address if it's not familiar to you; the shop is right off the rue du Faubourg St-Honoré. Open Monday through Friday, 10:30am to 6pm.

L'ANNEXE DES CRÉATEURS

19 rue Godot-de-Mauroy, 9e (Métro: Madeleine).

This shop is crowded and lacks charm, but is crammed with clothes and bolts of fabric. It has all sizes up to 44 (American size 12). You won't have to make a special trip; the location is close to many places in every woman's journey through Paris—halfway between boulevard Madeleine and the big department stores on boulevard Haussmann.

It tries to specialize in younger and kickier designers, such as Moschino and Mugler; pieces are a season old and therefore are sold at 30% to 40% off regular French retail. Stop in to check out hats and accessories as well—the good stuff begins at $100.

MENDÈS

65 rue Montmartre, 1er (Métro: Les Halles).

Mendès is a jobber who now owns the rights to make Yves Saint Laurent's Rive Gauche and Variations lines, as well as Claude Montana and Christian Lacroix. The shop is devoted to these brands, but don't start getting excited. I haven't found anything good here in years—and the prices are high.

It's very hard to characterize this shop, because both the quality and the selection of goods varies. Certainly don't buy from the Variations line just because it's YSL. Make sure you've really got a winner. There are a number of classics sold from the racks here. You can see their deriviation from the Rive Gauche line, and note the less expensive fabrications. But some of the stuff sold in this part of Mendès is, well, junky.

Upstairs is another story—this is where you'll find the *crème de la crème.* The *crème* just happens to be old. Possibly very old. There are ball gowns, sportswear separates, blouses, and accessories—even velvet bustiers. Sizes vary dramatically.

Just because this shop is on rue Montmartre, do not think it is in the famous section of Paris called Montmartre. It's not. It is about three blocks from the mall **Forum des Halles;** just stay on the rue Montmartre until you get there. The numbers should go down if you're going in the right direction. If you end up on the rue du Faubourg Montmartre, you went the wrong way. With its smoky glass doors, the store looks like an office building; keep your eyes out for the small sign. If you feel lost, ask in any of the jobbers nearby. They all know Mendès. Open Monday through Thursday, 10am to 6pm; Friday and Saturday, 9:30am to 5pm.

BABS
89 bis, ave. des Ternes, 17e (Métro: Porte Maillot).

I have had a love-hate relationship with Babs, in her many incarnations, for about 10 years. I never find anything when I'm seriously looking, but then I find things I've seen elsewhere, and they're less money at Babs. Babs seems to sell mostly business suits and good blouses to local ladies. I wouldn't go out of my way, but if you happen to be nearby, stop in.

TANGARA
92 Quai de Jemmapes, 10e (Métro: République).

This is a private shopper's club that anyone may join. In fact, after you join, you'll get mail from Paris that will warm your heart. The location is not in the regular tourist stream of things, but they're open Sunday, so you can always make time then. Tangara sells major big-name clothing for men and women, as well as shoes and handbags. I bought a Charles Jourdan summer bag for $100 here that I still use. Prices are 40% off French retail; and there are end-of-season sales and promotions. If you are not a member, you must go with someone who is a member or join up at the door. Membership was free when I signed up. You get an orange-and-white plastic membership card to present when you enter thereafter. Note that the clothes are expensive designer models. While prices are less than retail, they are still stiff.

Mi-Prix

27 blvd. Victor, 15e (Métro: Porte de Versailles).

This store is far from fancy. It's also far from central Paris.

But the bargains? Mi-Prix has a very weird combination of items—the junkiest of no-name merchandise, some very nice skiwear, a fabulous collection of Maud Frizon and Walter Steiger shoes (and boots), Bottega Veneta closeouts, and Philippe Model hats—at almost give-away prices. The store is packed with merchandise; much is current. The shoes are a different story. Some could be as current as last season, others as old as your grandmother.

If you are attending a trade show at the Porte de Versailles, this is a must. Also check the newspapers for *brocante* and antiques shows that may be held in this area, so you can combine agendas. It's hard to convince yourself to come all the way out here for one store, especially when it is a matter of hit-or-miss, but I've never been sorry I did. Walk from the convention center along boulevard Victor about two blocks; there are some other shops and discounters along here you may also want to check out.

BATH & BODY

My favorite French bath suds and soaps come from Annick Goutal, but I also buy numerous bath products in every *parapharmacie* I hit in France; I've been testing slimming baths (stop snickering) and *thalossotherapie* for a few years now. I can't tell you that either of these concepts works, but I'm having a good time. And I'm very clean.

Should you want to get into the swim of *thalosso-therapie*, there are a few firms you'll want to know about. **Phytomer** is the most famous, but only **Louison Bobet** has U.S. distribution. You can buy both in department stores and drugstores in Paris.

Finally, don't neglect the section in this chapter on makeup and perfume, as many of the stores listed there carry wonderful bed and bath products as well.

DARPHIN
97 rue du Bac, 7e (Métro: rue du Bac).

This is one of those very chic, almost secret beauty salons that do facials and treatments (hair is never done in a skin salon in France) and sell their own line of natural bath and beauty products. They're big on body shaping, as are all French cures, but also have many *hydroplus* (water-added) products to moisturize and balance.

OCTÉE
53 rue Bonaparte, 6e (Métro: St-Germain-des-Prés).

Known for its fragrance line, this small shop also sells color-coded perfume and soap. The gimmick is that the colors you prefer (no names) indicate your personality type. Honest.

OCCITANE
1 rue du 29 Juillet, 1er (Métro: Tuileries).

Home of the best 13 F gift (package of scented soap) in France, Occitane is a soap manufacturer from Provence that now has a few shops around France and is growing globally. There are numerous scented products for body, bath, and home. This is a must-do stop.

SAPONIFÈRE
16 rue Vignon, 8e (Métro: Madeleine); 59 rue Bonaparte, 6e (Métro: St-Germain-des-Prés).

This is a combination gift shop–towel shop–bath shop that sells tons of soaps. It has a chic, Provençal, yet beachy feel to it.

SANTA MARIA NOVELLA
2 rue Guisarde, 6e (Métro: Mabillon).

This is a very, very famous (to the point of cult worship for some) Italian pharmacy from Florence. It has begun to expand into international shopping cities only in the past few years. The Paris shop does not compare to the mother ship in a former convent in Florence, but if you can't get to Italy, stop in here. I buy the weekend soap, divided into three small bars for Friday, Saturday, and Sunday.

CHILDREN'S CLOTHING

· ·

If you're not the kind of Mom—or Grandma—who likes to drop a bundle on a single outfit for your little darling, don't forget about the department stores. Le Bon Marché and Galeries Lafayette are famous for their children's departments. If you like cheap, fun, throw-away things, try Prisunic or Inno. Each has a toy department and a good selection of inexpensive basics (underwear) and some acceptable ready-to-wear clothing. Not terribly classy, but if you need just a bathing suit or a sweatshirt, why pay more than you have to? If you must have an Yves Saint Laurent dress for your little princess, buy it at Galeries Lafayette, where you can save the receipt and qualify for *détaxe*.

BONPOINT
15 rue Royale, 8e (Métro: Madeleine).

BONPOINT SOLDES
82 rue de Grenelle, 7e (Métro: rue du Bac).

For classic styles, you won't find better than Bon point and its perfectly crafted outfits. You've never seen anything so superbly made in your life. An adorable romper costs $50; a simple smocked dress starts at $100, but prices can go to $300 for the grander stuff. If your child is over five, go upstairs where the fashions for older children are displayed. Parisian women of money and style swear by this resource.

There are several Bonpoint shops around town, by the way. Some specialize in kids' shoes; one has furniture only. There are freestanding stores in New York, London, and Milan.

If you're impressed with the clothing once you've seen the store, but can't hack the prices, perhaps you'd like to try the outlet store where last season's collection (or what's left of it) is sold for a fraction of the uptown price. Here you'll find that $300 little frock for a mere $60! They are closed on Saturday and Sunday. This outlet happens to be convenient to everything else on the Left Bank, so don't miss it.

TARTINE ET CHOCOLAT
89 rue du Faubourg St-Honoré, 8e
(Métro: Concorde).

French-style maternity dresses and layettes, both classic and nouveau. My own fave: the big pink hippo in pink and white stripes sitting in a play-pen, just begging to be taken home to someone's child. There are Tartine et Chocolat boutiques in the major French department stores as well. Some duty-free shops (like Silver Moon) sell the children's toiletry line. Any one of the items makes a nice gift.

PETIT FAUNE
33 rue Jacob, 6e (Métro: St-Germain-des-Prés).

Very original baby clothes in the nouveau style. Some even have matching shoes and hats. Everything is very, very small—up to size 2. The clothes are very American, and even the fanciest isn't in the classic style.

CHOCOLATE

Who makes better chocolate, the French or the Belgians? You'll just have to keep tasting until you decide. Designer chocolate is not inexpensive. Expect to pay about $100 per kilo. Of course, no one could eat a kilo, could they? Hmmm.

CHRISTIAN CONSTANT
37 rue d'Assas, 6e (Métro: St-Placide);
26 rue du Bac, 6e (Métro: Rue du Bac).

The more things change, the more they remain Constant, especially when you are considered one of the top chocolatiers in town. Constant also sells ice cream and other sweet treats. You'll pass it automatically as you shop the rue du Bac. Open Monday through Saturday, 8am to 8pm.

DEBEAUVE & GALLAIS
30 rue des Sts-Pères, 7e (Métro: Sèvres-Babylone).

This shop is on the part of Sts-Pères between the boulevard St-Germain and the river; many shoppers are more familiar with the other portion of this famous shopping street. This incredibly fancy chocolate shop sells unusual flavors. Note the chocolate postcards for $7.

LENÔTRE
49 ave. Victor Hugo, 16e (Métro: Victor-Hugo).

One of the older, more famous names in candy and sweets, Lenôtre is known for its chocolates and desserts, as well as its tea room. A nice place to go for a gift for your hostess—Parisian prestige in a box.

LA MAISON DU CHOCOLAT
8 blvd. de la Madeleine, 9e (Métro: Madeleine);
19 rue de Sèvres, 6e (Métro: Sèvres-Babylone).

If you read American gourmet-food magazines, you'll find plenty of mentions of this boutique, which wraps its *chocolats* much as Hermès wraps its goodies. They are famous for their truffles, which are so rich you can't eat more than three a day (breakfast, lunch, dinner). Chocolates are handmade, a rarity these days, and mavens claim you can get no closer to heaven.

MARQUISE DE SÉVIGNÉ
32 place de la Madeleine, 8e (Métro: Madeleine).

Since I like sweet chocolates, I send you here for the hazelnut praline. It has a picture of the marquise herself on the golden foil. There are other divine chocolates here; I'm just addicted to this one flavor. There is also candy for diabetics. Those who prefer dark chocolates and more heady stuff may pooh-pooh this as a source.

RICHART
258 blvd. St-Germain, 7e (Métro: Solférino).

This address is in the chic and tony part of the Left Bank. It serves the local wealthy residents with chocolates from Lyon. The most famous ones are filled with cremes of whiskey or champagne. They open Monday and Saturday, 11am to 7pm; Tuesday to Friday, 10am to 7pm.

COUTURE

· ·

Couture is considered the epitome of French style. It also has become an international statement of fashion and elegance. Haute couture translates as fancy seams; and when you're talking about couture and realize that you are talking about $30,000 garments, you'd better believe that you get very fancy seams.

Now then, about actually going to a couture house to shop. Some of them are very accessible; some of them are terrifying. Some of the houses have a retail boutique on the premises; others keep their couture business completely separate from their boutiques. If you are a true couture customer, you go in with an appointment and a letter of introduction (a fax will do) . . . or with Pamela Harriman at your side.

If you are just browsing, you might want to consider the houses on avenue Montaigne, all accessible to the public through their retail operations. It is more or less unheard of that madame should wander in off the street and want a couture fitting. If madame wants to see the earrings that are for sale, that's another matter entirely. This way, please.

Balenciaga, *30 ave. d'Iena, 16e.*
☎ 1/47-23-03-00.

Balmain, *44 rue François-1er, 8e.*
☎ 1/47-20-35-34.

Carven, *6 Rond Point des Champs-Elysées, 8e.* ☎ 1/42-25-66-52.

Chanel, *31 rue Cambon, 1er.*
☎ 1/42-86-28-00.

Christian Dior, *30 ave. Montaigne, 8e.*
☎ 1/40-73-54-44.

Courrèges, *40 rue François-1er, 8e.*
☎ 1/47-23-00-73.

Emanuel Ungaro, *2 ave. Montaigne, 8e.*
☎ 1/47-23-61-94.

Givenchy, *3-6-8 ave. George V, 8e.*
☎ 1/47-23-81-36.

Guy Laroche, *29 ave. Montaigne, 8e.*
☎ 1/40-69-68-00.

Hanae Mori, *9 rue du Faubourg St-Honoré, 8e.* ☎ 1/47-42-76-68.

Hermès, *24 rue du Faubourg St-Honoré, 8e.*
☎ 1/42-65-21-68.

Jean Patou, *7 rue St-Florentin, 8e.*
☎ 1/42-60-70-10.

Jean-Louis Scherrer, *51 ave. Montaigne, 8e.*
☎ 1/43-59-55-39.

Lacroix, *73 rue du Faubourg St-Honoré, 8e.*
☎ 1/42-65-79-08.

Louis Féraud, *88 rue de l'Arbre Sec, 1er.*
☎ 1/42-86-00-00.

Nina Ricci, *39 ave. Montaigne, 8e.*
☎ 1/47-23-78-88.

Paco Rabanne, *23 rue du Cherche-Midi, 6e.*
☎ 1/42-22-87-80.

Pierre Cardin, *27 ave. de Marigny, 8e.*
☎ 1/42-66-92-25.

Sidonie Larizzi, *8 rue Marignan, 8e.*
☎ 1/43-59-38-87.

Torrente, *9 rue du Faubourg St-Honoré, 8e.*
☎ 1/42-23-61-94.

Valentino, *17–19 ave. Montaigne, 8e.*
☎ 1/49-52-02-26.

Yves Saint Laurent, *5 ave. Marceau, 16e.*
☎ 1/47-23-72-71.

CONTINENTAL BIG NAMES

Despite the fact that the French think French fashion is the best in the world (many other people happen to agree), they have graciously allowed other designers to open up shop in Paris. Of course, the Italians have a good number of shops, representing some of the most famous names in fashion. And many of the world's biggest fashion names come from other countries, yet show their lines in Paris (Valentino, Hanae Mori), and so have come to be considered French designers.

Paris, like most of continental Europe, has gone crazy for the American look. Many U.S. firms have chosen to open branch shops; many local stores have put their reputation on the line in order to bring American styles to the French public.

For example, the entire Chevignon line has a Sante Fe–Wild West look.

AKRIS
54 rue du Faubourg St-Honoré, 8e
(Métro: Concorde).

ARMANI EMPORIO
25 place Vendôme, 1er (Métro: Tuileries);
149 blvd. St-Germain, 6e (Métro: St-Germain-
des-Prés).

BODY SHOP
Le Carrousel du Louvre, 99 rue de Rivoli, 1er
(Métro: Palais-Royal).

BORSALINO
368 rue St-Honoré, 1er (Métro: Concorde).

BOTTEGA VENETA
6 rue du Cherche-Midi, 6e (Métro: St-Germain-
des-Prés).

BURBERRYS
8 blvd. Malesherbes, 8e (Métro: Opéra).

CERRUTI 1881
15 place de la Madeleine, 8e (Métro: Madeleine).

DUNHILL
15 rue de la Paix, 2e (Métro: Opéra).

ERMENEGILDO ZEGNA
10 rue de la Paix, 1er (Métro: Opéra).

ESCADA
418 rue St-Honoré, 8e (Métro: Concorde);
51 ave. Montaigne, 8e (Métro: F-D-Roosevelt).

ETRO
66 rue du Faubourg St-Honoré, 8e (Métro:
Concorde); 177 blvd. St-Germain, 6e (Métro:
St-Germain-des-Prés).

FERRAGAMO
50 rue du Faubourg St-Honoré, 8e (Métro:
Concorde): 68–70 rue Sts-Pères, 6e (Métro:
Sèvres-Babylone).

GIANFRANCO FERRE
38 ave. George V, 8e (Métro: George V).

GIANNI VERSACE
*62 rue du Faubourg St-Honoré, 8e
(Métro: Concorde).*

GIORGIO ARMANI
6 place Vendôme, 1er (Métro: Tuileries).

GUCCI
*27 rue du Faubourg St-Honoré, 8e
(Métro: Concorde); 350 rue St-Honoré, 1er
(Métro: Tuileries).*

HOLLAND & HOLLAND
29 ave. Victor Hugo, 16e (Métro: Victor-Hugo).

JAEGER PF FRANCE
*5 rue du Faubourg St-Honoré, 8e
(Métro: Concorde).*

JOSEPH
*44 rue Étienne Marcel, 2e (Métro: Étienne-
Marcel); 14 ave. Montaigne, 8e (Métro:
F-D-Roosevelt).*

KRIZIA
48 ave. Montaigne, 8e (Métro: Alma-Marceau).

LA MAISON SELON VERSACE
41 rue François-1er, 8e (Métro: F-D-Roosevelt).

LAURA ASHLEY
*94 rue de Rennes, 6e (Métro: Rennes); 261 rue
St-Honoré, 1er (Métro: Concorde); 95 ave.
Raymond-Poincarè, 16e (Métro: Victor-Hugo).*

LAUREL
*402 rue St-Honoré, 8e (Métro: Tuileries);
52 rue Bonaparte, 6e (Métro: St-Germain-
des-Prés).*

LES COPAINS
*4 rue du Faubourg St-Honoré, 8e (Métro:
Concorde).*

LOEWE
57 ave. Montaigne, 8e (Métro: F-D-Roosevelt or
Alma-Marceau).

MARIELLA BURANI
412 rue St-Honoré, 8e (Métro: Concorde).

MAX MARA
265 rue St-Honoré, 1er (Métro: Concorde
or Tuileries); 100 ave. Paul-Doumer, 16e
(Métro: La Muette); 37 rue du Four, 6e
(Métro: St-Germain-des-Prés).

MCM
243 rue St-Honoré, 1er (Métro: Concorde).

MISSONI
43 rue du Bac, 7e (Métro: Rue du Bac); 1 rue du
Faubourg St-Honoré, 8e (Métro: Concorde).

MIU MIU
10 rue du Cherche-Midi, 6e (Métro: St-Germain-
des-Prés).

MOSCHINO
68 rue Bonaparte, 6e (Métro: St-Germain-
des-Prés).

MULBERRY
14 rue du Cherche Midi, 6e (Métro: St-Germain-
des-Prés); 45 rue Croix des Petits Champs, 1er
(Métro: Palais-Royal).

ROMEO GIGLI
46 rue de Sévigné, 4e (Métro: St-Paul).

SYBILLA
62 rue Jean-Jacques Rousseau, 1er
(Métro: Musée-du-Louvre).

TRUSSARDI
21 rue du Faubourg St-Honoré, 8e
(Métro: Concorde).

VERSACE JEANS
67 rue des St-Pères, 6e (Métro: Sèvres-Babylon).

VERSUS
64 rue des St-Pères, 6e (Métro: Sèvres-Babylon).

ZARA
2 rue Halevy, 9e (Métro: Opéra); 44 ave. des
Champs-Elysées, 8e (Métro: F-D-Roosevelt).

COSTUME JEWELRY
· ·

The essence of French fashion (aside from couture)
is simplicity—consider the basic black skirt and
white silk blouse—a staple of every stylish Frenchwoman's wardrobe. Of course, the way to spruce
up these basics has always been accessories. Hence
the importance of the Hermès silk scarf. Should
you care to go for something more glitzy, these
sources offer some of Paris's boldest statements; their
specialty is either in making copies of more serious
jewelry or in making originals that will have value
in the marketplace for years to come; originals
that reach beyond the basic defintion of "costume
jewelry."

BURMA
72 rue du Faubourg St-Honoré, 8e
(Métro: Concorde or Miromesnil).

If the real thing is beyond you, try Burma! There
are a few Burma shops in Paris; if you want to have
fun while doing this, shop at either the Faubourg
St-Honoré shop or the place Vendôme shop. That
way, you can fantasize that you can afford something on one of these two luxury streets.

LESAGE
21 place Vendôme, 1er (Métro: Tuileries).

Located in the Schiaparelli space on the place Vendôme, Lesage announces itself with discreet letter-
ing in the window (just below the pink "Schiaparelli"
sign). You could easily walk by without ever notic-
ing, but designer mavens have known for years that

Lesage is the house that does all the beading for the couture houses.

This shop, with its shocking interior, offers a host of accessories at the highest retail prices in Paris. You sit at a little table and trays of costume jewelry, handbags, and even some heavily beaded or embroidered clothing are brought to you. The work is sublime, but the price tags are not. We're talking investment chic.

YVES SAINT LAURENT
32 rue du Faubourg St-Honoré, 8e
(Métro: Concorde).

Saint Laurent shows us what he's made of by having the good grace to open a razzle-dazzle shop that allows us to smell the refined air of couture but still come away with a trophy we can afford. His shop for accessories has two levels of goodies, many of which are made of crystal and are meant to make your friends very envious that you've been to Paris.

Go upstairs for the serious shopping. While the store sells more than jewelry (shoes, sweaters, scarves, ties, and more), it's the jewelry that you should be buying. I recently blew my whole travel budget on one piece; prices can be several hundred dollars for the smallest of items. But it does say Saint Laurent on it.

SWAROVSKI
7 rue Royale, 8e (Métro: Concorde).

Over the years, this crystal maker has provided much of the glitter to Lesage and Chanel. Now, it has its own shop on the rue Royale selling diamondlike jewels made from their top-of-the-line crystals, as well as accessories (handbags with crystal clasps) and glassware. The store—the company's first retail effort on the international scene—is owned by the people who run the Ciro stores (also famous for faux baubles).

OCTOPUSSY
*255 rue St-Honoré, 1er (Métro: Tuileries or
Concorde).*

ANEMONE
*7 rue de Castiglione, 1er (Métro: Tuileries or
Concorde).*

I have two special resources for costume jewelry and
earrings in Paris that are reliable, year after year.
Since they are around the corner from each other,
they are easy to work.

The first, Octopussy, is on the rue St-Honoré;
the second, Anemone, is on the rue de Castiglione.
It's hard for me to differentiate between the two,
although I think I've been lucky more times at
Octopussy than at Anemone. Both carry a wide
range of designer lines as well as many no-name
works that are just enough ahead of the times to
be worthwhile. Earrings begin around $50 (this is
Paris, you know), but may prove to be the best buy
of your trip. They will allow you to save up your
receipts to qualify for the *détaxe*.

CLEOPATRE
1 rue du Renard, 4e (Métro: Hôtel de Ville).

Located across from BHV, this large shop sells
obviously fake jewelry and hot fashion looks for a
few francs. I'm talking teen-time here—really low-
end, but fun. They have hair ornaments, bracelets,
necklaces, pins, and more earrings than you can
imagine.

GAS
*44 blvd. Étienne Marcel, 2e
(Métro: Étienne-Marcel).*

This is a small store with very inventive pieces,
often made from odds and ends. More fun than
couture in terms of a look; possibly a good investment as a collectible.

NEREIDES
23 rue du Four, 6e (Métro: St-Germain-des-Prés).

This shop sells a very South of France look, sort of casual and fashiony and resorty, but with bigger pieces than you might wear to work. You'll find various sizes and shapes and a touch of brushed gold and Etruscan influence.

🛍 HAPPY DAYS
12 rue de Passy, 16e (Métro: La Muette).

If my rave about the fun you'll have while strolling the rue de Passy hasn't been enough to convince you to get over there, perhaps this will. Happy Days is no bigger than a large closet, but has tons of imaginative earrings, most costing in the $25–$30 range. They have other accessories, but I come here to try on earrings for an hour, and always leave with several pair. In spring, they bring out the resort collection, which has a very "South of France" feel to it. So, if you have vacation plans there, you may want to shop here first.

LES CRÉATEURS

. . . .

The French have an expression (don't they always?) for big-name designers who do not make couture. They are *Les Créateurs,* the Creators. Many are as rich and successful as the names who make couture; some more so. You tell me which name you recognize more quickly: Per Spook or Sonia Rykiel? Spook creates couture; Rykiel is a *créateur.*

The list below gives the address of each *créateur's* studio (which may or may not have a store attached—roughly half have stores). If you study the list, you'll also note that the times they are a changin'. Case in point: Claude Montana began as a *créateur,* became a couturier for Lanvin, and then left couture and is once again a *créateur.* Some *créateurs* have such a large following (and major international advertising campaigns to match) that they can be considered big names. So check "French Big Names," later in this chapter, if you don't find your favorite French designer's name below. Note that not all of these designers are French. Italian designer Valentino shows in Paris as well as in Rome. Several Japanese designers are actually considered French designers because they show in Paris. More and more English and Italian designers choose to show in Paris; even Oscar de la Renta, Spanish by birth and American by trade, currently does the Balmain line and shows in Paris.

For academic purposes, you may also want to know that *prêt-á-porter* (ready-to-wear) is made by the *créateurs*. They usually have various lines in order to cover multiple price points. Some of the designers below show with the couture; some show with ready-to-wear. The Oscar de la Renta that is shown in Paris is nothing like the Oscar de la Renta you buy at Neiman-Marcus. (Especially when it has a Balmain label on it.)

Angelo Tarlazzi, *29 rue du Faubourg St-Honoré, 8e.* ☎ 1/42-65-15-65.

Anne Marie Beretta, *1 blvd. St-Martin, 3e.* ☎ 1/42-72-16-11.

Azzedine Alaïa, *18 rue de la Verrerie, 4e.* ☎ 1/40-27-85-58.

Balmain, *44 rue François-1er, 8e.* ☎ 1-40-73-25-51.

Cerruti 1881, *3 place de la Madeleine, 8e.* ☎ 1/42-65-68-72.

Chantal Thomass, *100 rue du Cherche-Midi, 6e.* ☎ 1/45-49-43-43.

Claude Montana, *131 rue St-Denis, 1er.* ☎ 1/40-39-90-60.

Comme des Garçons (Rei Kawakabo),
16 *place Vendôme, 1er.* ☎ 1/42-97-57-77.

Dorothée Bis, *17 rue de Sèvres, 6e.*
☎ 1/42-22-02-90.

Emmanuelle Khanh, *39 ave. Victor Hugo,
16e.* ☎ 1/45-02-12-00.

Issey Miyake, *5 place des Vosges, 4e.*
☎ 1/42-77-07-17.

Jacqueline de Ribes, *50 rue de la
Bienfaisance, 8e.* ☎ 1/45-62-56-74.

Jean-Charles de Castelbajac,
16 ave. Robert Schuman, 7e.
☎ 1/45-55-23-29.

Jean-Paul Gaultier, *70 Galerie Vivienne, 2e.*
☎ 1/42-96-82-20.

Junko Koshino, *5 rue de Rigny, 8e.*
☎ 1/42-94-19-03.

Junko Shimada, *35 rue de L'Arbre Sec, 2e.*
☎ 1/42-60-30-09.

Karl Lagerfeld, *144 ave. des Champs-Elysées,
8e.* ☎ 1/43-59-57-50.

Katherine Hamnett, *144 rue de Rivoli, 1er.*
☎ 1/42-61-57-17.

Kenzo, *3 place des Victoires, 1er.*
☎ 1/40-39-72-01.

Martine Sitbon, *6 rue de Braque, 3e.*
☎ 1/42-03-91-00.

Matsuda, *4–6 rue de Braque, 3e.*
☎ 1/42-78-41-68.

Michel Klein, *45 rue de Richelieu, 2e.*
☎ 1/42-86-02-57.

Popy Moreni, *170 rue du Temple, 3e.*
☎ 1/42-74-53-56.

Sonia Rykiel, *175 blvd. St-Germain, 6e.*
☏ 1/49-54-60-00.

Thierry Mugler, *130 rue du Faubourg
St-Honoré, 8e.* ☏ 1/42-56-19-28.

Yohji Yamamoto, *155 rue St-Martin, 3e.*
☏ 1/42-78-94-11.

DEPARTMENT STORES

French department stores are for French people; only
Galeries Lafayette and **Au Printemps** make a serious attempt to woo American tourists. As a result,
Americans know about these two—which are next
door to each other and easily hit at once—but aren't
very familiar with the other department stores. Few
Americans even realize, for example, that there's a
rather large branch of the British icon **Marks &
Spencer** across the street from Galeries Lafayette.

The biggies offer a lot of bang for your time, but
they get incredibly crowded on Saturday, especially
in summer. If your time in Paris is limited, check out
the designer fashions and all the ready-to-wear clothing floors of a good department store, and you will
immediately know what's hot and what's not. Don't
forget to tour the housewares floors (or building, in
the case of Printemps) to see the latest ideas for
the home and table.

Galeries Lafayette has four different buildings
and Printemps has three (this is a total of seven
buildings of department store proportions!). There
are also scads of street vendors (selling goods from
the stores, by the way) outside these two stores as
well as in a nearby alley. In short, this area is overwhelming. It's not an easy browse, so it won't be
fun if you think you are going to tackle it all.

What you need is a plan. I suggest hitting **Galeries
Lafayette** first for fashion, then moving on to the
Galeries Lafayette supermarket (**Lafayette Gour-
met**). Afterward, I'd tackle **Monoprix** (the dime

store), and then **Bouchara,** the fabric store. I'd move on to **Printemps Maison** and **Prisunic,** which is behind Printemps. You can do all of this in three hours and have a ball; I suggest you limit your time here and enjoy it. Then go to either the **Café de la Paix** or **Le Grand Hôtel** (an Inter-Continental property) for tea.

However, if you are doing some very serious shopping, and it looks like you are going to be spending 1200 F (about $250), then do not divide your time between two different department stores. Buy everything from one store so you qualify for the *détaxe*. Allow at least 15 minutes for the *détaxe* paperwork, which you must commence in the department store. Expect it to take longer if it's the middle of the tourist season.

GALERIES LAFAYETTE
40 blvd. Haussmann, 9e (Métro: Chausée-d'Antin); Commercial Centre Montparnasse, 14e (Métro: Montparnasse/Bienvenue).

I have come to love Galeries Lafayette (GL) in my old age, mostly because it's easy. They sell everything here. If it's raining or you are in a hurry, you are in good hands. If you want an overview of all of Paris retail before you begin to shop, this is a good place to educate your eye. Come early in the day and take notes, if need be.

If you are planning on buying a lot, but it will be a lipstick here, some panty hose there, a blouse on two, and a toy on five, and the thought of writing up all those sales slips on an individual basis makes you nuts, you can use a "shopper's card," available at the **Visitor's Desk.** Your first purchase is rung up on a cash register and held at the desk, while your card is marked with the amount. You go around shopping all day, clutching your card in your hand. When you are finished, you pay for the grand total. This means you don't have to keep opening and closing your wallet and signing multiple sales receipts.

It's also one of the easiest ways to get your *détaxe*, since you pay and claim the credit all at once. There's only one problem: After you have paid, you must collect all of your packages. Arrangements may be made at some stores to ship your purchases directly home.

Foreign visitors get a flat 10% discount by showing their passports at the time of purchase. (Be sure to present yours before the sales clerk rings you up.) You can also receive a coupon for this 10% discount from your U.S. travel agent or hotel. The export discount is 13% after an expenditure of 1200 F. GL is open until 9pm on Thursday. I don't know about you, but this is my idea of heaven: Shop all day, have tea, and then shop into the night. Collapse back at your hotel for room service, or, better yet, go to GL's grocery store for a gourmet takeout *pique-nique*.

Galeries Lafayette offers a free fashion show on Wednesday throughout the year, and on Wednesday and Friday from April through October. Make reservations by calling 1/48-74-02-30. The show is in the Salon Opéra. Use the store's Auber entrance and head to the 7th floor.

Open Monday through Saturday, 9:30am to 6:45pm; Thursday, 9:30am to 9:00pm. Open on the five Sundays prior to Christmas.

Note: The Galeries Lafayette on the Left Bank is a small store catering to locals who work in the area. Its best feature: It opens early in the morning on weekdays. Its second best feature: It's across the street from **Inno,** my dime-store supermarket.

Au Printemps
64 blvd. Haussmann, 9e
(Métro: Chausée-d'Antin).

Printemps Nation
25 cours de Vincennes, 20e
(Métro: Porte-de-Vincennes).

PRINTEMPS ITALIE
30 ave. d'Italie, 13e (Métro: Italie).

PRINTEMPS RÉPUBLIQUE
*10 place de la République, 11e
(Métro: République).*

Most people call it merely Printemps, which means spring. You can walk in feeling like spring and come out hours later like a lion in winter. To an American accustomed to shopping everything from Saks to Limited Express, Printemps now looks like an old friend. The store was just redone in Le Look Americain.

Just like Galeries Lafayette, Printemps has a discount coupon that entitles foreign visitors to a 10% discount. Mine was in a stack of coupons at the concierge desk at my hotel. While I got the coupon during the winter season, it was valid for a full year. You present the card and your passport at the **Welcome Service** desk on the street floor of the main fashion store, and you will be given something resembling a credit card. The 10% discount offer does not apply to food, books, or already discounted merchandise. This has nothing to do with the *détaxe* refund; if you qualify for *détaxe*, you get an additional 13% off.

The main store is divided into three separate stores: **Brummell,** the men's store, which is behind the main store; the Home Store (**Printemps de la Maison**); and the fashion store, **Printemps de la Mode.** For some reason, perfumes are sold in the home store. Not to worry, go right up those escalators. Also note that directly behind Printemps is a branch of the dime store **Prisunic,** owned by Printemps. How convenient!

Printemps hosts a free fashion show on Tuesday every week of the year, and on Tuesday and Friday, from March through October. The show is held at 10am on the 7th floor, under the cupola. Commentary is in English and French; the show lasts

45 minutes. Open Monday through Saturday, 9:35am to 7pm. Open on the five Sundays prior to Christmas.

Bazar de l'Hôtel de Ville (BHV)
52–56 rue de Rivoli, 1er (Métro: Hôtel-de-Ville).

If you think this is a funny name for a store, you can call it BHV (pronounced *Bay*-H-Vay in French), or remember that the full name of the store tells you just where it is—directly across from the Hôtel de Ville. The store is famous for its do-it-yourself attitude and housewares. You owe it to yourself to go to the basement (SS) level. If you are at all interested in household gadgets or interior design, you will go nuts.

The upper floors are ordinary enough, and even the basement level can be ordinary (I assure you— I am not sending you to Paris to buy a lawn mower), but there are little nooks and crannies that will delight the most creative shoppers among you. I buy the brass lock pieces and string them on necklaces for gifts. Open Monday, Tuesday, Thursday, Friday, and Saturday, 9:30am to 6:30pm; Wednesday, 9:30am to 10pm.

Le Bon Marché
5 rue de Babylone, 6e (Métro: Sèvres-Babylone).

Bon Marché is the big department store on the Left Bank, close to the Hôtel Lutétia and close to my heart. While there are branches of some of the other French department stores on the Left Bank, this is the largest one here, and it is convenient to a good bit of Left Bank shopping. They also have a sensational grocery store (**Grand Epicerie**); look for me there.

Bon Marché is the connecting point between two fabulous neighborhoods—rue du Bac and Little Dragons. It's convenient not only to enticing little boutiques, but also to a collection of discount stores on rue St-Placide (see p. 131).

There are actually two Bon Marché stores across the street from each other. The smaller one is devoted to food and entertaining and antiques and connects through the basement to the main store. *Mais oui,* it has its own tiny flea market upstairs! Open Monday through Saturday, 9:30am to 6:30pm.

FRANCK ET FILS
80 rue de Passy, 16e (Métro: La Muette).

Franck et Fils is a specialty store. The store is elegant, easy to shop, uncrowded, and relatively undiscovered by tourists. It's currently being overhauled to copy Barney's! *Zut!*

You can find respectable, classical fashions in a well-bought atmosphere geared for madame. You'll feel very French if you browse, although you may get bored if you were expecting something hot or hip. I buy my Chanel-style camellias here, $10 is all each costs! Open Monday through Saturday, 10am to 5:30pm.

MARKS & SPENCER
33–45 blvd. Haussmann, 9e (Métro: Chausée-d'Antin); 88 rue du Rivoli, 4e (Métro: Hôtel-de-Ville).

From boulevard Haussmann, you can zigzag into the Garnier Opéra or go immediately into Marks & Spencer. Which would you rather do, really? The Marks & Spencer in Paris is amazingly like the flagship Oxford Street store near Selfridges in London. Locals depend on it, especially the fabulous grocery store on the first level. Go there not only for English snack foods, but for picnic supplies and sandwiches and ready-made foods to cut down on your dining costs in Paris.

Marks & Spencer is still a good place for underwear (try the private-label brand, St. Michael) and for good, sturdy, inexpensive kids' clothes. It is more elite to the French than to American tourists, but is not a must-do experience if your time is limited. Open Monday, Tuesday, Thursday, Friday, and Saturday, 9:30am to 6:30pm; Wednesday, 10am to 6:30pm.

SAMARITAINE
67 rue de Rivoli, 1er (Métro: Châtelet or Pont-Neuf).

It can be confusing to find your way around the separate stores and interconnecting basement here, but Samaritaine offers a distinctively French atmosphere to shoppers. Of the four buildings that make up the store, only one of them is even called Samaritaine. The most important shop is Store 2, which is behind Store 4. Store 4 has recordings, books, and art supplies. The sports department is in Store 3. But Store 2 is my favorite; it is also the only one with a bathroom. Locals use this resource as we would use Kmart or Target. In recent years, though, Samaritaine has made a concerted effort to take its image upscale. The best examples of this is the newly installed Inès de la Fressange home furnishings department and the *trés chic* new perfume department. It's not the obvious choice, but it makes you feel so much more French.

There is also a roof garden with a great view. Open Monday, Wednesday, Thursday, and Saturday, 9:30am to 7pm; Tuesday and Friday, 9:30am to 8:30pm. Dine at Toupary.

FABRICS, NOTIONS & CRAFTS

For those who sew, Paris, the home of fancy seams, offers plenty to get creative with. While fabric may not be less expensive than at home, the selection in Paris is so incredible that you are unable to think about price at all. Besides couture fabrics, you'll find the trendy fabrics—imitations of the hottest looks that Americans are still reading about in *Women's Wear Daily*. When the Gianni Versace–style prints went crazy a while back, I was able to buy a washable polyester with a silky hand to make a skirt. The total cost of the project was $25. No one in the U.S. had anything to compete.

Should you be somewhat interested in fabric, but not interested enough to spend much time tracking it down, stop by **Bouchara**. It's next door to all the big department stores in the 9e and has every imaginable fabric and notion—for reupholstering chairs or making your own clothing. Many are moderately priced.

If you want a taste of the world of couture, or just a silly adventure, you may want to spend a few hours in the **Marché St-Pierre** area in the 18th arrondissement, a neighborhood that sells fabrics and notions, almost exclusively. Couture ends are sold; shopkeepers are friendly. Some working knowledge of French will be helpful, and lots of cash. Take the *métro* to Anvers, or hail a taxi (a pricey ride), and go directly to **Sympa**. It has three locations—two on rue d'Orsel and one directly across from the Anvers *métro* stop, on the corner of boulevard de Rochechouart and rue du Steinkerque—you can't miss it; there are bins in the street.

After you've shopped the bins and been to as much of Tati as you can take, walk back one block to the fabric markets. This is a trip for the true and the strong, but I've rarely had a better day in Paris than the day that Pascale-Agnès and I spent here last winter. It was drizzling rain all day and we had a fabulous time. Need I say more?

For a few other couture fabric resources, try the following (all are famous for their fabric selections—Chanel, YSL, Dior): **Artisanat** in the Sentier, which also sells wool and yarn goods; **Sevilla**, right off Passy, which can be fabulous if you hit it right. Please remember that couture fabrics are not inexpensive—often they are $50 a yard for a silk that may not even be very wide. **Bouchara** carries the good stuff, but is more famous for its wide range of copycat fabrics at good prices. **Le Stand des Tissus** is a small shop in the heart of the textile markets. Pascale-Agnès has seen couture fabrics here; there were none when we looked last time. However, there were absolutely gorgeous English wools for about $20 a meter.

ARTISANAT TEXTILE
21 rue des Jeûneurs, 2e (Métro: Sentier).

BOUCHARA
54 blvd. Haussmann, 9e
(Métro: Chausée- d'Antin).

LA SOIE DE PARIS
14 rue d'Uzès, 2e (Métro: Rue Montmartre).

LE STAND DES TISSUS
11 rue de Steinkerque, 18e (Métro: Anvers).

RODIN
36 ave. des Champs-Elysées, 8e
(Métro: F-D-Roosevelt).

SEVILLA
38 rue de l'Annonciation, 16e
(Métro: La Muette).

TISSROY
97 ave. Victor Hugo, 16e (Métro: Victor-Hugo).

FOOD MARKETS

One of the difficulties of shopping in Paris is deciding which markets to visit and which to pass up. Unlike most other cities, which usually have one or two good markets, Paris is crawling with them. There are dozens of good ones, and it's impossible to get to them all unless you spend a month doing little else.

Most food markets are closed on Monday mornings; anything that is more or less open on a Sunday is not open on a Monday. The rue du Buci gets a slow start on Monday, but the action builds quickly.

With the exception of the Sunday market at Porte de Vanves and the *brocante* offerings at the place d'Aligre, most flea markets do not have food markets attached to them.

Years ago, the major wholesale food markets were in Les Halles; they have since moved to Rungis. This is a wholesale market, and tourists are not particularly welcome; you can go, but you should speak some French and know how to stay out of the way. It's best to sign up for a tour given by a professional, as the market really is "to the trade." To book a tour, call 1/41-80-80-82 or 1/40-15-04-57; tour costs vary based on the tour leader and can be as low as $10 per person or as high as $100 per person.

Markets selling organically grown vegetables and fruits are one of the newer trends in Paris; these are called *marché biologique*. There's one at the intersection of rue de Rennes and boulevard Raspail on Sunday on the Left Bank. I was not impressed.

When shopping markets, remember:

- Dress simply; the richer you look, the higher the price you'll pay. If you wear an engagement ring or have one of those wedding bands that spells "Rich American" in pavé diamonds, leave it in the hotel safe. I like to wear blue jeans and to try to fit in with the crowd; I also have a pair of French eyeglasses to complete my costume. Even though my French is atrocious, I speak French or mime my way through it.
- Ask your hotel's concierge about the neighborhood where the market is located. It may not be considered safe for a woman to go there alone or after dark. I don't want to be paranoid, but crime in market areas can be higher than in tourist areas.
- Have a lot of change with you.
- Don't touch the food, especially in the wholesale market. Ask for a taste or let the vendor choose for you. (Try flirting first for a better choice.)

- Food prices are usually fixed; you don't bargain as you might at a flea market. If the vendor likes you, he may throw in something extra after you've weighed in.

In Paris, many market areas are so famous that they have no specific street address. Usually it's enough to give the name of a market to a cabbie. Buses usually service market areas; but the *métro* goes everywhere and is usually your best bet. Food markets can be held any or every day of the week; flea markets are usually weekend events. Food markets alternate in various neighborhoods; you can often find a good one any day of the week. All of the food markets listed below are open on Sunday!

🛍 RUE DE BUCI
(Métro: St-Germain-des-Prés).

The rue de Buci is behind the church of St-Germain-des-Prés. This is a flower and food market that is colorful and quaint. Although it's located in a neighborhood with a number of antiques shops, the market does not sell *brocante*. If you go to only one street market in Paris, this should be the one. This is everyone's fantasy of Paris.

There are vendors on both the rue de Seine and the rue du Buci: There are fresh fruits and vegetables piled high on tables, buckets and buckets of brightly colored flowers, rotisserie chickens, even seashells and sponges. There are a few grocery stores and takeout food joints as well. Come hungry; leave very satisfied. Avoid Monday mornings, if possible, since not very much is open. Sundays are a special treat here.

🛍 RUE CLER
(Métro: Latour-Maubourg).

If you are tired of the rue de Buci, there is a less chaotic and possibly more authentic food street, which is also open on Sundays—the rue Cler. It's in a more residential part of the Left Bank, not that far from the Hilton and the Eiffel Tower.

The rue Cler is only about two blocks long, and it is jammed with the things that delight foodies. There are two local supermarkets; many small vendors who set up on the street; several branches of famous chocolatiers, including **Leonidas** (no. 39); and two famous cheese shops, one of which, **Barthelèmy,** has a rue de Grenelle address because it is on the corner (no. 51).

Tarte Julie (no. 28) is a great little place for dessert, tea or coffee, or Sunday brunch; they also have takeout.

Almost every store on the two-block stretch is open on Sunday (closed all day Monday), so you can buy many things, not just food items. This is a fabulous "We Are French" adventure. Stores open early Sunday—anywhere from 8:30am to 9am, and then close at 1pm for the day. Obviously, this is a morning excursion.

If it's a Sunday and you are looking for a nice stroll, you can leave the rue Cler via the rue St-Dominique, window-shopping as you stroll (sorry, the shops in and around here will be closed), and find yourself at the Eiffel Tower in no time at all.

PLACE D'ALIGRE
(Métro: Ledru-Rollin or Gare de Lyon).

The place d'Aligre has a covered indoor meat market, an open flower and vegetable market, several tables devoted to *brocante* dealers, and even a few shops along the way. Heaven, it's heaven. Furthermore, few tourists come here, so you are really getting a true picture of modern Paris, as there is a lot of ethnic diversity in the shoppers and some of the wares.

Betty, a discount source that hasn't impressed me for a few years, is right here (open on Sunday), so if you're curious, you can stop by. This used to be a great place to buy Léonard at discount; lately it has a lot of career clothes that don't do much for me.

The *brocante* is yard-sale quality; you may be annoyed you came so far if you expect much more. This market is open every day except Monday, but closes at about 1pm. While ready-to-wear is sold here, it is exactly what Grandma Jessie would call *dreck,* if you'll pardon her French. The yard goods are worthy buys from nearby factories. This market has a real-people Paris feel to it that will make you feel like an insider.

Please note that this area used to be in the boonies. Now, thanks to **Le Viaduc des Arts,** a new shopping attraction only a block and a half away, this is no longer the case. However, the stores here are not open on Sunday, which is a big mistake. The two can be combined on other days of the week, except for Monday.

FOODSTUFFS

If you are looking for an inexpensive gift to bring home, consider taking a small but tasty treat or even putting together your own food basket. Foodstuffs are not necessarily easy to pack or lightweight, but they can be rather cheap and look like a lot once you get home and put them in your own basket or wrap them up in a clever fashion.

My single best gift in this category is a jar of Maille's Provençale mustard. You can purchase a selection of four Maille's mustards (total cost in France, $6), which makes a great hostess or house-warming gift.

The easiest place to do foodstuff shopping, and probably the cheapest, is at Prisunic or Mono-prix. I've become an **Inno** convert and usually go there (place Juin 18, in the 14e) immediately after checking into my hotel. It's a direct shot on the *métro,* and a good job for someone with jet-lag. There's a **Prisunic** on the Champs-Elysées, another behind Printemps on boulevard Hauss-mann, and yet another at St-Augustin; all of these locations are central to most hotels on the Right Bank.

If your palate or your pocketbook is advanced, Paris has no shortage of food palaces. As far as I'm concerned, the grocery store next to Le Bon Marché (**La Grande Epicerie**) and the one above Monoprix on boulevard Haussmann (**Lafayette Gourmet**) are more reasonably priced than the more famous houses and more fun to shop. Don't forget the entire rue du Buci, with two grocery stores and many small shops. You cannot bring back any fresh foods; processed hard cheeses are legal, all others are not. Dried items (such as mushrooms) are legal; fresh fruits and vegetables are not.

If you plan on buying foodstuffs, save your plastic bags from your shopping adventures or bring a boxful of plastic bags with you. Wrap each jar or bottle in plastic and tie the top of the bag with a twist tie before you pack the item. If the cushion provided by your clothes doesn't protect the jar, at least you won't get mustard all over your new suede shoes. Many of the big food stores will ship for you, but beware: Foodstuffs usually are very heavy.

LA BOUTIQUE LAYRAC TRAITEUR
29 rue de Buci, 6e (Métro: St-Germain-des-Prés or Mabillon).

Here you can pick up anything from *boeuf bourguignon* to *pommes de terre au gratin* dished out in a container for your picnic. Few items are over $15. Who needs Tour d'Argent?

FAUCHON
26 place de la Madeleine, 8e (Métro: Madeleine).

Prices are high here, and many of these items are available elsewhere (have you been to a Prisunic or Inno lately?), but it's a privilege just to stare in the windows. The salespeople also are extraordinarily nice. There are three parts to the store: Fruits and dry goods are in a mini department store of many floors, prepared foods are next door, and the cafeteria is across the street. You buy a ticket, then pick up your purchases.

FOUQUET
22 rue François-1er, 8e
(Métro: F-D-Roosevelt).

If asked to pick the single best gift item in Paris, I just might say it's a Fouquet gift box. As heavy as they are famous, they are nonetheless wonderful. Too heavy to carry home with you? Not to worry: The store will ship for you. There's no problem finding lovely gifts in the $25 to $50 range; just bear in mind that the cost of shipping may double the price. Still, the boxes are so extravagant that it does seem worth it. Jars are filled with chocolates, jams, gingered fruits, nuts, and other assorted edibles.

G-20 COMESTIBLES
rue de Buci, 6e (Métro: St-Germain-des-Prés or
Mabillon).

More like a fancy supermarket, G-20 is right in the middle of all the French charm of the rue de Buci. Stock up from the vendors and have a marvelous picnic. This store is bigger than a 7 Eleven, but not as large as a supermarket.

GARGANTUA
284 rue St-Honoré, 1er (Métro: Tuileries).

Another of my regulars between the Hôtel du Louvre and Hôtel Meurice, Gargantua has cooked foods, wines, jars, and cans of fine eats. It's only a block from the Tuileries, so you can picnic in the garden if you like. This is a full-line shop, so you can get everything at one stop. They'll happily throw in free plastic knives and forks.

HÉDIARD
21 place de la Madeleine, 8e (Métro: Madeleine).

Conveniently located around the bend from Fauchon and Marquise de Sévigné (my favorite chocolate candies are bought here), Hédiard competes handily with Paris's other world-class food stores. It's been in the food biz since the mid-1800s, and there is little you cannot buy in this shop. They will also deliver, but room service may not be amused.

LENÔTRE
44 rue d'Auteuil, 16e (Métro: Michel-Ange Auteuil); 49 ave. Victor Hugo, 16e (Métro: Victor-Hugo); 5 rue du Havre, 8e (Métro: Havre-Caumartin).

Lenôtre will always mean chocolate and dessert to me, but the store is a full-fledged charcuterie. Pick up a picnic here. They're open on Sunday (quite unusual) and will gladly guide you through any pig-out. For a price, they will deliver to your hotel.

FLEA MARKETS

. . . .

Paris is famous for its flea markets, although I think only two big ones are worth getting hot and bothered over. I have found that many people think of the markets in St-Ouen as the only game in town, when, in fact, I think Vanves is better.

PUCES DE VANVES
(Métro: Porte de Vanves).

This market is not like any other market; it's more like a bunch of neighbors who all went in together for one of those big five-family garage sales. The garage sale just happens to stretch for a mile or so. The market is L-shaped: On the main part of the street are the licensed vendors who pay taxes to the city; on the branch part are the illegal, tag-sale vendors, who are, of course, the most fun. The tag-sale people's goods are of lesser quality than those of the pros, but together they make for wonderful strolling and browsing. If you don't have much time or can't stand the strain of St-Ouen, this is a neighborhood affair that is perfect for a Sunday or a Saturday. In fact, Saturday is considered the best day to shop Vanves. Early birds get the worms, of course.

The main part of the market is on the avenue Georges-Lafenestre. With the legal and the illegal guys, there are almost 200 vendors here. Prices are the best in town: I bought a plaster virgin for 10 F; an old postcard album (empty) for 50 F, and numerous *feves,* all for 10 F each. I splurged on a green glass necklace from the 1960s for 150 F. There's a crêpe stand at the bend in the road; the street market on Sunday enhances the experience. Start early: 9am is late for Saturday, but just right for Sunday.

THE MARKETS OF ST-OUEN
(Métro: Porte de Clingnancourt).

Also known simply as the Marché aux Puces, or the famous flea market, St-Ouen comprises several different markets, each with its own kind of dealers and each with its own special feel. Before I get into the complexities of the market, I might add that unless your French is first-rate, you may not be properly pronouncing this venue and may have difficulty getting directions or help. Get a lesson from your concierge before you set out.

Tip: It's pronounced "San-Twan." Honest.

The St-Ouen markets grew from a series of little streets and alleys. Today, over 75 acres of flea market sprawl through this suburb. The market most frequently bears the name of the street on which it rests—even though you may be hard pressed to find the original street sign. The markets themselves are usually well marked.

Usually the stalls open onto the street or a walkway but have some covered parts; these are not street vendors set up garage-sale style. Even the informal markets are sheltered. There is some amount of street action and selling off makeshift tables, but not a lot. There is, however, plenty of street action in terms of stalls, candy stands, and blue jeans dealers as you walk from the *métro* to the flea market. This is not the flea market you are looking for; these dealers should all be ignored.

Do remember there are plenty of places to eat on the premises, not as many places to go to the bathroom as you might like, and more pickpockets and rowdy boys than the French government would like to admit.

If you feel like you need to have a system for working this vast amount of space, try mine. Start with the big guns (Biron, Cambon) and the markets in that area, and walk your way back, so that Malik becomes one of your last stops. In fact, if you like Marché Malik as little as I do, you'll be happy to run out of there and call it a day.

To do it my way, you'll turn into the market streets on the rue des Rossiers (if your back is to the *métro* station you came from, you'll turn left). You'll work this street until the good stuff peters out, and cut to the left by shopping your way through the Marché Paul Bert. Then you'll go right on the rue Vallès until you've shopped it thoroughly. At that point, retrace your steps by cutting through Malassis. Note that there are freestanding antiques stores as well as the big (and small) markets.

Marché Antica: Just a little-bitty building refinished in the Memphis Milano teal-blue-and-crème look. This market is filled with cute shops selling small collectibles of good quality at pretty good prices. Actually a corner of the Marché Vernaison at the corner of rue des Rossiers and rue Voltaire.

Marché Biron: This is the single fanciest market in the place; it's one of the first markets you'll come to on rue des Rossiers. This should be the first stop for dealers who are looking for serious stuff. If you come here first and you are looking for fleas, you may be turned off. It's quite hoity-toity.

Marché Cambon: Another serious market but a little less refined—the dealers are usually busy hobnobbing with each other and may ignore you totally. You'll see furnishings in various states of refinish and find dealers in various states of mind—some know what they have and are very hard-nosed about it; others want to move out the merchandise and will deal with you. They are particularly responsive to genuine dealers who know their stuff and speak some French. The selection is less formal and more eclectic than at Biron, and there are rows of stalls along lanes or aisles. Next door to Biron.

Marché Dauphine: Newer village of some 300 shops opposite the Marché Vernaison on the rue des Rossiers, making it one of the first places you want to hit when you get to the market area. It's enclosed with a balcony and a factorylike high-tech atmosphere under a glass rooftop and industrial lighting. There is a shipping agency on hand. Some of the dealers are affordable here; I found a button dealer to buy from and a specialist in vintage designer clothing that flipped me out for *fripes*.

Marché des Rossiers: A very small market specializing in the period between 1900 and 1930. There are about 13 small stalls in an enclosed U-shaped building; fronts on the rue Paul-Bert.

Marché Jules-Valles: I like this one although it's small and junky; it's got reproduction brass items for the home mixed in with real antiques and real repro everything else.

Marché Malik: Ugh! It may be famous for its *fripes*—used clothes—but I find it seedy, disgusting, expensive, and dangerous. Need I say more?

Marché Paul-Bert: I saved the best for last. Are we having fun yet? If not, send the husband and the kids to the pizza place and go for it on your own—this is too good to not enjoy. This is the market that is more outdoorsy than the rest; it surrounds the Marché Serpette in three alleys forming a U. This market is both outside and inside, with lower-end merchandise, including art deco, moderne, and country furniture. Most of the items here have not been repaired or refinished. There could be some great buys here, but you need to have a good eye and know your stuff. Piles of suitcases, carts, dolls and buttons in bins. Yummy. If you do only one market or want to start with the very best, or you think the weather may turn on you, start here please.

Marché Serpette: This market is in a real building, not a Quonset hut. There is carpet on the floor, and each vendor has a stall number and a closing metal door. There also are nice, clean bathrooms on the second floor. It's on the edge of the Marché Paul-Bert, but you can tell the difference because this one is totally indoors and is sort of dark and fancy.

Marché Vernaison: I like this market a lot, although the new building puts me off a bit. There isn't that much I want to buy; I just like to prowl the various teeny showrooms. There are a few fabrics, textiles, trim, and needleworks mavens who always have things I covet. It sprawls to quite an extent and you may not at first realize that this market alone rather constitutes a village with its own streets and byways, all with stalls, of course. This is a good first stop because it has a lot of natural charm and many affordable places; it's also first if you follow my walking path.

PUCES DE MONTREUIL
(Métro: Porte de Montreuil).

I have included this market because I want you to know that I know it exists and that I've been here. But it's really only for die-hard flea market shoppers. It's a junk fair of sorts, so there are very few diamonds here—and those that exist are artfully hidden. You could hunt for hours before throwing up your hands in disgust, having found nothing.

This immense market has absorbed three other nearby markets and has a huge path of illegal vendors that stretches from the nearest *métro* station all the way across a bridge to the beginning of the market proper. There's a good selection of *fripes* (used clothes), Victorian bed linens, old hats, new perfumes (look, Mom, who needs *détaxe?*), work clothes, cheap clothes, records, dishes, junk, junk, and more junk. Did I mention there is a lot of junk? This is a really low-end market without any charm whatsoever. Dealers work this market very thoroughly—it runs a good 10% to 20% cheaper than St-Ouen. But it is 50% harder to find anything good. This is for those with a strong heart and a good eye; princesses and blue bloods need not apply.

FRENCH BIG NAMES

. . . .

AGNÈS B.
3 and 6 rue de Jour, 1er
(Métro: Étienne-Marcel).

An international chain of ready-to-wear shops selling casual clothes with enough of a fashion look to make them appropriate for big-city wearing. Jazzier than the Ann Taylor look. Near the Forum des Halles.

ANDRÉ COURRÈGES
46 rue du Faubourg St-Honoré, 8e
(Métro: Concorde); 40 rue François-1er, 8e
(Métro: F-D-Roosevelt); 49 rue de Rennes,
6e (Métro: St-Germain-des-Prés); 50 ave.
Victor Hugo, 16e (Métro: Victor-Hugo).

ANDRÉ COURRÈGES STOCK
7 rue de Turbigo, 1er (first floor)
(Métro: Étienne-Marcel).

Courrèges invented the mini-skirt and gave us all white patent leather boots. Despite his excesses of the past, Courrèges actually has a very traditional basic line, some dynamite skiwear, and very little that is weird or wacky. You still can find some stuff that is so reminiscent of the 1970s that you don't know if it's new or old merchandise.

The upstairs stock outlet is closed on Monday and opens at 10:15am otherwise.

AZZEDINE ALAÏA
7 rue de Moussy, 4e (Métro: St-Paul).

ALAÏA STOCK
18 rue de la Verrerie, 4e (Métro: Hôtel-de-Ville).

Tunisian-born Alaïa shocked Paris fashion with his skintight high-fashion clothes and his first boutique in the then up-and-coming Marais neighborhood. Now people expect the unusual from him; get a look at the architecture of this place and you know he'll never disappoint.

The clothes are only for the young, or those with figures like movie stars, but the man is on the cutting edge of fashion and retail. Like many shops in the Marais, this one opens at 11am.

The outlet shop is in the headquarters of the firm and not inconvenient to touristic haunts. You'll find end-of-season clothing, samples, pieces of this and that; all at 50% to 60% off regular retail. Even with last season's garments, you're looking at prices that begin around $200.

CACHAREL
34 rue Tronchet, 8e (Métro: Madeleine);
5 place des Victoires, 1er (Métro: Bourse).

CACHAREL STOCK
114 rue d'Alésia, 14e (Métro: Alésia).

Jean Cacharel made his name in America when he introduced charming clothes in precious prints. Thankfully, he has graduated from sweet along with the rest of us, and now does a wide line of separates that are moderately priced. I prefer Cacharel for children's clothes rather than for adult fashion; there is a discount/stock shop that sells the whole shebang.

CÉLINE
38 ave. Montaigne, 8e (Métro: F-D-Roosevelt or Alma-Marceau); 24 rue François-1er, 8e (Métro: F-D-Roosevelt); 26 rue Cambon, 1er (Métro: Tuileries); 58 rue de Rennes, 6e (Métro: St-Germain-des-Prés).

An old French name that was actually born right after World War II, Céline makes clothes and leather goods. New ownership has brought new direction to the house, as well as a new shop—with more branch stores anticipated in the world's best shopping cities. (There are already 83 stores around the world.) There is a horsey motif, similar to Hermès; scarves, bags, and ready-to-wear are the specialty. Prices are less than Hermès, but they are not modest.

CHACOK
Les Trois Quartiers, place de la Madeleine (Métro: Madeleine).

This is a French sportswear line with boutiques all over France; I have no idea why they haven't conquered the rest of the world. The clothes are usually bright and fun-filled, with a slight ethnic edge. For designer sportswear, the prices are moderate. I was tempted by a sweater coat for $400, but decided to wait for the sale. I love these clothes for restful weekends in the South of France. I don't know who wears them in Paris.

CHANEL
31 rue Cambon, 1er (Métro: Tuileries); 42 ave. Montaigne, 8e (Métro: F-D-Roosevelt or Alma-Marceau).

What becomes a legend most? The mother house, as it's known in French, which holds both couture and a boutique at this famed rue Cambon address, tucked behind the Ritz.

Two smaller boutiques are open across town on the tony avenue Montaigne; they are good to remember if rue Cambon is mobbed with tourists, as it often is. However, Cambon has a bigger selection.

There aren't a lot of bargains here, even on sale. You may be hard pressed to find sales help that is pleasant. But prices are less than regular retail in the U.S., and you will undoubtedly qualify for *détaxe* if you are a serious shopper. Sale prices in the U.S. may be surprisingly competitive.

A lot of the accessories—which are the only things that mortals can hope to embrace—are put away in black cases in the front of the store, so you have to ask to be shown the earrings and chains, which is no fun and puts a lot of pressure on you.

I happen to buy my Chanel at the duty-free store at JFK airport in New York; it's cheaper than in Paris and while you don't get a high-fashion selection, you can get simple gold-tone earrings for about $125 to $150.

If you're game, try a used Chanel suit. A classic is a classic is a classic, no? Check with **Réciproque, Dépôts-vent de Passy,** or **Didier Ludot.** Used suits are not cheap, since this is not a new trick; you'll pay around $2,000. Usually the blouse is sold with the suit at Ludot, but it brings the price of the suit up; at Chanel the blouse is another purchase. Expect to pay $3,500 or more for a new suit at Chanel. (*Note:* Used Chanel is less expensive in New York and in London.)

If by any chance you expect to find faux Chanel in French flea markets, you can forget it right now. France is very strict about copyright laws; Chanel is even stricter. You want a pair of imitation earrings for $20? Go to Manhattan.

CHARVET
8 place Vendôme, 1er (Métro: Opéra or Tuileries).

Although Charvet sells both men's and women's clothing, this is known as one of the grandest resources for men in continental Europe. Elegant men have been having shirts tailored here for centuries. You may buy off-the-rack or bespoke. Off-the-rack comes with only one sleeve length, so big American men may need bespoke. The look is Brooks Brothers meets the Continent: traditional yet sophisticated. American men like to come here for status appeal. The mini department store of the shop is filled with boiserie and the look of old money. A man's shirt, like all quality men's shirts these days, costs well over $100.

CHRISTIAN DIOR
30 ave. Montaigne, 8e (Métro: Alma-Marceau).

Although the real Christian Dior is dead, the line carries on his fashionable tradition. This large house has many floors for shopping—you can get ready-to-wear, costume jewelry, cosmetics, scarves, menswear, baby items, and wedding gifts, as well as the couture. In fact, several little shops are clustered around the main "house."

One of the best things about the House of Dior is that they seem quite aware that you want to buy from them and have gone out of their way to have items priced for tourists with taste. The gift department is exhaustive—local brides often register here. There are numerous $25 to $50 items that will be gift wrapped for you in the distinctive Dior wrappings that will make your gift list wilt with delight. I give Dior high marks for merchandising their famous name to make everyone happy; I give their salespeople high marks for carrying out the stereotypical haughty behavior that offends many.

CHRISTIAN LACROIX
26 ave. Montaigne, 8e (Métro: Alma-Marceau);
73 rue du Faubourg St-Honoré, 8e (Métro: Concorde).

You no longer need to be a couture customer to buy a little something from Christian Lacroix. I found a pin for under $100 worth writing home about. Clothes may be dramatic and expensive, but the accessories are wearable and affordable. Walk in to examine everything; the Montaigne space is a visual feast. Get a look at the front of the store. For color and sheer delight, this place should be on everyone's must-see list.

Now then, here's something I learned from *Paris Pas Cher*, a French guidebook to Paris for visitors on a budget: Upstairs at the Faubourg address is a room selling end-of-the-season goods and samples. If price tags of 4000 F don't frighten you, there are some virtual bargains here.

CLAUDE MONTANA
31 rue de Grenelle, 7e (Métro: Sèvres-Babylone); 3 rue des Petits Champs, 1er (Métro: Palais-Royal); 56 ave. Marceau, 8e (Métro: Victor-Hugo).

Montana may sound American to us, but these inventive stores and inventive clothes are utterly French. I just don't know how he gets away with it.

DEVERNOIS
255 rue St-Honoré, 1er (Métro: Tuileries).

This is an extremely French line that I can't imagine any American would know much about yet. It's somewhat similar to Rodier in that there are great knits that travel well, but much of it will appear a tad old lady-ish to a young American eye. There are shops everywhere. These are clothes that work well if you must mix with a European crowd and don't want to look too American.

DOROTHÉE BIS
46 rue Étienne Marcel, 2e (Métro: Étienne-Marcel); 33 rue de Sèvres, 6e (Métro: Sèvres-Babylone).

The woman responsible for getting this business off the ground was none other than the Duchess of Windsor. Sweaters and knits always have been the house specialty and continue as such. Prices are moderate to those of us used to outrageously high designer prices. There are several retail outlets: for men, for women, for sportswear, for discount.

EMANUEL UNGARO
2 ave. Montaigne, 8e (Métro: Alma-Marceau);
2 rue Gribeauval, 7e (Métro: Rue du Bac).

If you were to translate the colors of the rainbow through the eyes of a resident of Provence, you'd get the palette Ungaro is famous for. The couture house is a series of three chambers that connect on the rue Montaigne, so you can see many aspects of the line in one larger space. Don't be afraid to walk in and take a look.

If you are remembering the smaller boutique on the Faubourg, remember what I told you about the Faubourg? Ungaro moved that shop to a Left Bank location; it is a franchise.

FABRICE KAREL
39 ave. Victor Hugo, 16e (Métro: Victor-Hugo);
95 rue de Seine, 6e (Métro: St-Germain-des-Prés).

FABRICE KAREL STOCK
105 rue d'Alésia, 14e (Métro: Alésia).

If you were a fan of Sonia Rykiel way back when, you will appreciate the knits of Fabrice Karel, which are very similar to old Sonia clothes and more sophisticated than Rodier knits—great for travel. I would also like to tell you that Fabrice is not a woman's name; the line is designed by a man. (Imagine my surprise!) If you aren't familar with the line, put down this book right now and flag a taxi, please.

The stock shop (which is closed on Monday) has both old and current styles; old sells for very little money (how did I pass up that black knit skirt for

$40?), while the new collection is less than retail but not dirt cheap. If you wear a lot of navy and white, these knits are classics to collect. In the outlet, you can buy an entire suit for about $200 or something you love for about $50.

FAÇONNABLE
9 rue du Faubourg St-Honoré, 8e
(Métro: Concorde).

Façonnable has taken over the high street of every French city and moved into vacant space on the Faubourg St-Honoré. Under the auspices of Nordstrom, they have also come to the U.S. and even opened a store on Fifth Avenue in New York.

The clothes are simply preppy menswear. Navy blazers. Navy and white stripes for summer. Khaki trousers. Gray flannel trousers. Topsider shoes. You get the picture.

The Faubourg store is sort of like a fancy version of "the Gap goes BCBG"; the stores in Nice are nicer, if you'll excuse the expression. Maybe preppy just plays better at the beach.

GIVENCHY
3, 8, 29–31 ave. George V, 8e (Métro: George V);
66 ave. Victor Hugo, 16e (Métro: Victor-Hugo).

Hubert de Givenchy retired, and his couture is now designed by brash British upstart John Galliano. Shopping the stores can be confusing—there seem to be shops all over avenue George V—but it's really quite simple: The couture house is upstairs at 29–31. The men's store takes up three floors and sells everything. Women's accessories and ready-to-wear are housed in two separate shops.

 ## HERMÈS
24 rue du Faubourg St-Honoré, 8e (Métro:
Concorde); Hermès Hilton Hotel, 18 ave. de
Suffren, 15e (Métro: Bir-Hakeim).

While we're on the subject of status and power, well, I'm just forced to mention Hermès, perhaps the single best-known French luxury status symbol. The Hermès scarf is universally known and coveted; the handbags often have waiting lists. I've personally gone nuts for the enamel bangle bracelets that are much less expensive in Paris than elsewhere in the world. Since they cost about the same as a scarf, you may want to reprogram your mind for a new collectible. And the tie? Well, it's a power tie with a sense of humor, that's all I can say.

Remember, in order to get the best price at Hermès, you need to qualify for the *détaxe*. Plan to buy at least two of anything (or four ties). Unless, of course, you buy a saddle.

If you can't buy anything but want the thrill of your life, wander the store to educate your eye and then show your copy of this book at the scarf counter, where they will give you a free copy of a gorgeous booklet called *Comment Nouer Un Carré Hermès—How to Tie an Hermès Scarf*. It's all pictures, so don't worry if you can't read French.

You'll have trouble stopping at two items if you are talking scarves or bangles: There are thousands and thousands of choices. You'll also have trouble breathing as you battle your way through the throngs who gather at the scarf counter and the tie racks. If you are claustrophobic, go to the Paris Hilton and shop for Hermès in peace.

Final Tips: Don't forget to see if your airline sells Hermès scarves and ties in their on-plane shop; these usually cost slightly less than at Hermès (although the selection is often limited). If you want used Hermès, Didier Ludot is the most famous specialist (see p. 000).

JEAN-CHARLES DE CASTELBAJAC
6 place St-Sulpice, 6e (Métro: St-Germain-des-Prés).

Castelbajac may be too wild and too expensive for you to make a special trip to this off-the-beaten-path location (a new address). His creative mind continues to produce original works of art for when you want the world to notice you. Not for the shy or the short. His mother has a shop near the Marché St-Honoré.

JEAN-PAUL GAULTIER
6 rue Vivienne, 2e (Métro: Bourse or Palais-Royal).

JUNIOR GAULTIER
7 rue du Jour, 1er (Métro: Les Halles).

Gaultier fans can use Paris as an excuse to find the Galerie Vivienne. The boutique is the cornerstone of the Galerie Vivienne, a landmark *passage* near Victoire. Soak up the pleasures of the galerie itself, while you take in the high-tech shock appeal of Gaultier's unique mix of videotech, fashion, and architecture. The younger line (Junior) is less expensive and not appropriate for anyone over 40. Make that 30. It is sometimes sold at discount shops on rue St-Placide.

KARL LAGERFELD
17 rue du Faubourg St-Honoré, 8e
(Métro: Concorde).

Flagship store for Kaiser Karl and his non-Chanel and non-Fendi lines in snazzy, newly refurbished digs right on the Faubourg. It's extremely modern in the decor department, and you are to act shocked, like the rest of Paris.

KENZO
3 place des Victoires, 1er (Métro: Bourse);
Les Trois Quartiers, 23 rue de la Madeleine,
8e (Métro: Concorde); 18 ave. George V, 8e
(Métro: George V); 99 rue de Passy, 16e (Métro:
La Muette); Kenzo Studio (Espace Nouvel);
60–62 rue de Rennes, 6e (Métro: St-Germain-
des-Prés).

Yes, Kenzo does have a last name; it's Takada. Yes, Kenzo is Japanese, but he's a French designer. The clothes are sold in Galeries Lafayette, as well as all over the world, and are showcased in big high-tech stores designed to knock your socks off. The line isn't inexpensive—but there are great sales. If you're looking to make one moderate designer purchase, you can get a T-shirt for $30 that will make you feel like a million.

LACOSTE
372 rue St-Honoré, 8e (Métro: Concorde).

Lacoste, often called *le crocodile* in France, is one of those tricky status symbols that you assume will be cheaper here—after all, it is a French brand. But it isn't. You will pay $85 for a short-sleeve shirt in France, when the same shirt costs $65 at Saks Fifth Avenue in the U.S. It's because Lacoste is a tremendous status brand in France—more so than in the U.S.

LANVIN
15 rue du Faubourg St-Honoré, 8e
(Métro: Concorde).

The House of Lanvin is one of the oldest and best known of French couturiers, due mostly to its successful American advertising campaigns for the fragrances My Sin and Arpège (promise her anything . . .). In recent years, the line has been in transition as the house tries to find its place in the modern world. The men's store has a fabulous cafe on the basement level that is a must-do for any weary shopper. You can get a burger for less than $10, and some of the best scrambled eggs I've ever eaten were consumed right here.

LÉONARD
48 rue du Faubourg St-Honoré, 8e (Métro: Concorde); 36 ave. Pierre 1er de Serbie, 16e (Métro: Iena).

Léonard is a design house that makes clothes but is perhaps more famous for the prints the clothes are made of. Many pieces are made from a knitted silk; the prints are sophisticated, often floral, and incorporated in ties and dresses. A men's tie will cost about $100, but it makes a subtle statement to those who recognize the print. I can get it for you cheaper if you come to Italy with me; I've been to the factory shop.

The last time I was in Paris, Pascale-Agnès and I were walking past Léonard and admitted a terrible secret to each other: We now like Léonard. I don't know if we're getting older or the line is getting better (or both), but I do think this is a very chic, very French way to spend some money making a splashy entrance at just the right place.

LOLITA BIS
3 bis, rue des Rosiers, 4e (Métro: St-Paul).

Although she sounds like a Polish union leader straight from the docks, she is the darling of the hot set in Paris—and has been for several years. The Lolita Bis line is sold in this store; it's a less expensive (and less wacky) line than her signature collection (jackets in the $350 range). Accessories are extremely affordable and may even come in around $25. Anything from this designer has to be considered collectible by fashion mavens.

LOLITA LEMPICKA
*14 rue du Faubourg St-Honoré, 8e
(Métro: Concorde); 2 bis, rue des Rosiers, 4e
(Métro: St-Paul).*

LOUIS VUITTON
6 place St-Germain, 6e (Métro: St-Germain-des-Prés); 57 ave. Montaigne, 8e (Métro: Alma-Marceau or F-D-Roosevelt).

Louis Vuitton himself opened his first shop in 1854 and didn't become famous for his initials until 1896, when his son came out with a new line of trunks. Things haven't been the same since.

Nor will you ever be the same after you've seen the new Left Bank store, designed by Anoushka Hemphill. The front door alone is worthy of a half hour of silent, stunned appreciation. The store is on different levels, and you sort of weave up and down and around. Toward the front of the store is the house collection of restored but older LV luggage and steamer trunks; these are for sale. You may also bring in your old ones for repair or renovation.

The avenue Montaigne shop is brash, cold, and unfriendly. The Vuitton staff is there to take you by the hand and guide you to a purchase or two or three. There are set limits on how much you may buy. Worship on the Left Bank.

MARITHE ET FRANÇOIS GIRBAUD
38 rue Étienne Marcel, 1er
(Métro: Étienne-Marcel).

Masters of the unisex look, the Girbauds are still making the only clothes that make sense on either sex with equal style. While they have many lines, and you may never see everything these designers can do, their main store is a must because of the architecture. Discounted jeans can sometimes be found at **Le Mouton à 5 Pattes.**

NINA RICCI
39 ave. Montaigne, 8e (Métro: Alma-Marceau).

I think we can cut to the chase here. I mean, we all know Nina Ricci is a couture house. Let's go straight to the good stuff.

Downstairs is where the samples are sold. There is a large and incredible selection of evening gowns and a few day dresses and suits. If you don't need a ball gown but are looking for a gift to give someone you want to impress, consider the Ricci gift department, which is small enough to consider with one big glance. There are $25 gift items here that will be wrapped in Ricci wrap to ensure that they look like a million. Sale gift items will not be wrapped, by the way. The men's store is next door on the rue François-1er. This store is closed all day Saturday and from 1 to 2pm every day for lunch.

PHILLIPE MODEL
79 rue des Sts-Pères, 6e (Métro: Sèvres-Babylone).

Have you ever looked at those pictures of the fashion showings (couture and *prêt*) in your *WWD* or *W* and fallen in love with the hats that have been teamed with the clothes? If so, you'll be pleased to find Model, who makes many of the hats and is famous for his inventive, slightly crazy, and very stylish *chapeaux*. There are also shoes. This shop happens to be behind the Hôtel Meurice; there is a more accessible shop in Little Dragons on the Left Bank. Prices on sale are over $100 for a simple hat, but these are the things whimsy are made of. Pascale-Agnès's Mom saw a bunch of out-of-season hats at Miprix, the discounter, for reasonable prices. You just never know.

RODIER
Rodier Étoile, 15 ave. Victor Hugo, 16e (Métro: Victor-Hugo); Rodier Rive-Gauche, 35 rue de Sèvres, 6e (Métro: Sèvres-Babylone); Rodier Forum des Halles, 1er (Métro: Châtelet); Rodier Passy, 75 rue de Passy, 16e (Métro: La Muette); Rodier Kasha, 27 rue Tronchet, 8e (Métro: Madeleine).

Rodier makes knits that are ideal for travel. I wear a lot of their clothes on the road. Regular retail prices in Paris are no bargain, but can be good during sales. However, prices at French sales may not be as good as U.S. sale prices! Know your stuff before you pounce. Also note that some pieces in France are not available in the U.S.

There are 16 boutiques in Paris; the big news is the new home for their Kasha line. It's near place de la Madeleine, so take a look.

SONIA RYKIEL

70 rue du Faubourg St-Honoré, 8e (Métro: Concorde); 175 blvd. St-Germain, 6e (Métro: St-Germain-des-Prés). Inscription Rykiel, 6 rue de Grenelle, 6e (Métro: Sèvres-Babylon). Sonia Rykiel Enfant, 4 rue de Grenelle, 6e (Métro: Sèvres-Babylone). SR Stock, 64 rue d'Alésia, 14e (Métro: Alésia).

Sonia Rykiel began rewriting fashion history when she was pregnant and couldn't find a thing to wear; her children's line was born when she became a grandmother. Now her daughter Nathalie is also designing, so there've been big changes in the family real estate, with Sonia moving into a gorgeous new store and Nathalie taking over the older space.

It's Nathalie who is responsible for the new line called Inscription Rykiel, which is being sold in the former Sonia shop, now that Mom has moved into her new shop right on the boulevard St-Germain. Inscription Rykiel is a younger, more casual, less expensive line than what Sonia does, and is priced more moderately—though not moderately enough for my taste! Right next door is Sonia Rykiel Enfant. The baby clothes are quite sweet, but I just can't spend $50 for a little velour pull-on.

TEHEN

Les Trois Quartiers, place de la Madeleine, 8e (Métro: Madeleine).

Tehen is designed by Maria Cornejo, who made her name in the British fashion scene as the other half of the Richmond-Cornejo duo. She's now in Paris doing knits, short skirts, and Lycra jerseys that retail from $100 to $400. There are branch stores here and there; the most convenient address appears above.

THIERRY MUGLER
49 ave. Montaigne, 8e (Métro: Alma-Marceau);
10 place des Victoires, 2e (Métro: Bourse).

Count on Mugler for a certain look—both pure
and outrageous. The shops offer selling space
that could put a museum to shame. Walk down
a longish entry after you are inside and into a
salon of selling space. Along the way you'll pass
blue lights, modern art, and a few spare articles of
clothing.

VALENTINO
17–19 ave. Montaigne, 8e (Métro: Alma-
Marceau); 27 rue du Faubourg St-Honoré, 8e
(Métro: Concorde). Valentino Homme, 376 rue
St-Honoré, 1er (Métro: Concorde).

Valentino shows in Paris and takes his fashion very
seriously here. He renovated the shop rather recently
in order to hold his place of esteem among his couture neighbors. The Oliver line is also sold here, but
you won't find V or Night in this palace of beige
marble and glass.

YVES SAINT LAURENT
Rive Gauche, 19–21 ave. Victor Hugo, 16e
(Métro: Victor-Hugo); 38 rue du Faubourg
St-Honoré, 8e (Métro: Concorde). YSL Couture,
43 ave. Marceau, 16e (Métro: Alma-Marceau).
YSL Couture Accessories, 32 rue du Faubourg
St-Honoré, 8e (Métro: Concorde). L'Institut
Beauté Yves Saint Laurent, 32 rue du Faubourg
St-Honoré, 8e (Métro: Concorde). Variations,
9 rue Grenelle, 7e (Métro: St-Germain-des-
Prés).

For ready-to-wear that's less expensive than Rive
Gauche, there's the Variations line (although if you
are a Rive Gauche fan, you may find Variations is
too low-end for you). The full Variations line is difficult to find in the U.S. Check it out when you hit
the YSL discount store, Mendès.

Don't forget that Saint Laurent is also in the beauty biz. There is a beauty institute that does skin care, but not hair, next to the accessories shop on the Faubourg.

HAIRSTYLISTS

. . . .

I've taken to having my hair done when I travel—not only does it save on the stress of packing several hair dryers of different voltages, but it allows me into a new world for a few hours and a chance to see how the other half lives. I come away with a lot more than clean hair.

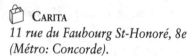

⬛ CARITA
11 rue du Faubourg St-Honoré, 8e
(Métro: Concorde).

Perhaps the most famous name in beauty in all of Paris, Carita offers an entire townhouse devoted to putting madame's best foot forward. The entrance is on the Faubourg, but off the street; the door is a wall of glass with an electronically controlled wave machine so that the ocean seems to separate you from the world beyond. Indeed, more than an ocean separates some of us from Carita's kind of style.

The great thing about this place, aside from the fact that the staff at reception speaks English, is that it's so organized you can be assured you'll be taken care of. Just walk to the appointment clerk (on street level to your left once you've parted the waves) and make an appointment. You can, of course, ask for a particular stylist, but if you don't, not to worry. You'll be in good hands, regardless.

The stylists are all dressed in white uniforms; the patrons are wearing expensive clothes and carrying the best handbags in Paris. You are given a paper number when you check in; don't lose it. This is your client number, which stays with you until you pay the bill.

Note: You receive your number when you check your coat and/or belongings and pick up your smock. Patrons do not take off their clothes here; the smock is put directly over what you are wearing.

The cost of the pampering is the going rate for ultra-fancy in Paris; you can do better price wise, but never experience wise. I consider each trip to Carita a souvenir for myself. I come away with a memory and a good do. A shampoo and blow-dry, which includes service, costs about $60.

Beauty products and accessories are sold at the back desk at street level. Call or fax ahead for an appointment if you wish. ☎ 1/44-94-11-00; fax: 1/47-42-94-98.

ALEXANDRE DE PARIS
3 ave. Matignon, 8e (Métro: Matignon),
☎ 1/43-59-40-09; Les Trois Quartiers, place
de la Madeleine, 1er (Métro: Madeleine),
☎ 1/49-26-04-59.

Alexandre is legend. The aura lives on within the house; there is cachet attached to just whom at Alexandre does your hair. In fact, you are to know to book Charlie and that Charlie is a woman! (Charlie does Catherine Deneuve.) Of course, Charlie will charge you $400 to $500 for your coif.

Indeed, Alexandre may be the most famous of the old-school hairdressers. The name is so well known that there's a separate hair accessories business, with shops all over the world.

JACQUES DESSANGE
37 blvd. Franklin D. Roosevelt, 8e
(Métro: F-D-Roosevelt).

Still famous after all these years, Dessange has a number of shops in Paris and other locations. Not as fancy as Carita, but with a big-time reputation nonetheless, Dessange attracts a younger client than

Carita. Hollywood's Jose Eber started here. Sometimes you can run into a promotional package where the shampoo, cut, and dry costs 195 F! They may also give you a free makeup consultation. There is a beauty and makeup line, which is sold at the salon and at pharmacies. ☎ 1/43-59-31-31 for the salon nearest you. There are literally hundreds of salons in France; they are expanding throughout the U.S.

L'ORÉAL CENTRE TECHNIQUE
281 rue St-Honoré, 1er (Métro: Tuileries or Concorde).

I love this very notion. If you are in Paris and feel like a hair fling, but are watching your budget, you can pay about $15 and be a guinea pig for color or a cut. The price is actually 70 F. They are closed for lunch from noon to 2pm, but otherwise you can drop in. The location couldn't be better. ☎ 1/40-20-97-30.

MANIATIS
35 rue de Sèvres, 6e (Métro: Sèvres-Babylone), ☎ *1/45-44-16-39; 18 rue Marbeuf, 8e (Métro: F-D-Roosevelt),* ☎ *1/47-23-30-14.*

Still one of the hot shops for models and runway stars, Maniatis has three salons in Paris (one is in Galeries Lafayette) and a beauty school. The beauty school, at the Forum des Halles, has a service that offers free haircuts to those clients who are willing to let a student practice on them. To get information about the training sessions, held on Wednesday evening, call 1/40-39-90-95. Men, women, and teens may participate.

If you want to go for a regular Maniatis session, pay attention to your location and the day of the week. The Right Bank salon is open on Monday; the Left Bank salon is not. If you are doing this up proper, forget about going to GL. I mean, really.

HANDBAGS & LEATHER GOODS

. . . .

DIDIER LAVILLA
15 rue du Cherchez-Midi, 6e (Métro: St-Germain-des-Prés).

Every once and again I wander into a store and find a resource that is so exciting that I want to tell the world. This teeny-tiny shop is such a place. I thought it was my personal find until I found it written up in *Madame Figaro*. Clearly, the word is out, but the prices have not yet gone up.

Lavilla makes nylon handbags in various fashion colors that are so chic you can barely stand it. And with prices in the 360 F to 400 F category, they're easily affordable. There are also belts, gloves, and hats.

DELVAUX
18 rue Royale, 8e (Métro: Concorde).

Straight from Belgium and stunning, the Delvaux line of handbags is deluxe yet practical, with many bags large enough to fit into an active American woman's lifestyle. Prices are in monumental range, and can only be considered a saving if you were thinking about a bigger splurge at Hermès. A fine status tool for the person who wants something no one else at home can get. Frankly, $500 is the top of my budget, not the opening bid, so I only stare here and drool.

DIDIER LAMARTHE
219 rue St-Honoré, 1er (Métro: Tuileries);
19 rue Danou, 2e (Métro: Opéra).

If you are looking for something drop-dead French—elegant and *sportif* and totally different from the other big names sold in duty-free shops and American department stores—head for one of this designer's shops. Lamarthe sells luggage, handbags, and small leather goods (wallets and much more) at high but not top-of-the-line prices to those who buy only the best and crave fabulous color. When I'm rich and famous, I shall have a bag in every color.

MAKEUP & PERFUME

For tips on buying strategies, see page 66.

🛍 ANNICK GOUTAL
14 rue de Castiglione, 1er (Métro: Tuileries or Concorde).

This tiny shop on the rue de Castiglione is a Paris landmark, but there are actually a number of outlets for Annick Goutal in Paris and elsewhere in the world. For example, it's sold at Bergdorf's in New York and Harrods in London. So what's so special? Just step into the Belle Époque–style salon and sniff the house brands, which include perfumes, lotions, and house scents. If you are looking for a special gift for someone who understands the meaning of the word *sublime*, search no further. Be sure to look at the firm's logo, which is spelled out in a mosaic on the sidewalk in front of the store. I'm addicted to the soap called l'Hadrien, which happens to be the house soap for hotels in the Concorde chain. I like it so much I've been known to pay cash for it. *Zut!*

GUERLAIN
68 ave. des Champs-Elysées, 8e (Métro: F-D-Roosevelt), ☎ 1/47-89-71-00 (for treatment appointments); 2 place Vendôme, 1er (Métro: Opéra); 93 rue de Passy, 16e (Métro: La Muette); 29 rue de Sèvres, 6e (Métro: Sèvres-Babylone); 35 rue Tronchet, 8e (Métro: Madeleine).

GUERLAIN INSTITUTS DE BEAUTÉ
68 ave. des Champs-Elysées, 8e (Métro: F-D-Roosevelt); 29 rue de Sèvres, 6e (Métro: Sèvres-Babylone).

Perhaps the most famous name in fragrance in France, Guerlain has two different types of boutiques in Paris: Some sell products only, while others have salons on the premises.

Some insider's information: Guerlain has been bought by a large purveyor of luxury goods. Soon the Guerlain name will be attached to many other luxury products. They already have scarves. Who knows what else is to follow. Perfumes are now sold only through Guerlain stores and are not discounted; the brand is rarely found at a duty-free store. If you see it at a duty free, chances are there is no discount. This may change in the near future, but the new owner wants to protect the name value, so it's unlikely. Some of the Guerlain fragrances you'll see in France are not sold in the U.S.

PERLIER
8 rue de Sèvres, 7e (Métro: Sèvres-Babylone).

This beauty line is made with honey and is widely sold in the U.S. In fact, sometimes I can buy it at Marshall's and save on French prices. The nicest thing about the line is its large number of small items that make adorable gifts (like the honey bath balls!). There's all sorts of beauty products, though—shampoos, bath gels, body lotions, night creams, morning creams—you're getting the idea. I'm addicted to the vanilla-scented line.

SEPHORA
70 ave. des Champs-Elysées, 8e (Metro: F-D-Roosevelt); Forum des Halles, 2e (Métro: Châtelet or Les Halles); 50 rue de Passy, 16e (Métro: La Muette); 66 rue de la Chausée d'Antin, 9e (Métro: Trinité); 38 ave. du Général Leclerc, 14e (Métro: Alésia).

This is a chain of cosmetics shops all over France. It is one of the best things about shopping in France. The Champs-Elysées store is open seven days a week.

About Bourjois

You've heard of Chanel, but Bourjois? Bourjois is the name of the company that owns the Chanel line of makeup and perfume; it makes a lower-priced line of makeup under the Bourjois name—at the same factories where Chanel is manufactured! This doesn't mean that the two lines are identical, but if you can't afford Chanel and want to give this line a whirl, you may be pleased with the investment (about 50% to 75% less than Chanel).

Bourjois is hard to find in the U.S., but it's not hard to find in Paris—if you know where to look. You can buy Bourjois at any branch of **Prisunic**, **Monoprix**, or **Sephora**, or at any big French department store, such as **Galeries Lafayette**. Prices are the same in all retail outlets; it's two francs less at a duty-free store.

What makes the line so special? For starters: many, many, many shades of eyeshadow sold in big containers that can last you forever. The nail polishes and lipsticks are also good. Their rouge colors are excellent.

Sephora gives only the *détaxe,* not the duty-free price. Who cares?

SHU UEMURA
176 blvd. St-Germain, 6e (Métro: St-Germain-des-Prés).

He's one of the most famous makeup artists in the world, and you can buy his makeup products in every world capital. He's a cult hero in his native Japan. Color is the name of the game here. The hues are spectacular. If you consider yourself an aficionado of cosmetics, to be in Paris and not go to Shu Uemura is a sin. Yes, it's even better than Bourjois; more expensive, too. A single square of color costs about $16. Splurge. This high-tech shop is filled with samples and mirrors and brushes, just encouraging you to come in and make up your face again and again.

SALON SHISEIDO
142 Galerie de Valois, Jardin du Palais-Royal, 1er (Métro: Palais-Royal).

If you think this is one of those stores that caters to Japanese tourists, you can forget it right now. This happens to be not only one of Paris's best-kept secrets, but one of the must-do addresses any serious shopper (I mean, sociologist) should seek, merely from an academic standpoint.

First, a quick history lesson. Shiseido *is* a Japanese makeup firm, true. A million years ago they hired the most famous makeup artist in Paris, Serge Lutens, and let him explore his creativity. This tiny shop, with the most glorious decor in Paris, sells the private inventions and designs of Mr. Lutens and is best known for his custom-made perfumes. And note that everything is a perfume—there are no derivatives. A bottle of scent costs about 550 F. Beware the stopper; it's not set in too well, so you must pack your fragrance carefully or hand-carry it onto the plane.

Now then, about the location. The location is simple and easy for all; it's the address that may confuse. Pay no attention to the address and follow my directions. Get yourself to the Comédie-Française (next to the Palais-Royal *métro*); walk behind it and into the garden of the Palais-Royal. First you'll see creative modern sculpture that will make you think you are at a *métro* station on Mars. Then you will see the many centuries-old gardens. On both sides of the gardens there is an arcade, crammed with shops. Each arcade has a name. Ignore the names. The Shiseido salon is in the far arcade across the garden.

PATRICIA DE NICOLAI
80 rue Grenelle, 7e (Métro: Rue du Bac).

A nose is a nose is a nose; this is the granddaughter of the Guerlain family, out on her own. Fragrance, candles, potpourri, and more. Note the odd hours. It's closed for lunch every day from 2 to 2:30pm.

POUDRE LECLERC
10 rue Vignon, 1er (Métro: Madeleine).

Barney's helped establish this old-timey French loose face powder as the hottest thing in America; trendies can buy theirs in many shops in Paris, at several *parapharmacies*, or at this, the brand headquarters, a block from place de la Madeleine. There are assorted pale colors to even out skin tone as well as many neutrals.

Makeup & Perfume Discounters

Remember, *discount* is a dirty word in France. Even a source that discounts, and has done so for years, suddenly is now terrified to use that word. Also note that because of the change in the *détaxe* law in 1996, there is still some confusion among different vendors as to how to implement changes (see p. 42).

CATHERINE
6 rue de Castiglione, 1er (Métro: Concorde or Tuileries).

If you've never been to Paris before, listen up. Catherine is my duty-free shop of choice. I do shop at other duty-free stores, believe me, but this is where I do the bulk of my shopping—when in Paris.

That's because Catherine is one of the few duty-free shops that will give you the discount up front. It works this way: Let's say you have had no trouble at all spending 1200 F (I have no trouble doing it; I think I can count on you). Now you qualify for a 40% to 45% discount. Your credit card will be charged with the discount in place! This is highly unusual. A second imprint is made with the 15% tax difference written on it. Should you fail to file the proper *détaxe* papers, you will pay the 15%. If you do what you need to do, when Catherine receives your paperwork, your second chit-slip will be destroyed.

A few other details about Catherine:

- The store is very tiny, so go early in the morning. There is room for no more than three customers at a time.
- I always work with Patricia, but the store is run by the Levy family; Patricia is one of the sisters. She and her sister Fanny and their mother, Madame Levy, all speak perfect English. Monsieur Levy makes me speak French so he can laugh.
- If you do not buy 1200 F worth of goods at first, but later return and buy more items, as long as the period is within six months (as required by law), Catherine will let you tally up all the receipts and get the *détaxe* when you reach 1200 F.
- There is a flat 25% discount if you don't reach the 1200 F level on all brands except Chanel and Christian Dior, which allow only a 15% discount. If you show your copy of *Born to Shop*, you will get a 20% discount on those two big names.
- Mail orders are taken by fax or phone, but require a $100 minimum purchase. The store's fax number is 1/42-61-02-35; ☎ 1/42-61-02-89.

🛍 PARFUMERIE DE LA MADELEINE
9 place de la Madeleine, 8e (Métro; Madeleine).

I recently discovered this duty-free shop and like it because I anonymously dished out a lot of trouble, which they handled relatively well. The store is large, by Paris standards, has many brands and some accessories. I bought some Christian Lacroix earrings here, which were slightly less money than in a Lacroix boutique. Their discounts vary with the brand, which they tell you up front. This makes it harder to know exactly what you are doing price-wise; some duty-free shops offer an across-the-line flat discount. On the other hand, they had an enormous discount on all Sisley products, which I use, and they steered me to this part of the store. If your purchases don't reach the 1200 F mark, they will allow you to save up several receipts until you qualify for a tax rebate.

SILVER MOON-LIZ
*Trois Quartiers, 23 blvd. Madeleine, 1er
(Métro: Madeleine).*

I can't help but be attracted to Silver Moon, even though I'm not sure why. Essentially it's no different from any other place in town, yet the mere fact that it's spacious makes an American feel at home. They offer only a 10% discount and a *fidelity* card (star card). This location, in the mini-mall Trois Quartiers, gives you a reason to see the mall, although Silver Moon is a large chain with stores all over town. You can easily go from one to the next and use your star card to run up another 5% discount.

They sell big names in fragrance but also lots of treatment lines, skin and hair care products, and some dime-store makeup, including Bourjois. They also publish a very nice magazine with prices that makes an excellent reference guide if you want to compare French prices to U.S. prices.

MALLS & SHOPPING CENTERS

Slowly, Paris has been going mall mad. The shopping center of your teen years does not exist in great abundance in Europe, but Paris is trying out every kind of mall you can imagine. The larger mall structures are often called "commercial centers." The success of **Les Trois Quartiers** has brought about the *intime* mall—sort of American in feel but smaller and therefore less intimidating. There are new entries constantly, all with very good addresses. Don't forget that the French had the original version of the mall, 150 years ago, with their *passages* and *galeries* (see "*Passages*," below).

FORUM DES HALLES
11 bis, rue de l'Arc-en-Ciel, 1er
(Métro: Les Halles or Châtelet).

The Forum des Halles was built to rejuvenate a slum and serves as an exciting monument to youth, style, and shopping. It's a huge square with a courtyard. The atmosphere is rather American and sterile, and it's easy to get lost once you are inside. You'll find it conveniently located directly above a *métro* stop, Les Halles, and down the street from the YSL discount store, Mendès. It's also a stone's throw from the Beaubourg, which you may want to visit. There are fast-food joints in the *métro* part of the complex and real restaurants among the shops in the regular complex.

A series of escalators zigzags between the floors; there are master maps throughout the mall to help you find your way. Although a number of designers and upper-priced bridge lines have stores here, the stores are often not as charming as the boutiques on the street can be. The Forum was built in stages; be sure to see the newest part of the mall, which stretches underground. Most of the stores in the Forum des Halles open Tuesday through Saturday between 10 and 10:30am and close between 7 and 7:30pm. All stores are closed all day Sunday and Monday morning, opening for business again at noon on Monday. All stores take credit cards.

LES TROIS QUARTIERS
23 blvd. de la Madeleine, 1er (Métro: Madeleine).

This is what I'd call a mini-mall. It's nothing to write home about, despite the fact that locals love it and find it very American. The stores are small (with the exception of **Silver Moon**) and well integrated.

I like the mix of designers and upscale suppliers. This is a good way to see a lot of shops fast. Designer shops range from **Kenzo** to **Chacok;** there's a little of everything thrown in, including **The Body Shop** and a few English chains. Also, the famed hairdresser **Alexandre** has a branch salon here.

The success of this mall has made the surrounding area one of the hottest in Paris retail; there's a new mall-like structure next door, Le Cedre Rouge, and a rehabbed *passage* across the place de la Madeleine.

LE CARROUSEL DU LOUVRE
99 rue de Rivoli, 1er (Métro: Palais-Royal).

This is an American-style shopping mall. While it isn't very big, its construction revolutionized Paris retail and brought on a new surge of mall-building within landmark sites. The mall is attached to the Louvre and has many entrances and exits.

For the easiest access, enter from the rue de Rivoli, where there is a small banner announcing the space. This entrance is not particularly prominent, so you may have trouble finding it. The mall itself is on two subterranean levels; enter and take the escalator down one flight to the food court. Go down another level and you are in a mall like any other in your neighborhood, except that this one has **Lalique, The Body Shop, Esprit,** and **Virgin Megastore.** There are just over a dozen stores down here as well as a branch of the French Government Tourist Office.

I can't tell you that any of these shops is fabulous or that there's something here you haven't seen before (most of the stores are branches of famous French, American, or British chains), but it's still fun to see what our increasingly homogeneous culture has come to. This is also a great way to shop through a Sunday, since everything is open on Sunday.

Through one of the mall walkways, you connect to the basement of the Louvre (underneath the

I.M. Pei pyramid) and many artsy gift shops, including one that sells items from museum stores all over the world.

PLAZA PASSY
53 rue du Passy, 16e (Métro: La Muette).

It sort of looks like a redone deco-style apartment complex in South Beach, without the blue stucco, but this new mall helps you get a lot done in one neighborhood and has a very upper-class feel to it, especially when you glance around at your fellow shoppers. It's not a big mall or a very special one. It's just that it's easy and still French. Many of the retail tenants are French chains . . . or American ones, including the Gap.

   I am not embarrassed to tell you that I think it's super here; it's not terribly French, but it is very much a part of the new French retail scene—global, man, global. I also love the grocery store, **Champion,** on the lower level. Boutiques are open daily, 10am to 7:30pm; the grocery store is open Monday through Saturday, 8:30am to 8:30pm.

MUSEUM SHOPS

. . . .

Almost all Paris museums have gift shops; and as there are about 50 museums in Paris, that's a lot of museum gift shops. Some are even organized into their own chains with branches in various museums; the Louvre has its own special shopping bags for all its gift shops. Some shops just sell slides, prints, and a few high-minded books or postcards. But several are really with it.

MUSÉE DES ARTS DÉCORATIFS
107 rue de Rivoli, 1er (Métro: Musée-du-Louvre).

There are actually two shops, on either side of one corridor. One is the gift shop, the other sells books and paper goods. Both are wonderful, but the crafts and reproduction gift items in the gift shop are especially great. Prices aren't low, but you'll find unique gift items, even a copy of the very first scarf Hermès ever created. Some of the merchandise is tied to traveling exhibits and therefore changes regularly.

Closed Monday and Tuesday. Sunday shoppers, note: Hours are noon to 5pm.

Musée du Louvre
Palais du Louvre, 1er (Métro: Musée-du-Louvre).

There's a gift shop under that glass pyramid, and it is a beauty, with two levels of shopping space. The store sells books, postcards, and repro gifts. *Beaucoup* fun. You do not have to pay admission to the museum to gain entrance. After walking into the pyramid, take the escalator down, and you will be in a lobby reminiscent of a train station. Glance around, read a few signs, and you'll soon see the gift shop—it's straight ahead.

Musée d'Orsay
Gare d'Orsay, 7e (Métro: Orsay).

The gift shop isn't as wonderful as the architecture, but you can buy prints and some reproductions, as well as a scarf or two. Good selection of postcards.

Centre Georges Pompidou
Centre Georges Pompidou, 4e (Métro: Châtelet).

The gift shop takes up much of the first floor and is a wonderful source for posters, books, and postcards.

Musée Carnavalet
29 rue de Sévigné, 3e (Métro: St-Paul).

This museum is in the heart of the Marais and documents the history of the city of Paris; the gift shop sells reproductions of antique items, many of which are owned by famous people. I have the Georges Sand stemware. Closed on Monday.

MUSIC

· ·

It all started when Mike, my husband, bought me a single Johnny Hallyday cassette; I've gone nuts for Johnny Hallyday and have bought a number of his tapes and CDs. They're are zillions of them (the man's career spans decades), but they can be pricey. I've paid 99 F, considered a bargain price, and I've paid 350 F for a multi-CD pack (it was worth it).

For the most part, music is not a good buy in France, but if you like French artists, you have little choice. I shop at any branch of **FNAC** I happen to pass (usually the one on rue de Rennes) or at

Jean-Louis Ginibre's Jazz Picks

Paris is my friend Jean-Louis's hometown. He's American now, but he still goes to Paris to buy jazz. His fave, for LPs and secondhand jazz and blues recordings, is **Paris Jazz Corner.** He also suggests that fans check out the stalls at the **Marché Malik** in the flea markets at St-Ouen (see p. 176), which are open only Saturday, Sunday, and Monday.

CROCODISC
64 rue de la Montagne Ste-Geneviève, 5e (Métro: Luxembourg); ☎ *1/46-34-78-38.*

LIBRARIE GILDA
36 rue des Bourdonnais, 1er (Métro: Châtelet); ☎ *1/42-33-60-00.*

PARIS JAZZ CORNER
5 rue de Navarre, 5e (Métro: Monge); ☎ *1/43-36-78-92.*

the **Virgin Megastore** (either the one at 52 ave. des Champs-Elysées or the one at Le Carrousel du Louvre). There are also music stores at all the Paris airports.

PARAPHARMACIES

. . . .

These uniquely French places—essentially fancy drugstores selling everything from aromatherapy essences to products made with retin-A—all carry virtually the same lines of goods, but I haven't found one I could resist. These are great places to purchase bath and beauty gifts for friends back home and to try new French cures and beauty products.

PARIS SANTÉ BEAUTÉ
161 blvd. St-Germain, 6e (Métro: St-Germain-des-Prés); 23 rue Tronchet, 8e (Métro: Madeleine).

The Right Bank shop opens Monday through Saturday at 9:30am; the Left Bank shop opens at 10am—both shops are open until 7:30pm, so there's no excuse to miss out. Not the largest, but chock-full of goodies. The Left Bank store has a location that you can't miss.

EURO SANTÉ BEAUTÉ
37 rue de la Boetie, 8e (Métro: St-Augustin).

This is one of the larger shops; it has a mezzanine and a lower level so you can shop all three floors and have a ball. They also publish a price list, which you can pocket and use to comparison-shop. There are over 200 brands on sale here; I consider it one of the better *parapharmacies* in town.

SELECT BEAUTÉ SANTÉ
4 rue Duphot, 1er (Métro: Madeleine).

This happens to be my regular *parapharmacie*, mostly because of the location—it's not that far from the Hôtel de Crillon. The store is enormous; I have a *fidelity* card that entitles me to 200 F off once I spend 2000 F.

PASSAGES
. . . .

A *passage* (it rhymes with "massage") is a shopping area, exactly like an arcade in London. Today, *passages* are the French equivalent of American mini-malls and are cut into a building's lobby like a throughway. In the early 1800s, new buildings were large, often taking up a block. To get from one side of a building to another, a *passage* was built. Since it's inside the building, it's totally covered. Doorways lead through the original structure.

There are lots of *passages* all over Paris. One of the most famous is the **Galerie Vivienne.** One doorway is on the rue Vivienne, the other is on the rue des Petits-Champs. The *passage* is not surrounded by a greater building but is directly across from the National Library and near the Palais-Royal; it has a number of cute shops, a **Gaultier** boutique, and a lost-world ambience that makes it very much worth exploring.

The shop owners in a *passage* usually organize themselves, at least informally. Together they will decide if their shops will be open or closed during lunchtime. (The Galerie Vivienne is open during lunchtime.) *Passages* have cheaper rent than regular commercial space, so usually you'll find relatively mundane enterprises (like a printer or bakery) or young designers who are just starting out but may be moving fast.

Also check out **Cour du Commerce St-Anne** (59–61 rue St-André-des-Arts, 6e; *métro:* St-Germain-des-Prés or Odéon), which is nestled into the Left Bank. The famous restaurant Le Procope is located in this tiny alley, but there's also a tea salon that I suggest for shoppers, called **Cour de Rohan,** and a few shops. It's not that the shopping is so great; it's that the charm is heart-stopping.

Others to check out, if only for the architecture and not the actual stores within: **Galerie Véro-Dodat,** 19 rue Jean-Jacques Rousseau; **Passage des Panorama,** rue St-Marc; and **Passage Verdeau,** 31 bis, rue du Faubourg Montmartre. **Le Passage du Havre,** 109 rue St-Lazare, is a modern *passage.*

RESALE & VINTAGE

The French pride themselves on being a practical people. They rarely throw anything away; they buy only the best quality and use it forever; they hate waste of any sort. But if someone in the family dies or if someone should fall on hard times, he or she can sell his or her fine possessions at a *dépôts-vent.* Or, knowing that good merchandise is being sold, he will frequent a *dépôts-vent.* No one in Paris is ever ashamed to be seen buying used items. They think it's smart. I do, too.

Do note that designer clothing that you may not consider purchasing at regular retail can be sale priced at the end of a season at virtually the same price you might pay at a *dépôts-vent. Dépôts-ventes* traditionally sell used clothing of current styles, while vintage shops sell older clothing. These days, with so many retro looks in vogue, it's hard to tell one from the other anyway. The two big flea markets, St-Ouen and Vanves, each have dealers who sell vintage clothing. The term *fripes* generally refers to nondesigner used clothing from the 1970s—not vintage Chanel or Balenciaga.

RÉCIPROQUE
89, 95, 97, 101, and 123 rue de la Pompe, 16e (Métro: Pompe).

Réciproque has grown at an alarming rate—there are now more storefronts bearing this store's name along rue de la Pompe than ever before. The main shop, no. 89, has two floors, so don't forget to go downstairs. There are racks and racks of clothes, all of which are clean. You'll find separates, shoes, evening clothes, and complete ensembles. You must look through the racks carefully and know your merchandise, although the labels always are in the clothes. Not everything is used, or seriously used—many designers sell samples here. Every big name is represented; this is the best single resource for used couture clothing. A Chanel suit will cost over $2,500—so prices are not dirt cheap.

🛍 Dépôts-vent Passy
14 and 25 rue de la Tour, 16e (Métro: Passy).

Another contender in the used-designer-clothing wars, Catherine Baril has two shops with top-drawer stuff—YSL, Chanel, the works. One shop is for women, the other for men. They are a few yards from each other. There is a fair amount of samples. On my last visit, I found tons of Chanel straight from the runway. The prices were generally high, but I found a few bargains. A Chanel suit (summer weight) for $1,500 seemed like a good buy, whereas a Chanel camisole for $200 was overpriced, at least to me.

The best part about this shop is its location. You can easily combine a stroll along the rue de Passy with a shopping spree here and have a fabulous time. Open Tuesday to Saturday, 10am to 7pm; Monday, 2 to 7pm. In July, Monday to Saturday, 2 to 7pm.

🛍 Didier Ludot
24 passage de la Galerie Montpensier, Palais-Royal, 1er (Métro: Palais-Royal).

Be still, my heart! Do I have a favorite hangout for used Chanel or what? Do I come here just to stare? Do you want to do the same?

This shop is not easy to find, so have patience and remember that it is on the gallery side of the building, not the street side. It is a very tiny shop run by a man who really cares about the clothes he carries and their history. He tries to sell only top-of-the-line used designer goods, specializing in Hermès, Céline, and Chanel. You may find old Hermès bags from the 1930s, as well as vintage Vuitton luggage. This store is a standout for old-clothes junkies. Prices are high for quality items, but not unfair: a Pucci in perfect condition, just over $1,000; a wool Chanel suit (no blouse), $2,000.

The easiest way to get there is via the Palais-Royal *métro*. Zig to the right into the open arcade, then hug the lefthand side of the arcade (where it is covered). Shops line the walkway. Ludot is here.

SHOES

Shoe freaks will find the Little Dragons neighborhood on the Left Bank (see p. 125) a treasure trove of little shoe stores belonging to famous designers and hoping-to-be-famous designers. Weave along these streets and you can't go wrong. Be sure to stop at the many shoe shops on the rue des Sts-Pères (there's even a branch of **Ferragamo** here), and then make your way onto rue du Four, where there are more shops for the teens. Don't forget to shop rue de Grenelle as well. For something truly unique or French, try some of these resources.

CHRISTIAN LOUBOUTIN
Vero-Dodat (arcade), 19 rue Jean-Jacques Rousseau, 1er (Métro: Musée-du-Louvre).

One of the new shoe darlings for those with diamonds on their souls (or soles), Louboutin has made his mark with wacky designs—think heels that look like handcarved trees. Prices begin at $300; many celebrity clients.

CAMILLE UNGLIK
66 rue des Sts-Pères, 6e (Métro: Sèvres-Babylone).

My notes on this shop are very simple. They say: Fab shoes!!! The store is small; it's in the Little

Dragons area. The shoes are inventive and whimsical. If you buy only one thing in Paris to show off at home, these shoes are it.

FRANÇOIS VILLON
58 rue Bonaparte, 6e (Métro: St-Germain-des-Prés).

This store is on the corner. The number is not well marked, and the store looks rather ordinary from the outset. Very little prepares you for the fact that this local shoemaker fits the stars, from Brigitte Bardot to Catherine Deneuve. I got the address from Princess Grace. (Honest.) Aside from the custom work, there are regular shoes in classical styles.

HAREL
8 ave. Montaigne, 8e (Métro: Alma-Marceau or F-D-Roosevelt).

These are truly the most exquisite shoes I have ever seen in my life, in terms of style, color, skins, and workmanship. The prices match. Flats begin around $500, while heels are more like $700. Still, press your nose to the glass just to understand all that Paris can be.

REPETTO
22 rue de la Paix, 2e (Métro: Opéra).

This is basically a supply house for ballerinas, but it offers much in terms of fashion, including dresses that would be great for black-tie events. This is the firm that introduced "le ballet" into fashion as a shoe rather than a dance item.

SOUVENIRS

Paris is loaded with souvenir shops. They congregate around the obvious tourist haunts (Notre-Dame, Champs-Elysées, etc.) and line the rue de Rivoli from Concorde all the way up to the front gate of the Louvre. They all sell more or less the same junk at exactly the same prices. Yes, folks, those prices are nonnegotiable. The only way you can get a break is to deal on the amount you buy. If you buy a few T-shirts, you might get a few francs knocked off. The price of T-shirts fluctuates, by the way, with the dollar: The price in francs varies (note the handwritten signs), so the T-shirts always cost $10. No dummies here. Naturally, there are T-shirts that cost more, but you'll have no trouble finding acceptable gifts for $10.

Some of my favorite things to buy at a souvenir stand include a toothbrush with your name in French, or some similar name in French; a breakfast bowl sponged in blue and white, also with your name in French; boxer shorts with various Parisian motifs; T-shirts with French universities; key chains with all kinds of possibilities—miniature Eiffel Towers, street signs, Napoleon, and more; scarves with kitschy tourist haunt designs that are so bad they are fabulous.

TEENS

Teens will have no trouble spending their allowance, and all future allowances, when it comes to Paris. Many will like the tourist traps along the **rue de Rivoli,** with sweatshirts and boxer shorts; others will go for the *fripes* and vintage clothing sold in markets. Any young woman over the age of 11 will be mad for any branch store of **Prisunic** and **Monoprix,** the two big French dime stores—both have tons of fashion at pretty fair prices, although the quality isn't much to brag about. Those with strong hearts may search the bins at **Tati** and come away with glad rags.

Most of the Left Bank is awash with stores that cater to students, some more fashionable than others. American-style clothes are in vogue with the French, so be careful. You could end up at the Gap or some place like **Chevignon,** which makes clothes that look like American clothes. For hot, body-revealing looks, check out **Kookai** at 1 rue St-Denis, 8–10 place St-Opportune, and 15 rue St-Placide; and **Morgan** at 165 rue des Rennes on the Left Bank and 81 rue de Passy on the Right Bank.

PRO MOD
67 rue de Sevrès, 6e (Mètro: Sevrès-Babylone).

This French chain is somewhere between the Gap and Ann Taylor. In summer, the clothes are perfect for any beach destination. In fall, they are more serious and businesslike, copies of current styles. Everything is priced so you can wear it one season and forget about it the next year. Many branches.

AU VRAI CHIC PARISIEN
8–10 rue Montmartre, 1er; 47 rue du Four, 6e (Métro: St-Germain-des-Prés).

The Left Bank shop is tiny, but exactly what you want in a Left Bank store: small and cozy, with great stuff at moderate prices. On sale, you'll want to buy armloads of these quasi-teen/quasi-adult fashions.

VESTS
. . . .

There is a certain look going around Paris, mostly for dress-up, but I've also spotted it on waiters at chi-chi restaurants: a brocade vest made from jacquard silk that would make Marie Antoinette feel right at home.

L'ESCALIER D'ARGENT
42 Galerie de Montpensier, Jardin du Palais-Royal, 1er (Métro: Palais-Royal).

I found this shop because it's very close to the vintage clothing store Didier Ludot; it's also close spiritually—this store specializes in textiles that were made in the 18th century. They mostly make ties and vests; ties cost about $60. The location only reinforces the magic of the goods in the store; this is Paris at its best.

FAVOURBROOK
Le Village Royal, 25 rue Royale
(Métro: Madeleine).

This is actually an English firm that has moved into this French fabric trend and gone wild for Regency this and that, including men's vests, but also accessories for men and women and all sorts of sumptious creations. With a business suit, one of these ties would make a very powerful statement.

Chapter Ten

. . . .

PARIS HOME STYLE

FRENCH STYLE

. . . .

Over the years, American home design has been tremendously influenced by French style. While country French is now considered classic, my grandmother's idea of decorating had to do with draped silk swags, watered silk, and reproduction Louis. Maybe she knew which Louis it was; surely I did not. Yet today I live with a jumble of her Louis and my Souleiado. I'm not alone.

Those going to Paris in search of home furnishings and accessories not only can choose between these two styles, but also can check out the newer French designs—everything from the sleek modern designs inspired by Philippe Starck's work to Jacques Grange's modern Shaker look. For the first time in perhaps a hundred years, new home furnishings and decorating ideas are coming out of Paris, led in large part by Andrée Putman (who's been hot for almost 50 years) and her protégés. The latest design rage is called "French Forties," and it bears not the slightest resemblance to reproduction Louis or Souleiado. It's closer to art nouveau, but reminds me of the decor and lines of a sleek ocean liner from the 1930s and 1940s. However one describes it, it'll open you up to a whole new way of seeing.

When shopping for the home in Paris, you can choose French antiques, *brocante,* table linens, or merely candles (wait till you see what the French can do with candles!). For listings of antiques shops, antiques events, *brocante* fairs, and even flea markets, see chapter 9. For everything else, flip this way. You need not do over the house or change your personal style, but please, make room for one lasting souvenir.

SMELLING FRENCH STYLE

Just before I left for Paris, I asked four different girlfriends, as I often do, "Is there anything you need from Paris?" All four of them asked for the same thing—a home scent. Despite all the aromatherapy available in the U.S., each woman wanted a different French brand.

Since they are such affordable gifts, I think you'll want to know about them, too. Jill wanted **Guerlain** liquid potpourri, which is sold in all Guerlain shops but is not available in the U.S.

Michele wanted the most interesting item of all— a lamp with scent from **Lampes Berger.** They have their own small store (14 rue Duphot, 1er; *métro:* Madeleine), although their products are also sold in the big department stores. Theirs is a staggering business just beginning to be imported to the U.S.

Lampes Berger makes oil-burning lanterns, not unlike fashionable genie lamps. They come in about three dozen styles and range from $40 to approximately $60 to $100. You buy the scented liquid oil separately for approximately $15 per bottle. Michele uses Greenwood, I use Océan. There are over one dozen different scents, each with a scratch-and-sniff label, so you can spend a lot of time trying to figure out which one you like best. The process of using this product is more complicated than lighting a simple aromatherapy candle, but then, this one works. If you smoke, look into this product immediately. Your colleagues at work will be much more fond of you after you set one up in your office.

One of my favorite suppliers is a firm called **Estéban,** which opened its first retail shop last year. Up until then, Estéban was a brand name that you could find only sporadically. Head over to the Left Bank to check their freestanding beauty: Estéban, 49 rue de Rennes, 6e (*Métro:* St-Germain-des-Prés).

SMART SHOPPERS' HOME STYLE
· ·

Let's face it, very few people with any smarts at all go to Paris to buy fine and formal antiques. Okay, maybe you're Lord Rothschild and you go to Paris for a few finishing touches for Spencer House. If you're playing in the big leagues, ignore this paragraph. There's no question that Paris has top-of-the-line resources; but the truth is, if you have ever cast a wary eye at the bottom line, you know that Paris has top-of-the-line prices as well. Even Parisians leave town to buy antiques.

People who have price in mind work the wide network of antiques shows, *brocante* fairs, auctions, flea markets, and weekends in the country that provide not only wonderful entertainment, but far better prices than you'll ever find on the Faubourg St-Honoré. Note that there are a number of annual events that charge an admission price of about 40 F. Don't be turned off by the admission fee; it's usually the sign of a worthwhile event.

While Paris has very serious antiques, real joy—even for those who are shopping to ship—is found in flea markets and alternative retail. Do note, however, that prices may be no lower than at big-time dealers—especially if you don't know what you are doing. People who really want to save money buy their antiques in Belgium (a train ticket to Brussels costs $50). See chapter 12 for details.

If you're a serious shopper and plan on doing some big-time buying, keep the following tips in mind:

- Buy from a reputable dealer with an international reputation.
- Prices are usually quoted in dollars once the sales tag is over $5,000.
- There is now a value-added tax on antiques; ask for a *détaxe* form.
- Make sure you are provided with the appropriate paperwork so that your purchase can leave the country. The French are not going to let any national treasures slip through their fingers.
- Insure for replacement value, not cost.

LE LOOK

Paris has its share of home-style shops that are similar to Pottery Barn—they sell a Euro look at a fair price, and it includes bed linens, textiles for the home, dinnerware, foodstuffs, and tabletop. Prices might not be any better than at home (in fact they could be higher), but you'll find style galore, not to mention items you can't find elsewhere. I am constantly amazed by this Euro look, because it was first mastered by the Englishman Sir Terence Conran. His ability to translate country and contemporary concepts and make them suitable for England, France, and Italy in his Habitat and Conran's stores paved the way for these French home-style boutiques and stores.

LE CEDRE ROUGE
5 rue de Médicis, 6e (Métro: Odéon);
25 rue Duphot, 8e (Métro: Madeleine).

A chain with shops outside Paris, Le Cedre Rouge tends to focus on a country garden look. Affordable style for the masses, but quite classy. Everything is beautifully displayed.

MIS EN DEMEURE
27 rue du Cherche-Midi, 6e (Métro: St-Germain-des-Prés); 66 ave. Victor Hugo, 16e (Métro: Victor-Hugo).

Sort of a hipper, more French Conran's. On my last visit, there were lots of country tabletop looks (items made with twigs) and papier-mâché Christmas ornaments. Some items border on the fabulous; others are rather ordinary. But when you first step inside and see all the glassware, linens, furniture, and lamps displayed together, you will think it's quite *extraordinaire*.

GENEVIÈVE LETHU
95 rue de Rennes, 6e (Métro: St-Germain-des-Prés); 12 rue de Passy, 16e (Métro: La Muette).

This designer has a boutique in Printemps Maison, Galeries Lafayette, and Bon Marché, or you can check out any of her several freestanding stores in Paris. Did I say several? There are about a dozen in Paris and maybe 50 shops scattered across France. There are also shops in the Far East and much of Italy. As of yet, there's only one in North America, and it's in Montreal. So shop in Paris or buy a franchise to this tabletop and kitchen shop and bring her to America.

Lethu does what I consider to be some of the most refreshing tabletop in Paris: Her use of color is bold and extravagant, and her prints are exotic, without being beyond the pale. She mixes contemporary tabletop and country looks so elegantly, that even a formal setting will work. The tablecloths are my favorite, but there's much more to choose from.

Last year I bought one of my best buys ever from Lethu: a wicker water bottle cover, 39 F. It's meant to fit a large-size bottle of Evian water. Surely, the gift for the person who has everything.

THE CONRAN SHOP
rue du Bac, 7e (Métro: Sèvres-Babylone).

Despite the fact that this is a British shop, Sir Terence Conran is an expert on French design. The store is filled with tons of whimsy and charm. Just browse and breathe the magic.

HABITAT

12 blvd. de la Madeleine, 9e (Métro: Madeleine); 45 rue de Rennes, 6e (Métro: St-Germain-des-Prés); CC Montparnasse, 14e (Métro: Montparnasse).

Although both were developed by Sir Terence Conran, Conran and Habitat are not the same store. In fact, these days they are no longer even similar. Habitat sells lower-end goods and is not my idea of something you'll want to plan your trip to Paris around.

SPECIALTY LOOKS

There are a number of chicer-than-thou shops that are so unique and so fabulously French, you have to visit them, if only to browse.

TERRITOIRE

30 rue Boissy d'Anglas, 8e (Métro: Madeleine).

I'm not at all certain how to categorize this shop. It sells a look that evokes English breeziness, lighthouses along the French Atlantic coast, and American summer cottages with Adirondack chairs on the lawn. Many Parisians summer on the French Atlantic coast. This is their shop. There are books and gifts and some tabletop. It's a terrific store in a great part of town. Enjoy it.

MAISON DE FAMILLE

29 rue St-Sulpice, 6e (Métro: St-Sulpice or Mabillon).

What I love about this store is what it looks like and what it feels like. What I don't like is that a lot of the merchandise is British, American, or imported from elsewhere. I can easily find similar goods at home for less. But put it all together and you have a serious browse.

La Tuile Loup
35 rue Daubenton, 5e (Métro: Cencier Daubenton).

Just trust me on this one. This shop is brimming with country French charm. It's worth the slightly out-of-the-way location, since you can easily wander into the 6th arrondissement from here. You may wish to call first to be sure they're open before making the trek. ☎ 1/47-07-28-90.

Rosemarie Schultz
30 rue Boissy d'Anglas, 8e (Métro: Madeleine).

This shop is quite close to Territoire, so be sure to see them both. Emotionally, however, the two shops are worlds apart. Schultz is a German designer and possibly a florist—her shop sells fabrics, pillows, sachets, and flowers. This is one of the most imaginative and truly special shops I've ever been in. Once I found this little gold string tied with shells and paper flowers, which may sound silly as I describe it, but is the most beautiful piece of whimsy I've ever seen. I hang it from my front door every spring.

There are "dream pillows," which are silken and almost medieval in look and feel; they cost between $30 to $50 apiece. Everything in the shop has texture and can be experienced through multiple senses: touch, smell, and sight. There are even items for under $10. If you check out only one new address this trip, this is it.

Agnès Comar
7 ave. George V, 8e (Métro: Alma-Marceau or George V).

This is another perfect shop with much to see and touch. There's a great deal of bedding, but tabletop is also in abundance. Very "in" with ladies who live in this part of Paris.

FABRIC SHOWROOMS

If you are a member of the trade or simply want to view showrooms, you are welcome to browse in decorator showrooms to get ideas. Don't be surprised if many of the home furnishings fabric suppliers want nothing to do with you unless you quickly brandish a business card that proves you are a designer. Most showrooms have U.S. representatives or distributors, and they do not want to undercut their own agents.

This leads to an even bigger point to bear in mind: You may find these same items are the same price (or even less) in the U.S. Mom, who ran a design firm in Manhattan, always traveled with business cards, which she presented—not when browsing—but during final negotiations on price or when the bill was presented. In flawless French, she then asked for a 10% trade discount. It usually worked.

You may also want to negotiate for the *détaxe* refund, for which you must qualify when you arrange to ship outside the country. Many firms will not ship to the U.S. at the risk of offending their American agents. Ask when you are talking turkey. Finally, remember that a huge amount of "French style" is actually British. Some of the best fabric showrooms in Paris showcase British goods! If you discover that your favorite item is British, buy it in the U.K., not France, if you want to save.

Check out some of the following showrooms to get a feel for the system:

BOUSSAC DÉCORATION
27 rue du Mail, 2e (Métro: Sentier).

One of the most famous names in fabric in France, Boussac has a complete line for home furnishings and for couture. This showroom sells the home furnishings fabric only. Yves Saint Laurent uses the wools from the other line, which is not called *décoration*. It's just called *cher*.

MANUEL CANOVAS

5–7 place Furstemberg, 6e (Métro: St-Germain-des-Prés).

Our living-room furniture is upholstered in Canovas, but I wasn't smart enough to buy it in Paris. While this showroom will not ship to you, you can take delivery in Paris (come back for your yardage in six to eight weeks), and then arrange for a shipper to receive the delivery. That way, you'll receive a magnificent 30% saving over U.S. prices.

While Canovas is known as a fabric house, it also sells gift items, ceramics, and even bathing suits (for kids, too) in the gift shop next door. This is the place to go for a fast injection of French style. The showroom is very much a trade kind of place; the gift shop should be on everyone's must-see list. Expect to pay dearly.

JAC DEY

1 rue de Furstemberg, 6e (Métro: St-Germain-des-Prés); 3 rue Jacob, 6e (Métro: St-Germain-des-Prés).

You can count on Jac Dey for really good fabrics for upholstery—choose from traditional light geometrics, jacquards, florals, and French patterns. Although there is a Dey showroom at 979 Third Avenue in New York, the prices here are better—a good 20% below what similar goods would be if bought in the United States. But the cost of shipping probably would equal the *détaxe* discount.

ÉTAMINE

3 rue Jacob, 6e (Métro: St-Germain-des-Prés); 63 rue du Bac, 7e (Métro: rue du Bac).

If all the French Laura Ashley shops haven't convinced you that the French love the English country look, one minute inside Étamine will. This is a crowded, fabulous shop filled with papers and paints and stencil kits and veddy, veddy English everything. They are the French agents for Colefax & Fowler, Collier & Campbell, Designer's Guild, Osborne & Little, and Charles Hammond. The trade showroom is very trade-sy (6e), but the shop on rue du Bac is more consumer-oriented. I found incredible tabletop gifts here, at moderate prices, the likes of which have never been seen in the U.S.

PIERRE FREY

2 rue de Furstemberg, 6e (Métro: St-Germain-des-Prés); 47 rue des Petits-Champs, 1er (Métro: Palais-Royal); 48 rue St-Dominique, 7e (Métro: Invalides).

This is a boutique of fabrics, wall hangings, towels, bed quilts, luggage, purses, boxes, and table linens in an explosion of paisleys that is reminiscent of India, yet very French—all at the same time. I consider this look fancy country French formal, if you can imagine such a thing: It's sold at Bergdorf Goodman. Try the scented candle.

I find the fact that there is a Patrick Frey and a Pierre Frey in the same business a little confusing, because the designer name and/or labels sometimes don't match. Rest assured, it is the same firm.

LELIÈVRE

13 rue du Mail, 2e (Métro: Sentier).

Lelièvre's bright colors, formal textures with heavy weaves, and jacquards effect a striking yet traditional look. This is an international showroom with offices in New York and all the major European fashion centers. The address should tip you off to something. Yes, there are several fabric showrooms along the rue du Mail.

NOBILIS
29 and 38 rue Bonaparte, 6e
(Métro: St-Germain-des-Prés).

A classic showroom, Nobilis is one of those airy, modern spaces that could be anywhere in the world, selling what it sells best. There are pads of paper and pencils, boards of fabrics and wallpapers—it's all just as you know it—but it's open to the public and is in the best location in Paris, right behind the church of St-Germain-des-Prés. In short, you do not have to be a decorator to buy. The fabrics are gorgeous, running from the palest of pastel cottons to the most brilliant silk moirés. There is furniture just down the street—another good source. Shipping is no problem.

ZUMSTEG
4 rue de Furstemberg, 6e
(Métro: St-Germain-des-Prés).

Although there really is a Mr. Zumsteg, the name refers to the fabric house that became famous when Yves Saint Laurent revealed that he chose many of his fabrics here. There also is a Zumsteg interiors line, which comes from the main offices in Zurich but can be bought in Paris for much less than in the United States. Most of the fabrics are extremely expensive and sophisticated. Those in the know know about this source.

GAMME
13 rue du 4 Septembre, 2e (Métro: 4 Septembre).

If you are redoing the family castle and you've decided against Italian silks to complete the medieval look, then only French will do—this is your resource. Actually, the silks are so incredible that I have considered buying some for evening gowns. If you are a fabric freak, don't miss it.

PASSEMENTERIE

I buy bits of *passementerie*—fringe and braid—at the flea markets, but if you are decorating your home and willing to splurge on the best, Paris has several serious sources.

PASSEMENTERIE DE L'ILE DE FRANCE
11 rue Trousseau, 4e (Métro: Ledru-Rollin).

This is just past the Bastille, but right on Napoleon in terms of style. They open at 9am but are closed Saturday and Sunday.

AU BON GOUT
1 rue Guisarde, 16e (Métro: La Muette).

This store's name means "With Good Taste"; they aren't kidding. They sell braids and buttons and all the things I love. You'll find them at the low end of the Passy district, so combine a visit here with a trip to the neighborhood. Couture buttons are sold here, but there are no CC buttons.

CLAUDE DECLERQ
15 rue Étienne Marcel, 2e
(Métro: Étienne-Marcel).

This designer makes new *passementerie* following old color schemes and methods; he will do custom work to match.

MARIE-PIERRE BOITARD
8 place du Palais-Bourbon, 7e (Métro: Invalides).

Good resource for simple *passementerie* in a chic, totally Parisian environment.

DECORATOR SHOWROOMS

I can't get too carried away with the idea of sending you to a decorator showroom in Paris—with one possible exception—Hilton McConnico. This

American in Paris is not only the talk of the town, but the darling of every European design magazine editor. I see pages and pages of his work almost monthly in every design magazine I read. Stop in and soak up the look.

HILTON McCONNICO
28 rue Madame, 6e (Métro: St-Sulpice).

I keep telling my Hilton friends that they have to hire this guy, so I can write "Hilton Does Hilton." Surely, Hilton has done every other big name in Europe. Now you know. There are ashtrays, lamps, and select tabletop. Nothing is inexpensive, mind you.

TABLETOP & GIFTS

Every place you look in Paris, there's another adorable shop selling gifts or tabletop. No one sets a table like the French. The department stores often have exhibits or even classes in table arts; you can take notes—or pictures.

MURIEL GRATEAU
Galerie de Valois, Jardins du Palais-Royal, 1er (Métro: Palais-Royal).

Muriel once designed ready-to-wear for Charles Jourdan; now she's nestled into her own place. There are linens in more colors than the rainbow and beautiful textiles. Her linen napkins come in 36 different colors!

EVERWOOD
96 ave. Paul-Doumer, 16e (Métro: La Muette).

This is a small shop in the Passy neighborhood that smells like success—the kind of which retail giants are made. Catherine Painvin, the designer/owner, came from the fabulous children's retail line Tartine et Chocolat, so I rest my case.

The look of the merchandise (and the shop) is very country French; on my first visit, I couldn't believe the goods come from Paris. Her look is totally different from Souleiado. She uses more solid fabrics and bigger patterns (checks and plaids), and lots of pale yellow or soft blue. Nothing busy or peppy—just loads of quiet country charm. There are total table settings as well as gift items, towels, and even boxer shorts. Utter charm. Buy your franchise now.

EN ATTENDANT LES BARBARES
50 rue Étienne Marcel, 2e (Métro: Étienne-Marcel or Palais-Royal).

Great shop for cutting-edge chic gifts. I'm most impressed with the items (especially candlesticks) made from resin. Stop by if only to gawk. At Victoires.

DINERS EN VILLE
27 rue de Varenne, 7e (Métro: Rue du Bac).

If you take my advice and stroll the rue du Bac, you will find this store on your own and congratulate yourself for being such a clever bunny. This is a small, cramped, crowded two-room store filled with the kind of French tabletop you and I adore. There isn't anything in this store I wouldn't buy. The address shouldn't throw you. It's on the corner of rue de Varenne and rue du Bac.

ART DOMESTIQUE ANCIEN
231 rue St-Honoré, 1er (Métro: Tuileries).

This is an antiques store specializing in kitchen and household items—it's fabulous. It's also a little bit hidden; you must walk into the courtyard in order to find it. It's worth doing.

AUX ÉTATS-UNIS
229 rue St-Honoré, 1er (Métro: Concorde or Tuileries).

This small, esoteric shop has nothing whatsoever
to do with shopping in the U.S. or with American-
made products—despite its name. It's mostly a luggage store, specializing in leather goods, but it also
sells travel gadgets and (go figure) porcelain dishes
for dogs. Since treating the dog as if he were a member of the family (he is, he is) is a French tradition,
you may want to see this rather unique pet selection—and pick up a souvenir dish for *le chien* . . . or
le chat.

LA DAME BLANCHE
186 rue de Rivoli, 1er (Métro: Tuileries).

Nestled between the tourist traps on the rue de
Rivoli is this tiny shop selling reproduction faience,
Limoges boxes, and Louis-style porcelains.

LAURE JAPY
34 rue du Bac, 7e (Métro: rue du Bac).

One glance at the windows of this tony shop in the
7th arrondissement, and you'll know why so many
designers feel the need to walk the Paris streets: There
are more ideas and inspiration here than you can
get in a week in your hometown mall. After you've
memorized the windows, step inside. You'll be overwhelmed by the Parisian chic of the tableware and
linens.

The first time I saw this shop I mentally wrote it
off as another Geneviève Lethu shop. Don't make
that mistake! Just because the store specializes in
color, it's not the same as Lethu! This shop is more
upscale, more sophisticated, and, *mais oui*, more
expensive.

SIÈCLE
24 rue du Bac, 7e (Métro: Rue du Bac).

It took me two trips to Paris to find this shop, not
that it's hard—I just walked the wrong direction
from the rue du Bac *métro* stop and had so much

fun, I never found my way back. The shop is between the river and the *métro,* so you can actually
walk across the bridge on rue du Bac and never go
near the *métro* station. It's a small shop, not one I
would have found on my own. I discovered it while
browsing the pages of *Elle,* looking for a present to
give my girlfriend (and former editor) Linda. *Elle*
featured a photo of the most wonderful pair of salad
servers and gave this shop as a resource for where
to buy them. Although the servers cost over $100,
they were so French, so chic, and so fabulous that I
just knew they were perfect. Everything else in this
store falls into this category. I saw another set of
salad servers that I liked more, but they were pale
green sharkskin and sold for over $500. Rarefied,
but fabulous.

MARÉCHAL
*232 rue de Rivoli, 1er (Métro: Concorde or
Tuileries).*

At first glance, this looks like a tourist trap selling
perfume, and not a particularly memorable one at
that. Still, there's a reason to stop in. Downstairs,
there's a great selection of Limoges boxes. Ask for
their catalog, which guarantees the French bargain
price and includes mailing to the U.S.

KITCHEN STYLE

Paris is rightfully renowned for its table arts;
luckily for tourists, there are a number of kitchen
supply houses within a block or two of each other,
so you can see a lot without going out of your way.
Price is not the object here; selection is everything.
Please note that most of the kitchen shops open at
9am (sometimes earlier), so you can extend your
shopping day by beginning with these resources. The
"kitchen neighborhood" is a matter of a block and

a cross street; you can easily start at one and walk to the others.

🛍 A. SIMON
36–38 & 48 rue Montmartre, 2e (Métro: Étienne-Marcel or Les Halles).

A major supplier of kitchen and cooking supplies for over 100 years, this store is conveniently located down the street from the Yves Saint Laurent outlet. You can buy everything from dishes to menus here; I buy white paper doilies by the gross—they have many sizes and shapes not available in the U.S.—at fair prices. Touch everything; this is a wonderland of gadgets and goodies. Remember, rue Montmartre is not in Montmartre; it is near Forum des Halles.

🛍 DEHILLERIN
18–20 rue Coquillière, 1er (Métro: Musée-du-Louvre or Les Halles).

Perhaps the most famous cookware shop in Paris, Dehillerin has been selling cookware for over 100 years. They mostly sell to the trade, but you can poke around and touch the copper, cast iron, tools, gadgets, and more. Or someone may even help you— try out your French; it goes a long way here. And they open at 8am! They're closed for lunch, so get here early.

LA CORPO
19 rue Montmartre, 1er (Métro: Étienne-Marcel or Les Halles).

This one isn't my favorite, but it, too, has a vast selection of kitchenwares, including much equipment. While you may be tempted, remember that electric gadgets are a no-no. Still there are lot of pots and pans and supplies that are very enticing.

🛍 DUTHILLEUL & MINART
14 rue de Turbigo, 1er (Métro: Étienne-Marcel).

This shop sells professional clothing for chefs, kitchen staff, waiters, etc. It would be a great resource for creative fashion freaks or teens. You can buy anything from kitchen clogs to aprons; a *toque* costs $12 while the *veste chef* is $30. There are various styles of aprons (which make good gifts) and many wine-related items. You'll find it right round the corner from the other kitchen shops and right at the Étienne-Marcel *métro* stop.

MORA
13 rue Montmartre, 1er (Métro: Étienne-Marcel or Les Halles).

Similar to A. Simon, but with more utensils (over 5,000 in stock), Morda has a salon for bakery goods that sells *fèves* in small (and large) packages. It has a huge papergoods section as well.

CANDLES

One of the first stores in Paris that ever bowled me over with just how clever the French can be was a candle shop, **Point à La Ligne.** Now that line is available at any French department store and in the U.S. Still, when you wander Paris, you will find extravagance and wit, often at an affordable price, at shops selling candles.

I now travel with aromatherapy candles, which I light in the bathroom while I soak in the tub or place by my bedside while I read. Do remember to snuff out the candle before you go to sleep! I used to buy **Rigaud** candles at my favorite duty-free shop, **Catherine,** but I now use other brands as well. Rigaud was the leading brand of scented candles when no was else was into this notion, and they are still at the top of the market in terms of status and quality. Most of the big fragrance houses (**Guerlain, Manuel Canovas**) sell scented candles in addition to perfume. For more home scent resources, see "Smelling French Style," earlier in this chapter.

POINT À LA LIGNE
67 ave. Victor Hugo, 16e (Métro: Victor-Hugo);
25 rue de Varenne, 7e (Métro: Rue du Bac).

Probably the most famous of the contemporary candle makers in Paris, Point à la Ligne has candle sculptures as well as ultra-skinny, enor-mously chic long tapers that make sensational birthday or celebration candles on a cake. In sum, they have all sorts of fabulous things. Their products can be found in all French department stores.

DYPTIQUE
34 blvd. St-Germain, 6e (Métro: Maubert-Mutualité).

This store sells the chic candle of the moment, partly because they are so sensual and partly because they are sold for sky-high prices in the U.S. Please note that this shop is not located along the touristy part of the boulevard. It's worth going out of your way to visit.

DELUXE LOGO STYLE

. . . .

Want a chic souvenir? Purchase something from a famous French address. There are several shops, cafes, and even tourist attractions selling attractive logo merchandise in Paris.

SALON DU THÉ BERNARDAUD
11 rue Royale, 8e (Métro: Concorde).

This is tricky, because there's an entire Bernardaud china shop at this address. What I'm suggesting you purchase are the Bernardaud logo souvenirs, in porcelain, that are sold at the front counter of the tea shop. I have the white, gold, and celadon ashtray, 50 F.

🛍 BOUTIQUE CRILLON
Hôtel de Crillon, 10 place de la Concorde, 8e
(Métro: Concorde); 17 rue de la Paix, 2e
(Métro: Tuileries or Opéra).

The Crillon is one of the most famous hotels in Paris. Even if you aren't staying here, you may want to visit for tea. Or to shop. Because the hotel is part of a chain of hotels (Concorde) that's owned by a famous French family (heard the name Taittinger before?), their gift shop sells products made by other companies in which the Taittinger family has an interest. Accordingly, you'll find an amazing array of French luxury goods—Annick Goutal and Baccarat, to name just a few. They also have Crillon logo goods that you wouldn't dare steal from your room—robes, slippers, note cards, etc.

The Crillon actually has two boutiques: one in the hotel and one along the rue de la Paix. The merchandise ranges from glassware and porcelain to handbags. Some items are decorated with the hotel crest; everything is beautiful to look at. Prices usually begin around $30, but wait: They have napkin rings for $10. Gorgeous ones, too.

Even without its association with the Hôtel de Crillon, this would be a good group of shops. Better yet, the gift shop located within the hotel is open on Sunday and stays open late during the week.

BOUTIQUE DU CAFÉ DE FLORE
26 rue St-Benoît, 6e (Métro: St-Germain-des-Prés).

The Café de Flore is one of the three famous Paris bistros on the Left Bank (the other two are Les Deux Magots and Brasserie Lipp), but so far it's the only one that's opened its own gift shop. The tiny store is around the corner from the cafe, and just adorable. You get a free chocolate when you wander in (you may buy a box), and you can choose from dishes, serving pieces, paper goods, and all sorts of gift items.

COMPTIOR DE LA TOUR D'ARGENT
2 rue du Cardinal Lemoine, 5e (Métro: Maubert-Mutualité).

La Tour d'Argent is one of the most famous restaurants in Paris and has withstood the comings and goings of new rivals. Whether you eat there or not, you may want to shop next door where you can get a picnic to go or a gift basket to take home. There are also ashtrays, crystal, china, and more.

CHINA, CRYSTAL & SILVER

French crystal and porcelain have been the backbone of French luxe for centuries. Prices can be fair in France, but the shipping will kill you. Come with a price list from home because a sale in the U.S. may wipe out any French savings.

BACCARAT
30 bis, rue de Paradis, 10e (Métro: Château d'Eau); 11 place de la Madeleine, 8e (Métro: Concorde).

Baccarat has two headquarters—its factory in the 10th arrondissement, which has a museum and a gigantic shop (no seconds, sorry), and the boutique amid the high-rent district of the 8th arrondissement. Prices are the same at either venue.

Finding the shop at the factory can be confusing the first time you try it, since you must walk through the company's offices and head up some stairs to reach it. Once up the stairs, the shop is to your left. It's hard to distinguish it from the museum that sprawls in front of you. In both, long tables are laid out with merchandise in rows—you may touch. You can even try on the earrings. Whether or not you can walk out with your choice is up to the gods. Baccarat is often six to seven months behind in its orders, so if they don't have what you want in the shop, they will send it to you . . . someday.

Prices are not negotiable. They ship anywhere in the world and will mail-order. If there is breakage in your package, Baccarat will replace the item. The selection in the sublimely located rue Royale/place de la Madeleine shop is not as overwhelming, so you won't have as much fun.

BERNARDAUD
11 rue Royale, 8e (Métro: Concorde).

If you're making the rounds of the hoity-toity table-top houses, don't miss Bernardaud, which means Limoges china. Especially impressive are the newer contemporary designs, with their art deco roots. If you don't have to ship, you can save over New York prices. The tea shop is located farther back in the *passage*.

ROBERT HAVILAND ET C. PARLON
CRISTALLERIES ROYALES DE CHAMPAGNE
Village Royal, 25 rue Royale, 8e
(Métro: Madeleine).

This shop is a little bit hidden, and very, very fancy. It's best not to bring the kids. Check out the way in which the printed patterns are mixed and matched— it's the essence of French chic.

CRISTAL LALIQUE
11 rue Royale, 8e (Métro: Concorde).

One glance at Lalique's crystal door and there's no doubt that you've entered one of the wonders of the world. Get a look at the Lalique-designed Olympic medals created for the 1992 Winter Games. The rue Royale headquarters is sort of like a museum: People come to stare more than they shop. The prices are the same as at factory sources on the rue de Paradis, by the way, so don't think you may beat the tags here. Besides, you get to apply for *détaxe*, and everyone is friendly and speaks English, and they ship to the United States.

DAUM
4 rue de la Paix, 2e (Métro: Opéra).

There's a lot more to Daum than large-size lead crystal cars, and this two-level shop is a great place to discover how much more. The extra room allows them to display inventive glass art and colored-glass pieces that will surely become collector's items one day.

PUIFORCAT
2 ave. Montaigne, 8e (Métro: Alma-Marceau).

If you believe in studying only the best, here's where you can get your graduate degree in fine French silver. Puiforcat was founded in 1820 and dedicated since that date to making shoppers swoon and the most collectible pieces are currently from the late 1920s and 1930s.

PARADISE & MORE
. . . .

The street for wholesale crystal, china, and tabletop in Paris is the rue de Paradis, where the headquarters of many big names are located. There are just a few catches: This is a low-rent district, but prices are no different than in the high-rent districts. It's a bit of a walk from the nearest *métro* stop in a not-so-interesting area (but it's not dangerous), or a $8 taxi ride from the 1st arrondissement. It's fun, true, but you might prefer a quick visit to Cristal Vendôme instead.

If you decide to head for **rue de Paradis,** be sure to take in the **Baccarat Museum.** Then just browse from one shop to the next. Prices are generally fixed by the factories; there is little negotiation. After a few shops, they'll all look alike to you. Many of the stores carry other European brands; all have a bridal registry.

CRISTAL VENDÔME
1 rue de Castiglione, 1er (Métro: Concorde).

Right underneath the Hôtel Inter-Continental on rue Castiglione is a factory-direct store that will even ship to the U.S. (You can phone in an order once you have bought in person, a service the factory will not offer.) Various lines are sold here, which makes the shopping easy: Baccarat, Lalique, Daum, and more. The store offers tax-free prices, which means they are the same as at the airport. I priced a Lalique necklace and found it to be almost half the U.S. price.

EDITIONS PARADIS
29 rue de Paradis, 10e (Métro: Château-d'Eau).

This is an enormous source with so much stuff that you'll be nervous if you are carrying a big floppy handbag. It's fancy, with table settings on display to give you ideas. And, of course, they carry small Limoges boxes—the perfect collectible.

LA TISANIÈRE PARADIS
21 rue de Paradis, 10e (Métro: Château-d'Eau).

A country-style resource on a street filled with more traditional showrooms, this porcelain shop has stacks of kitchenwares and tabletop at prices that are fair. Some promotional items are downright cheap. Much fun.

LIMOGES-UNIC
58 rue de Paradis, 10e (Métro: Château-d'Eau).

In spite of the name, this factory does not sell Limoges exclusively. It's merely one of the bigger, better-stocked traditional stores on the rue de Paradis. Locals consider this the anchor of the neighborhood, although there are other similar shops. They will ship; of course, you may apply for the *détaxe*.

PROVENÇAL FABRICS

· ·

If you aren't headed for Provence, Paris has a selection of traditional country French prints.

🛍 SOULEIADO
78 rue de Seine, 6e (Métro: Mabillon); Forum des Halles, 1er (Métro: Châtelet); 85 ave. Paul-Doumer, 16e (Métro: La Muette).

You have to be a real Pierre Deux freak to know that Pierre Deux is the name of the American franchise for these prints, but *is not* the name of the company in Europe. So remember the name Souleiado—which will get you happily through France.

The flagship rue de Seine shop, a great shop, is everything it should be. You will be in country French heaven. Be sure to see all parts of the shop (there are two separate rooms); the main shop winds around another showroom in the far back, where more fabrics are sold by the meter. There is a showroom for the trade next door. The Passy shop on avenue Paul-Doumer is almost as good, but is not quite as quaint. Nonetheless, it is chockablock with the look we love—plenty of fabrics plus ready-sewn clothing and all the tabletop in the world.

🛍 LES OLIVADES
1 rue de Tournon, 6e (Métro: St-Sulpice or Odéon); 25 rue de l'Annonciation, 16e (Métro: La Muette).

I have been told that Les Olivades was started in the mid-1970s when someone in the Souleiado hierarchy departed and started a new firm. Indeed, Les Olivades reminds me of the Pierre Deux/Souleiado look, although the colors are more muted, pastels and the like. Les Olivades sells much the same merchandise—fabric by the yard, placemats, tablecloths, napkins, umbrellas, travel bags, etc.

While the goods are not cheap, they are about 30% less expensive than Souleiado in France. The Right Bank store is small and a little hard to find— it's on a small street directly behind the rue de Passy. The Left Bank shop is almost directly across the street from Souleiado.

BED LINENS
. . . .

The sizes of continental beds differ from their American counterparts and are measured in metric, but why should that stop you? Just bring your tape measure. Or, if price is truly no object, have Porthault custom-make your sheets.

📖 D. PORTHAULT
18 ave. Montaigne, 8e (Métro: Alma-Marceau).

Porthault was making fancy bed linens with pretty colored flowers on them long before the real world was ready for patterned sheets or the notion that a person could spend $1,000 on their bedclothes and still be able to sleep at night.

There are two Porthault lines of goods for sale in America: One is identical to what you can buy in France and just costs more in the United States; the other is contracted by the Porthault family and is available only in the United States. The French laminated products are not sold in the U.S.; the American wallpaper is not sold in France. One Porthault saleswoman swore that our pattern was not "theirs" because she was unfamiliar with the American wallpapers. The Montaigne shop does have a whopper of a sale in January, during which they unload everything at half the retail price, or less! You cannot phone in orders from the U.S.

You may think that Porthault is totally beyond you and hurry by to avoid temptation; I beg you to reconsider. There are many little accessories and gift items that are affordable and fun and speak volumes when presented. I always travel with my

Porthault shower cap ($20) because it makes me smile and beats those plastic jobs supplied by hotels. I gave my niece a traditional Porthault bib when she was born: $25. You have to know the Porthault name to appreciate items like these, but for those in the know, this could be your gift headquarters. They wrap.

DESCAMPS
44 rue du Passy, 16e (Métro: La Muette).

Descamps no longer has its own stores in the U.S., but their products are sold in higher-end American department stores. You may not find prices much better in Paris. Still, every time I visit Paris, I buy a few items (those oblong terry-cloth bath mittens) that aren't available in the U.S. I also buy my Primrose Bordier (that's the designer's name) home scent here. Check out the starfish for 48 F. It's a perfect small gift to give yourself. There are truly hundreds of Descamps shops in France; there's one in every trading area in Paris.

YVES DELORME
Le Louvre des Antiquaires, 2 place du Palais-Royal, 1er (Métro: Palais-Royal).

Yves Delorme makes linen that's sold under the Palais-Royal label in the U.S., and has his own boutique on the street level of the Louvre des Antiquaires, along with shops in Monaco and Lyons. This is luxury linen that isn't as wildly priced at other premium French luxury linens (such as Porthault and Descamps) but is still chic and mildly (not wildly) expensive. Bed linen freaks won't care about the prices; there's a certain French charm to the total look that makes it a must-have.

OLIVIER DESFORGES
26 blvd. Raspail, 7e (Métro: Sèvres-Babylone).

This is Descamps main competitor, with fewer stores in France, and none (to my knowledge) in the U.S.

Sometimes, the line has a country look to it. There are other locations in Paris; this one's can't miss. A true winner.

CHIFF-TIR
1 rue Duphot, 1er (Métro: Madeleine).

This is a bargain basement selling mostly everyday linens. Often, you can find something unique enough that it will look right in your home. Once taken out of the context of the junky store, the item may sparkle. This is a chain, with other stores around Paris; I usually go to the one that's closest to Madeleine.

BLANCORAMA
12 rue St-Placide, 6e (Métro: Sèvres-Babylone).

This tiny shop is a regular haunt of mine because I always like to see what's in store at the discount shops that line the street. While there is bed linen in the shop, I buy bath mats here—very traditional French rugs for 50 F each.

Chapter Eleven

. . . .

PARIS SHOPPING TOURS

This tour not only takes you by most of the best shopping in Paris, but gives you a good workout as well. Since some of these stores are quite expensive, you may find yourself mostly window shopping. If that's the case, you can complete this tour in half a day.

Begin the tour at **Printemps Maison** on boulevard Haussmann. They open at 9:35am. Remember to save your purchase receipts so you can claim your *détaxe* at the end of the shopping tour. Don't mind the perfume and makeup on the street level, just get a free spritz and take the escalator up. Shop the three floors of housewares, being careful to ignore the non-French merchandise, of which there can be much.

Now head over to **Galeries Lafayette.** Check out the stained-glass ceiling, the souvenirs (why not?), the new tabletop and housewares area, and the designer floors. You might want to take notes on the new styles and trends you see.

Your next stops should be chosen according to your personal interests. I recommend that you stop at one of the dime stores, either **Monoprix** or **Prisunic,** and then pop into **Lafayette Gourmet,** a super supermarket, before hitting **Bouchara,** a fabric store. All of these shops are on boulevard

Haussmann, except for Prisunic, which is located in an alley behind **Printemps.** I can spend the better part of a day in these resources alone, but I can also trim it down to a quick few hours and be out by lunchtime. It's your call.

Next, hit rue Tronchet and walk toward the Seine; you are headed toward place de la Madeleine, which you will reach in a block. There are a number of fancy food shops around here; surely you have time to press your nose to the glass at **Fauchon** (26 place de la Madeleine) and **Hédiard** (no. 21).

If it's lunchtime, or even a little before (beat the crowds), try the famous tea room **Ladurée** on the rue Royale. After you pass the place de la Madeleine, the rue Tronchet becomes rue Royale. Ladurée looks like the kind of tea room your grandmother would take you to; they have desserts galore, but also salads and omelettes at moderate prices—plus a great-looking clientele.

From there, it's time to hit an American-style mall that's filled with small, fancy boutiques, **Les Trois Quartiers.** It may lack authentic French charm, but it gives you a quick look at some fast fashion. I like **Chacok, Tehen,** and even **The Body Shop.**

There's a tiny little knife of a street that runs alongside Les Trois Quartiers called rue Duphot. At no. 25, right across the street from the mall, is **Le Cedre Rouge,** a French country-style home furnishings store that's worth a peek.

Cross over to the far side of the place de la Madeleine, where the famed **Lucas-Carton** restaurant is located. At no. 9 place de la Madeleine is the **Parfumerie de la Madeleine,** a fragrance discounter I like to visit. This shop is on the outside of a *passage*. If you walk through the *passage,* shopping as hard as you can, you'll soon reach the rue Boissy d'Anglas, another tiny Parisian street known only to locals. There are several great stores back here, among them **Territoire** (no. 30).

Shop your way to the rue du Faubourg St-Honoré, and *voilà,* you are at the door of **Hermès!**

This is one of the swankiest streets in Paris; you will want to window shop, if nothing else. Be sure to see the door with the ocean in it at **Carita** (no. 11). About two blocks past the Elysée Palace, turn left on avenue Matignon and proceed to **Anna Lowe** (no. 35), where big-name clothes (Chanel) from last season are sold at a discount.

Follow avenue Matignon to the avenue des Champs-Elysées, and stroll on this famous street (toward the Arc de Triomphe) to your heart's content. Cross the street, then walk toward Rond Point, where the Champs-Elysées meets the avenue Montaigne.

Turn right onto the avenue Montaigne and stroll the entire length of the avenue (only two or three blocks). I like the side of the street away from the Arc de Triomphe, since it has more shops, but you should plan on prowling both sides of this street. Don't miss **Inès de la Fressange, Christian Lacroix,** and **Porthault.**

When you get to the end of avenue Montaigne, you have choices: You can either double back and hit the other side of the street, ending up at Rond Point; or you can follow the signs to the *bateau mouche* and collapse on a boat tour of Paris. Or you can hop on the *métro* at Alma-Marceau, conveniently located right at the end of avenue Montaigne. Luckily, there's a cafe inside the Joseph Store (no. 14), so you can sit down and think it over before deciding what you want to do.

You've chosen the other side of the street (smart move); don't forget that downstairs at **Nina Ricci** there's a bargain basement filled with couture gowns. After shopping your heart out and absorbing so much visual splendor, take a peaceful walk through the green paths that lead toward the American Embassy and the place de la Concorde. Now it's time for your reward for not buying too much: tea at the **Hôtel de Crillon.** Don't forget they have a hotel gift shop right by the front door. Go ahead, buy yourself a bathrobe and some slippers. Or what about those absolutely stunning napkin rings, just tassels of colored silk, that cost $10 each?

If you're not staying at the Crillon (well, maybe next trip), you'll note that a few meters beyond the hotel's entrance is the Concorde *métro* stop.

TOUR #2: THE ALL-DAY BARGAIN & DISCOUNT TOUR

This tour uses a lot of taxis, which may seem antithetical to bargain shopping. But when you see how much time they save you, and the kind of bargains you can get on designer and big-name merchandise on this tour, using this mode of transportation may strike you as positively thrifty by the time you're finished.

Begin your day with a croissant or two loaded with jam (you'll need the sugar) and a strong café au lait. Wear your most comfortable shoes and take the *métro* to Trocadéro. Give yourself time for a quick glance at the Eiffel Tower, but don't take too long. Remember, you're in Paris to shop!

Head for the **Dépôts-vent de Passy** and visit Catherine Baril's shop on the rue du Tour—a resale shop specializing in designer clothing with an emphasis on Chanel. You could shop the rue Passy from there, but this is the bargain tour, remember?

Take a taxi to **Réciproque,** the grandmother of Paris resale shops. Now you are French. Réciproque begins at 95 rue de la Pompe; don't miss their other shops up the street, or the fact that there are clothes upstairs and downstairs in this temple to designer resale. Prices are average to high, depending on the age and condition of the garment and the designer. There's a virtual library of Sonia Rykiel on one rack.

If you can manage all of your packages, hail a taxi now. If not, head back to your hotel, unload, and grab a bite to eat.

Have a taxi take you to **Eglise d'Alésia-Saint Pierre de Mantrouge.** Walk along the rue d'Alésia, where you will find the **Sonia Rykiel** outlet store almost immediately (no. 64). Check out the kids clothing at **Cacharel Stock** (no. 114), **Fabrice Karel Stock** for fabulous knits (no. 105), **Stock 2** for Daniel Hechter clothing (no. 92), and a few of the other stock shops. Ignore the regularly priced stores; this is the bargain day.

Get another taxi (think of all you're saving on clothes!) to **Mendès,** 65 rue Montmartre, where there are Yves Saint Laurent, Christian Lacroix, and Claude Montana discounts on two floors. If it's a bad day at Mendès (it happens), you'll be out of here in five minutes. If you have the time and the energy, you can explore a couple of other discount shops on this street as you head toward the mall Forum des Halles. There are rows of jobbers; some will sell to you—some won't. You are also deep in kitchen territory, so try some of these showrooms, such as **Mora** (no. 13) and **A. Simon** (no. 48).

All these kitchen goods leave you feeling hungry? You are in a great location for crêpes or fast food, as Mendès is near the Forum des Halles and the Centre Georges Pompidou. The rue Montmartre will dead-end into the Forum des Halles. You can promenade along the outside walkway, picking and choosing among the fast-food eats.

Hop onto the *métro* at Les Halles, make a connection at Odéon, and get out at Sèvres-Babylone. Dash into the indoor flea market at Le Bon Marché, the department store, to round out your bargain hunting by negotiating with a few of the 35 antique dealers here. Or you can walk along the rue St-Placide, which is filled with even more stock shops. Be sure to check out **Mouton à Cinq Pattes** (nos. 8, 14, and 18), with three different shops selling kids', men's, and women's designer clothes at discount. Things are in bins or crammed onto racks, but there are big names and big savings to be had.

You'll end up at the rue de Rennes, which has the magnificent, cheapo department store **Tati.** Some consider the day a total failure if they don't go to Tati. Others can't stand it. If you are feeling the least bit cranky, believe me—Tati is not for you. Only the strong can take this hodgepodge of junk. There are treasures here, they're just hard to find.

From Tati, walk one more block on the rue de Rennes toward the Commercial Centre Montparnasse, which you will pass as you head into **Inno.** This dime store, with a grocery in the basement, has afforded me some of my best bargains in Paris. Picky people with maps may wish to note that the rue de Rennes becomes the rue Depart after you've crossed the boulevard Montparnasse at the base of the Commercial Centre.

Now it's time to pop into the *métro* at boulevard Montparnasse and take it to Concorde. After you've alighted, walk two blocks along the rue de Rivoli until you get to rue Castiglione. At no. 6 is **Catherine**—my regular perfume discount shop. Well, who says a discount day can't end on a top note?

TOUR #3: LEFT BANK IN A DAY TOUR

The best way to see the Left Bank is to live there. Failing that, try to spend the best part of a day there. Get an early start, as from noon on its neighborhoods take on the hustle and bustle of any busy part of town. Early morning has a slowness to it that allows you to absorb the vibes.

Here's an optional pretour tour for the early birds in the group: Any early morning but Monday, start off at the street market in the rue de Buci, right behind the church St-Germain-des-Prés. Get out of the *métro* at St-Germain-des-Prés and hang a left on the rue de Seine. This will take you right into the thick of the street market. After you've spied all the wonderful fruits, vegetables, and fresh flowers, grab a table at **Café de Flore.** The awnings have the name clearly marked; you can't miss it. There's a kiosk just past it if you need your morning newspaper. There isn't much of a crowd for breakfast—all the better for you, my dear. You may eat outside, even if you don't see other people outside. Certainly sit near the glass walls, if you are indoors. The reason you come here is to watch the parade. Since most stores won't open until 10am, and some won't open until 11, you can still sit and sip, write postcards, read the news, and watch the world go by. This is what you came to Paris to do; take your time and enjoy.

When you're finished, head back toward the rue de Seine and catch the street market at the rue de Buci, if you didn't see it before. If you've already seen it, cut onto the rue Jacob, making sure not to miss the tiny place de Furstemberg, and walk the narrow streets, full of antiques shops, behind the church. Take the rue Jacob to the rue Bonaparte, and turn right. Shop, shop, shop.

Now, take the rue Bonaparte all the way back toward the church (this is all of two short blocks). Before you get to Deux Magots, hang a quick right onto a street that's only half a block long. Get a good hard look at the art nouveau tile-front cafe on the corner to your right, then turn left so you can shop at the retail store alongside the **Café de Flore.**

You have now come full circle and are on the boulevard St-Germain. Cross the street and head downtown toward the Musée d'Orsay. But don't go that far; you're stopping at **Sonia Rykiel** (no. 175). Just beyond here, turn left onto rue des Sts-Pères and begin to work the shoe stores. Segue from rue des Sts-Pères onto the rue Dragon, which hits it at an angle, and work your way through more boutiques. Take the rue Grenelle (more Sonia) when you reach it, and you'll eventually end up on the rue de Rennes.

Walk up one side of the rue de Rennes (toward the black office building you see in the background) and down the other side. Be sure to get as far as **Geneviève Lethu** (no. 95), and then head back toward St-Germain-des-Prés. If you have a good sense of humor, you may want to visit **Tati** as well. For details, see Tour #2 above.

Back on the rue des Rennes, look for the lefthand fork once you reach rue du Four; you'll see **La Bagagerie** (no. 41) as you turn. Explore all the trendiness you can stand. Then, turn right onto rue Bonaparte—a street filled with the sights you came to Paris to enjoy. At the corner of rue du Vieux Colombier, you'll see the church of St-Sulpice. Turn left. There's a little store for religious articles and *santons* here, **Georges Thuiller** (8–10 place St-Sulpice), and then you'll bump into a string of designer boutiques.

Leave place St-Sulpice via the rue St-Sulpice and pass a few wonderful shops. Eventually, you'll come to the new mall **Marché St-Germain** and rue de Tournon. There's a **Souleiado** shop here. Rue de Tournon becomes the rue de Seine on the other side of the street, so take the rue de Seine toward the Seine. It dead-ends at the quai Malaquais.

Hang a quick left for a block to reach the quai Voltaire and some fancy antiques shops you missed previously. Follow the quai uptown toward the Cathédrale de Notre-Dame. The antiques stores will peter out, but the stalls along the riverfront sell wonderful, touristy jumble—postcards (old and new), books, prints, and old magazines. Stop at a few, and don't forget to make a wish as you stare into the Seine.

TOUR #4: CROSSTOWN PARIS

This tour resembles the tours above, so it's best to read the others first. The advantage of this one is that it walks you across Paris quickly, covering only the best and the brightest shops. It's a very tony tour.

Begin at the duty-free shop **Catherine**, 6 rue Castiglione, in the 1st arrondissement. This shop is very tiny and gets crowded during the day, so get here first thing in the morning. Ask them to hold your purchases for you, since you have a big day ahead and don't want to schlep too many heavy bottles. If you've bought only a few small items, consider asking them to mail them to you in the U.S.—you'll get a bigger duty-free discount, and the postage may not be as expensive as you think.

From the rue Castiglione, walk toward the Tuileries (half a block) and hang a left to walk along the rue de Rivoli. This gives you ample opportunity to shop at every tourist trap in Paris. When you see the gold statue of Joan of Arc in the middle of the road, right before the Hôtel Regina, turn right and walk alongside the Musée de Louvre. Cross the river (on a bridge) and turn right onto rue du Bac. Welcome to a very fancy and private part of the Left Bank.

Prowl every inch of the rue du Bac, even though it twists and turns a little bit. You will pass the Hôtel Port-Royal, where the road curves a little, but don't let it throw you. The first blocks of rue du Bac are a tad slow, with just a few antiques shops and real-people places. By the time you hit the Port-Royal, things are sizzling. But before the sizzle, there are some quiet statements of style that shouldn't be over-looked, such as **Beauvais** (no. 14), one of the oldest engraving and print shops in Paris, and **Laure Japy** (no. 34), for stylish tabletop designs. Japy doesn't open until 10:30am, so take your time and don't rush to get here. At no. 38, you'll find **Myrène de Trémonville,** a designer who sells hipper-than-thou clothing to Henri Bendel and Barney's in the U.S.

At no. 43, I have a specialized find that may not be for everyone. **Deyrolle** (upstairs) is where you go to buy dead stuffed chickens. Don't stand there snickering. They happen to be gorgeous and fabulous (and expensive) and very country French. And, no, I have no idea how to get yours home with you. At least you won't ruffle any feathers at U.S. Customs, since the animals are quite dead. They do close for lunch, so don't spend too much time in the previous stores if you plan to stop here.

Very shortly, you will be at the crossroads of boulevard St-Germain. To your right, on the corner, is a leather shop that began in 1815. Called

Atelier Schilz, it's like Hermès without the hype. They sell a gorgeous handbag for 4450 F, which isn't cheap, but does enable you to get a *détaxe* refund and is less than Hermès.

Cross St-Germain and continue along the rue du Bac. Note there is a *métro* stop (rue du Bac) here. But as you walked crosstown, you don't need it, do you? Smart you. At this junction, the street gets even better, so if you must modify this tour, you can start here (which, of course, means you can use the *métro*, if you wish).

Walk along rue du Bac, enjoying every minute of it. Note that a number of these shops close for lunch, so you may want to do the same. Otherwise, keep on prowling—check out **Étamine** (no. 63), a fabulous home decor shop, and **Olivier de Sercery** (no. 96), for engraved stationery. But my favorite of them all is **Irena Grégory** (no. 130). I love it for two reasons. One, it's a great shop with cutting-edge yet classic looks that make every woman look snappy. Second, their business cards are printed on condoms. You read that right. Clothes start at $200; condoms are free.

You are still walking on the rue du Bac and having the time of your life. If you need a spiritual moment, tuck into **Chapelle Nôtre-Dame de la Medaille Miraculeuse,** where you can buy medallions at the gift shop and say a prayer in the chapel. This is as magical as it sounds.

Once back on the street, you are a half block from the big department store, **Le Bon Marché.** You can spend the rest of the day at Bon Marché, shopping its boutiques, eating lunch at **Le Grand Epicerie,** and checking out the antiques market upstairs. Just be sure to keep up your strength, because you must must make time afterward to hit the rue St-Placide. It's across the street from Bon Marché and to your left one block.

St-Placide is only a block long (for you, anyway), but it houses several discount designer shops where you may snap up a big-name designer garment for a few hundred francs. Because the rue St-Placide is very dumpy and can be depressing, you'll need a pick-me-up once you're finished. Walk one block along the rue de Sèvres right into the lobby of the **Hôtel Lutétia** and plop yourself down in the art deco lobby for a glass of champagne. Then you can face the *métro* ride back to your hotel. You're staying at the Lutétia? Clever you.

Chapter Twelve

· · · · · · · · ·

WEEKEND IN BRUSSELS

WELCOME TO BRUSSELS

· ·

Chocolate aside, I fell in love with Brussels not as an alternative to Paris (there is no alternative to Paris), but as an add-on condition.

I'll take Brussels as a suburb of Paris, a small hop, skip, and a jump to more shopping delights than you've ever imagined. Now that a high-speed TGV-style rail link exists between Paris and Brussels (and the Chunnel makes a jaunt from London possible), there's no reason that Brussels shouldn't be part of your European shopping excursions. In fact, I recently spent a week in Europe and easily made it to London, Paris, and Brussels in a week: the Golden Triangle of Shopping.

Brussels is the other woman. Brussels is the secret I've been holding out on you. Brussels is worth a weekend. Maybe even a week. But that's another book. However you plan it, don't miss the chance to check out the best-kept secret of Europe, where the antiques shops and flea markets are cheaper, where there are more Michelin-starred restaurants than even in Paris, and where there's fantastic beer and affordable chocolate galore. If you're thinking that Belgium may be nice, but you're not convinced: I welcome you to a new education.

I welcome you to the country that launched Diane von Furstenburg, Jean-Claude Van Damme, and

Tintin. I welcome you to a country with the hottest designers in ready-to-wear, where the names that make news are on the tongues of only those in the know: names like Ann Demeulemeester and Dries Van Noten, designers who show in Paris and are well known to European buyers and American hotshots. I welcome you to a country filled with secrets that I am about to share.

THE LAY OF THE LAND

Brussels lies at the midpoint between London and Paris in a triangulated right-hand position; it is now only two hours by train from Paris and is now easily accessible by Chunnel from London (approximately a three-hour journey).

Because of its location, Brussels is being promoted as the new transportation hub of the European Union (EU). The fast train networks all now connect to Eurostar and often use Brussels as their hub. By train, you can connect to almost all of Europe through Brussels; and several train passes are available to make this easier (and cheaper) for you.

The country of Belgium itself is not very big and has been fought over, divided, and subdivided throughout history. Even today, when you strike up a conversation with strangers in a restaurant or hotel in Brussels, you get an earful of politics just about the language they speak—French or Flemish! Then you'll meet people who will argue which town has more charm: Brussels, Antwerp, Ghent, or Bruges. It is nothing short of amazing how much is going on in such a small piece of real estate.

As the capital of the European Union, Brussels has come into its own as a business mecca. If you are visiting on business, you'll quickly discover that the city sprawls quite a bit, but the best shopping districts are compact and centrally located. The greatest beauty of downtown Brussels is its size—everything can be reached on foot. This is a city for walking while you are shopping. After big, fast, and powerful Paris, Brussels feels like an intimate village by comparison. Even the Grand' Place, one of Europe's most breathtaking central squares, feels small compared to Paris. Brussels is a big city that feels like a village; therein lies its charm.

GETTING THERE

. . . .

From the U.S.

One of my best tricks for getting to Paris is to go by way of Brussels. I learned this trick the year I tried to buy bargain airline tickets to Paris for my family on American Airlines, and all possible dates on which we wanted to travel were sold out. I simply booked the same carrier at the same low price through Brussels and got exactly what I wanted.

Several U.S. carriers (**American Airlines** and **Delta** among them) fly from various American gateway cities to Brussels and Paris. The Belgian national carrier, **Sabena** (☎ 800/955-2000), has a code sharing agreement with Delta that doubles their impact on the home market. In addition, Sabena frequently offers promotions that allow you to save on visits to more than one European city on the same trip. Most often, those cities are London, Paris, and Brussels, but there are promotions that include others as well. Sometimes there are promotional rates to Brussels that are lower than those to Paris, since there is less tourist traffic to Brussels. During those times, it pays to connect to a nearby destination, such as Paris. Sometimes you can get the connection for free!

From Paris

I always take the train. Everyone takes the train. With the new THALYS line (similar to TGV trains in France) the trip takes a quick two hours. Seats come with an automatic reservation and cost the same as the older trains, about $50 in second class and $70 in first class. There are promotional rates that can lower the price dramatically.

THALYS trains run every hour between Paris and Brussels, beginning at 6:37am from Paris and 6:30am from Brussels. They stop running at about 8:30pm, at which time you must revert to the slower train system . . . or spend the night.

Like all European trains, there are so many different price categories and promotions that you can get a headache trying to figure out the best deal. Ask your travel agent. Tickets can be booked from the U.S. through **Rail Europe** (☎ 800/4-EURAIL). You may also want to check out their **Web site** (http://www.raileurope.com) because it sometimes offers discounted tickets only to net surfers. Imagine my shock and dismay when I paid $99 for my Chunnel ticket from Brussels to London only to find that the same ticket cost $79 when bought on the Web!

In addition, there are a number of transportation passes you can purchase. One includes your train fare to and from Paris and Brussels and your transportation costs within Belgium. There is even what the French call *Le Billet Weekend en Belgique,* which is good Thursday through Monday and offers special fare reductions.

Don't forget about fare breaks that depend on your age or the age of your traveling companions: Kids under age 6 ride for free; kids up to age 12 ride half-price; and there are discounts for students up to age 25 and for seniors over age 60. A weekend ticket with a Saturday and Sunday overnight costs less than a nonrefundable ticket.

From the U.K.

The Chunnel, which everyone thinks just connects London to Paris, also connects London to Brussels via Lille. Call 800/677-8585 in the U.S. for fare and schedule information. Note that there are bargain round-trip fares; you can't change the tickets, but they are virtually half-price. Tickets may also cost less if bought in Europe rather than in the U.S.

British Rail has several passes available in the U.K. and/or the U.S. that allow for maximum train travel between not only the U.K. and Belgium, but on any routes that connect through Brussels, Amsterdam, and Paris.

ARRIVING IN BRUSSELS

Should you arrive in Brussels by air, you can connect to downtown by taxi or public transportation. Most taxi firms offer a fabulous deal if you buy a round-trip taxi fare from them—25% off the total fare. Furthermore, you can pay by credit card, a wonderful convenience if you do not happen to have local currency on you. Some drivers will even accept French francs.

After you pay the round-trip fare, you are given a voucher for your return fare. You can either book the taxi for your return trip to the airport at the time you pay or have your hotel concierge do it whenever you are ready. If worse comes to worse and you totally forget that you have the voucher, you can always use it on your next trip to Brussels. A taxi to the airport from the Royal Windsor Hotel (without the discount) costs about $40. Of course, you might not want to get into a taxi too quickly. The newly redone airport includes a few shops run by Antwerp's diamond dealers—right in the arrivals hall. While you wait for your luggage, you can shop for a girl's best friend.

If you arrive by train, there are taxi stands at the train stations, too, of course. If you come on a day trip and have no luggage, you can easily take public transportation to within a block of the Grand' Place. If you've come specifically for the flea markets, you'll do best to take a taxi directly there. While the Midi train station is downtown, it is not really within walking distance from the shopping and tourist places you'll want to visit. It's not far, but you need to save your strength for coping with all that chocolate. If you come to Midi Station on a day trip, simply take a taxi to either the Grand' Place or the place du Grand Sablon. Taxis charge an extra supplement between 10pm and 6am—about $3 more.

GETTING AROUND

You can get to almost any place downtown on foot. There is a *métro* system, which, while not extensive, certainly helps; a single journey costs 50 BF no matter how far you travel. If you choose your hotel by location, you should be able to save a bundle on cab and *métro* fares by walking everywhere.

If you want to get to some of the nearby towns (Antwerp is only one half hour away), there are commuter trains, or you can rent a car. If you choose to rent, it's always cheaper to book your car in the U.S. before departure. (Renting a car in Europe on the spur of the moment averages about $150 per day for a midsize car.) If you plan ahead from the U.S. and book with any agency that offers a prepaid plan, you'll get an even better deal. *Born to Shop* British correspondent Ian Cook and I always book with **Kemwel** (☎ 800/678-0678 in the U.S.). After you've placed your order on the phone, they fax you a voucher. You may find this pretty astounding, but the three-day rental from Kemwel in Belgium came to a total of $42!

Should you want to drive from France to Belgium or vice versa, you can still rent from Kemwel, but the rules and the prices are a little stiffer. Only one-week rentals are available, and they cost $279 for a B class (midsize) car. The cost is higher, not because of a drop-off charge (there is none), but because you are driving across borders. Whenever you cross a border in Europe, it costs more.

ABOUT ADDRESSES

I wasn't kidding when I said you can find people who will get huffy about whether they are French or Flemish speaking. This problem has been going on for centuries. Hence most street signs and store addresses are in two languages. Announcements at the train station are also made in two languages— and English is not one of them. In this book, I generally give street addresses in French only.

You may experience some confusion when reading a map; ask your hotel concierge for help. I get so confused reading addresses in Brussels that I tend to nickname the streets by semi-translating them. Thus, I can easily tell you where Chicken Street, Butter Street, Cheese Street, and Herb Street are located. (Don't laugh!) I'll try not to confuse you with my shorthand, but heed my warning: Unless you come up with your own system, you may be tongue-tied and totally disoriented. Speaking of tongue-tied, not as many shopkeepers speak English as you may think. Brush up on your French!

MONEY MATTERS

The monetary unit in Brussels is the Belgian franc, written BF or BEF. I find it awkward to make precise currency conversions in Belgian francs in my head, so instead I use the following rules of thumb: $1 (30 BF), $10 (300 BF), and $100 (3000 BF).

If you are in Brussels for only a day or a weekend, I also suggest that you calculate your expenses as closely as possible and use a lot of credit cards, so that you can keep the amount of cash you convert to a minimum. If you are in and out of Brussels frequently, you won't find this much of a problem, but if you don't know when you'll return, you don't want to be stuck with too many Belgian francs at the end.

Small denominations of traveler's checks will help you here. I further suggest that you avoid three-way conversions. Have dollars on hand. Don't change from dollars to French francs to Belgian francs, because you will lose money on each transaction!

There are numerous currency exchange booths dotted throughout the streets around the Grand' Place; some stores will also change money for you after you buy from them. There are a number of ATMs, one located a sneeze from the Grand' Place (No. 5 Grand' Place, to be exact) and another conveniently located on the best shopping street, so you can insert your bank card and withdraw funds from your American bank account in Belgian francs. **American Express,** 2 place Louise, also has a quick cash machine and offers travel service to cardholders.

TAX REFUNDS

. . . .

The amount needed to qualify for a VAT refund in Belgium is 5001 BF, or about $150. This is less than in France. If you are making any purchase that may not total $250 in France, buy those items in Belgium, rather than France, and benefit from the easier tax laws. VAT in Belgium is 21%.

TIPPING TIPS

. . . .

Service (usually 16%) is most often included in restaurant bills in Belgium, just as in France. You may want to leave some extra change for spectacular service. Taxi drivers seem genuinely surprised and pleased if you simply round out the fare.

The best tip for a bellhop is a 100 BF note; it is worth approximately $3 and takes care of all the bags—provided you've got only a few. I leave 500 BF for the concierge and front desk staff if they have been particularly helpful—made dinner reservations or got train tickets.

PERSONAL NEEDS

While downtown Brussels has its share of stores, pharmacies, and mini-marts, it's better to plan ahead, especially if you're in town only for the weekend. The downtown area does not cater to personal emergencies during off-hours. Most hotels do not have a shop that sells sundries.

Pharmacies are marked with a green neon cross but are rarely open late at night. There is a pharmacy at the Midi train station. Despite the fact that you may think of Belgium as a suburb of France, when you get to the pharmacy, do not expect to see the same products. I was told that my French eye drops, bought easily over the counter in any French pharmacy, required a prescription in Belgium. Condoms are sold in the train stations and pharmacies and some hotels and mini-marts.

CALLING AROUND

The country code for Belgium is 32. The city code for Brussels is 2. To call Belgium from France, dial 00 to get an international line, then 32, then the phone number. To call France from Belgium, dial 00 then 33. To call the U.S., dial 00-1, plus the area code and number.

To access AT&T USADirect Service, dial 0-800-10010 in Belgium.

SLEEPING IN BRUSSELS

Because all those EU businesspeople need hotels during the week, Brussels is filled with good downtown hotels. Better yet, each hotel has weekend promotional rates. I have inspected every hotel in downtown Brussels with the hope of finding something special for you, and have come away convinced, more than ever before, that you need to be careful where you place your trust and your reservations.

There are two hotels that are absolutely beautiful to look at in the middle of nowhere. There are two grand hotels that think they have been refurbished and are ready for prime time. I beg to disagree. **Le Meridien** (☎ 800/543-4300) has opened an absolutely stunning property in downtown Brussels, and they offer weekend promotional rates, but they aren't the best you can do. The weekend rate for two in a superior room is about $200 per night, but I can get you a better rate elsewhere, so read on!

For shoppers and weekenders, these are the best deals:

🛍 ROYAL WINDSOR HOTEL
5 rue Duquesnoy, Brussels.

Ever been to a property that features the best location in town for both businesspeople and shoppers, possesses a great and truly famous kitchen (one Michelin star), and offers low rates to boot? Add to that a health club, a perfectly nice decor, some rooms that are absolutely charming, a cute pub for a snack or a beer, and you've got my Brussels home, the Royal Windsor.

The Royal Windsor is not a palace hotel like the Hôtel de Crillon, but it is one of the best hotels in Brussels. At $150 a night (the special *Born to Shop* weekend rate), well, you simply can't do better.

As elsewhere, room rates vary with the season. Should you happen to stay here during the low season (July 1 to September 3), you can get a double room, guaranteed in U.S. dollars, for $150 a night, a price that includes tax, service, and breakfast. This is simply half the rack rate guests pay during the week during the high season, and is available every day, not just weekends.

If it's not summer, and you are looking for a rate frozen in dollars on a weekend basis only, you may fax the general manager directly and get a *Born to*

Shop rate of $150. If he has the availability, he'll let you stay over Thursday night for that rate also. Since the regular rate on these rooms is $450, you've got yourself a terrific deal.

Other pluses include the Chocolate Tasting weekend, during which a small ceramic dish is placed on your pillow. In the dish is a card, which you take to Godiva (one block away) and have filled with the chocolates of your choice. There's no charge at Godiva; the gift is included in the promotional price, $170 per night. Fax the hotel's general manager, Paul Van Wijk, and ask for specifics.

In addition to its affiliation with **Leading Hotels of the World** (☎ 800/223-6800 in the U.S.), the Royal Windsor is a member of the **Warwick** hotel chain (☎ 800/223-3652 in the U.S.). The hotel's direct phone and fax numbers are as follows: ☎ 32/2-505-5555; fax: 32/2-505-5500.

BRUSSELS HILTON
38 blvd. de Waterloo, Brussels.

The Hilton is on the fanciest shopping street in Brussels but not on the Grand' Place like the Royal Windsor. Never you mind. If you get one of their $99 rates, you can laugh all the way to the chocolatier. Like other Hiltons, the hotel is a cold, modern obelisk, but its reputation is among the best of any Hilton in Europe.

Promotional rates are competitive; you can get a dollar rate only occasionally. Should you luck into the summertime deal of $99 a night for a double room, grab it. (This rate does not include tax and service!) Also note that there are several deals with Sabena (and other airlines) as well as promotions with other hotels, so if you're planning to visit Antwerp or Paris, you can save by booking Hilton hotels there.

There's a coffee shop for a quick meal and a one-star Michelin steak house, Maison de Boeuf, if you want a fancier meal. (The steak house also serves fish and lighter fare, if steak is not for you.) There's even a branch of Godiva in the lobby. For reservations in the U.S., call 800-HILTONS. Local phone: ☎ 32/2-504-1111; fax: 32/2-504-2111.

SHOPPING HOURS

. . . .

Regular stores open at 10am and close around 6pm, except on Friday, when they stay open until 7 or 8pm. Stores that cater to tourists do not close for lunch; Mom-and-Pop shops do. Most stores are not open on Monday morning. Exceptions include tourist traps and small food stores. The stores at Sablon open at 10:30am.

While most retail stores are not open on Sunday, there are still plenty of opportunities to shop, particularly flea and food markets. You'll need a car and a good map of Brussels in order to make it to half of the Sunday markets.

THE SHOPPING SCENE

. . . .

The reason you don't associate Brussels with the other great shopping cities of the world is simple— it isn't. The best shopping in Brussels is very category-specific; if you fall out of those categories and look at the overall picture, you may not be impressed.

Yet Brussels has some easy-to-shop characteristics that will quickly addict you to the local lifestyle. I almost think of designer shopping in Brussels in the same category as suburban shopping in the U.S.: There's a branch of everything. It may not be Paris, but everything's at your fingertips and is very clean and easy.

If you are looking for cutting-edge high fashion, you may want to stay in Paris. (However, I have one shop, Kaat Tilley, that will slay you and is worth the trip alone!) If you are looking for branch stores of all the big designers, French and otherwise, they are all here, but may not have the same panache as their counterparts in Paris. Not to worry, *cherie*.

You'll qualify for a VAT tax refund faster in Brussels than you will in Paris, so designer clothing can take on a whole new meaning in Brussels, if you live outside the EU. That said, I would not send you to Brussels to buy Armani. (However, there is a very nice Armani shop, right near the Hilton Hotel.) Consider Armani an extra if you luck into it. I send you to Brussels for the funky, not the fancy.

Brussels is for three categories of shopping:

- Foodstuffs
- Antiques
- Anything you don't have time to buy in Paris.

Brussels cannot be considered the poor man's Paris. It is the smart shopper's attic. And pantry. If you have lots of time in Paris, when in Brussels you can ignore the boutiques selling country riding clothes, handmade leather gloves, and cheap teen fashions. Buy tabletop, home style, goodies to eat that you can take home (but don't pack beer in your suitcase, please), vintage clothing, and antiques. We'll talk about lace later.

BEST BUYS IN BRUSSELS

Chocolate: It's not only better than anywhere else in the world; it's cheaper! A pound of quality chocolate costs between $10 to $15 in Belgium. See page 000 for the best brands, the best stores, and the best prices.

Cookies: Dondoy (say "Dan-dwa") is dandy.

Beer: There are 482 different brands of Belgian beer. You can start sampling them now. Some brands are packed in travel boxes for easy transport back home.

Mandarine Napoléon: This is a tangerine-based liqueur mixed with Cognac Napoléon and made in Belgium; it is readily available in the U.S. It's a bit sweet, but ideal for those who like Grand Marnier and Cointreau; try it over ice. I buy mine at G.B. for 530 BF; it costs 650 BF at the Brussels duty-free store. The price in the U.S. is between $25 to $30, so it may not pay to schlep the bottle home with you. Nevertheless, it makes a great gift. You can bring in two of them and be right on top of your liquor allowance for U.S. citizens.

Fun & Formal Antiques: I call them fun, someone else might call them junk. Whatever you call it, Brussels is a lot more informal about its antiques . . . and a good bit less expensive than Paris. There's also a serious antiques business that is lower priced than Paris. In my mind, these are two different categories of antiques, and few people are shopping for both. Luckily, Brussels gives you lots of choices.

BUYER BEWARE

Although Belgium is one of the lace capitals of the world, I'd have to ask you to think twice before buying lace in Brussels, or in Belgium, for that matter. For the most part, lace that is sold to tourists is machine-made and comes from the Far East.

The good stuff is put away. If you insist on buying lace, be prepared to pay a high price and make sure you buy from a reputable dealer. You may want to buy lace in Bruges, which is also touristy but has some serious lace shops. Brussels does have serious lace, but you have to ask to see it. Don't expect bargain prices.

SHOPPING NEIGHBORHOODS

Brussels is a big city with a lot of neighborhoods and suburbs; many of them have names I can neither spell nor pronounce. Happily, the downtown shopping area is very compact and changes personality rapidly, giving you a chance to see a lot of different looks within a relatively short walking distance. Indeed, Brussels' neighborhoods can change drastically in a matter of blocks.

While locals divide the city into uptown (the new city) and downtown (the old city), I've created my own names and my own boundaries for the city's neighborhoods to make things easier for you, the visitor. For example, I call the shopping area around the Hilton the "Hilton Hillside," since there's a big hill there.

I have whittled down my directory of neighborhoods to just the best ones for someone visiting for a weekend; there's way more than this to discover, I promise.

Grand' Place

The heart of downtown Brussels is the 1,000-year-old Grand' Place, a plaza surrounded by incredibly gorgeous gilt-edged townhouses, all built by medieval trade guilds way back when. While the Grand' Place is grand, it has such a small, intimate scale to it that it seems to set the tone for all of Brussels.

At night, the buildings are lit and a few cafes and pubs serve until late hours. During the day, there are flower merchants selling potted petunias and geraniums from the central cobblestones. Much of the retail space on the Grand' Place is devoted to either tourist traps or chocolatiers. It's the tiny streets and alleys leading to and from the Grand' Place that give real delight.

Ilot Sacré

There is a local name for the warren of tiny streets directly behind the Grand' Place—**Ilot Sacré**—the sacred island. I'm not so sure about sacred, but it's got my vote for fabulous, picturesque, charming, and, more important, what it *should* be. The street that runs the long way alongside the Grand' Place is the rue des Bouchers, which is not a street of butcher shops, but a divine little street with cafe after cafe after cafe, each with a more bountiful display of seafood piled high in the street. Major photo op.

If you find it too hard to choose one of these cafes for your daily lunch, go with reputation: **Aux Armes de Bruxelles** (no. 13) gets my vote for charming tourist trap *avec frites*—it's cute to look at, has a huge menu, but also serves the must-have dish: mussels and fries.

There are actually very few stores on this street; however, the little warren of medieval alleys surrounding it does have shops. Furthermore, if you walk straight across the top of the Grand' Place and don't turn left onto the Butcher Street, you will end up in a series of two *galeries,* each filled with stores and officially named **Galerie Saint-Hubert;** a *galerie* in Belgium is the same as in France, a covered passage or mini-mall, invented way before there were malls. There are two such *galeries* in the heart of Brussels.

The first is **Galerie de la Reine;** the second, **Galerie du Roi,** and both house various cafes and legendary shops—some with international reputations, such as the chocolate shop **Neuhaus** and the handbag maker **Delvaux.** Thankfully, there is a branch of the French firm **Longchamp** just a few feet away from Delvaux, because after you see the price tags at Delvaux, you will either faint or flee. There's also **Gallery 34,** which sells handmade bags that are a little more affordable—they have a Kelly copy at $400 that is simply sensational.

There are more back street wonders that weave away from the Ilot Sacré. Running parallel to the Grand' Place and the Butcher Street, in between the two, is the street that begins as Grassmarkt, becomes Marché aux Herbes, and then becomes the Chicken Street, Marché aux Poulets. There are a few branches of mass merchants, there's a toy store for kids, a hairstylist or two, some shops selling socks, some selling shoes, and some selling inexpensive hair accessories. I follow this street all the way to G.B., where the neighborhood changes. This area is a little more commercial but still great.

Real-People Midi

You'll know you're in a different neighborhood once you get to the boulevard Midi, one of the main arteries of the city. Around the Bourse, this area is packed with stores. Most service the local community, so the area is less touristy and much more commercial than the back streets you now have to your rear.

Here the architecture is utilitarian, and the charm is either real or forgotten. I've found greengrocers here that I thought offered genuine charm and excitement (oh, those fresh-picked chanterelles, I'll never forget them), whereas the stores seemed relatively average. Again, please note that the rue du Midi will change names in this area, but it's still the same street. I happen to like to wander in this area because it makes me feel not only European, but like I know where I'm going and what I'm doing (rarely the case).

The heart of the real-people shopping here is on the rue des Fripiers (which is what Midi becomes) and the boulevard Anspach, one street over. In these two blocks there are tons of real-people clothing shops, a few branches of the chocolatier **Leonidas,** and even a mall or two. I can't claim to like these malls (they're ugly and modern), but they serve a purpose. The mall at 28 blvd. Anspach (which actually extends through the block to the Fripes Street) is named **Anspach Center** and houses **Virgin Megastore.**

There are also some bookstores in this area, so if you are looking for English books or magazines, **W.H. Smith** is right at hand (71–75 blvd. A. Maxlaan).

Manneken Pis

I don't insist that you visit the *Manneken Pis,* but since he's rather centrally located, you won't go seriously out of your way to see this little bad boy (didn't his mother teach him any manners at all?). If you're a fashion freak, you may want to make note of what he's wearing. You see, the little guy has several hundred different outfits and is changed more regularly than you ever changed your Barbie doll.

The two-block stretch of rue d'Estuve is cheek to jowl with tourist traps selling everything from lace and chocolate to beer steins and beer bottles. With beer in them. There's every conceivable postcard of you know who, as well as every type of chocolate, every lollipop (that boy again), every piece of fake Delft (we're not even in Holland!), and scads of lace, much from Hong Kong, thank you.

Here's the worst part: I actually like this street. It makes me laugh. I also like the souvenir chocolate places because I've found particular candies here I haven't seen anywhere else, like the chocolate cameos. This is a good neighborhood for getting your silly shopping out of the way, a good area for buying postcards and inexpensive gifts.

Sablon

Sablon is more than a location of a flea market and a home to a church in which I always light candles, it's a state of mind and a state of grace. Sablon is one of the reasons to come to Brussels for the weekend.

The place du Grand Sablon is a small square that is actually just a parking lot during the week. On weekends, the lot is emptied for the famous flea market. Meanwhile, there's tons of action along the sidewalks and in the side streets. **Emporio Armani** just opened here, sharpening the image of the area even more.

Surrounding the square are several little streets (I call them "The Sablon Secrets") with antiques shops, clothing boutiques, and home furnishing designs. Aside from the zillions of perfect little cafes, one of the most famous restaurants for serious dining is on the corner (**L'Écailler du Palais Royal**).

The Sablon Secrets poke off at angles from the central square; take a look at the tiny rue de Rollebeek if you want a peek at retail heaven. This street is only one block long (no cars); both sides are lined with adorable stores. There's not a loser here. About half the stores are antiques and junk stores, but there are some boutiques as well. One of my favorite stores for ready-to-wear is here: **Charlotte aux Pommes.** Here you can buy Issey Miyake and Euro-Japanese sweaters for $350. Hmmmm.

If you explore the rue des Minimes, you'll find a row of antiques stores. Some of these are fancy; a few are funky. My absolute favorite is called **Galerie des Minimes** (no. 23)—it's like a big garage filled with the best things that could have come from Grandma's attic. They are even open on Sunday to catch the drift from the Sablon market.

Segue halfway down the hill, toward the Grand' Place, to the rue Libeau, where you'll find a street of antique booksellers. The whole neighborhood is crawling with the kind of stores you want to browse. The *place* itself is surrounded on both sides by retail stores, antiques arcades, and cafes. Be sure to walk into doorways. Some lead to shopping strips and secret tea rooms; I found one alley that led to a discount china shop. While I doubt that you care to pack a few sets of dinner plates with your chocolates, **La Vaisselle au Kilo** offers a cute browse. And they did have some mass-produced faience that I actually considered buying.

Most of the shops here are open Sunday from 10am to 1pm to service the flea market crowd, but closed Monday. The rest of the week, stores open at 10:30am.

Hilton Hillside

While I don't suggest you make a habit of it, you need to walk to the Hilton at least once, following the shopping path up rue de Namur. From the Grand Sablon, work your way up the place Petit Sablon and then up the hill.

I'm wild for a women's clothing store called **Natan,** but there are plenty of European multiples back here, including **Laura Ashley.** This area is only the size of the back side of a hill, but I don't want you to miss it.

Boulevard Waterloo

Once you get to the Hilton, you are on the boulevard Waterloo—the basic Fifth Avenue of Brussels. If you taxi to the Hilton, you'll miss the hillside neighborhood, and instead will find yourself on a modern boulevard that houses little charm and many malls. The Hilton isn't gorgeous, but it's your uptown friend—it's a great pit stop for anything you need, including lunch or dinner or a bathroom.

Nearby, there are branches of **Armani, Hermès, Polo/Ralph Lauren, Ferragamo, Nina Ricci, Chanel, Gianni Versace,** and **Gucci.** In short, there is an overwhelming opportunity to blow it all in one block in uptown Brussels. Across the street, there's a series of malls that lead to even more shopping. Cut through the Galerie Louise to get to the famous avenue Louise, another tony shopping street (see below).

Rue de Namur

There's the rue de Namur and the Porte de Namur, and then there's the *métro* stop Namur—all within a few meters of each other. The rue de Namur is the street that runs up the back of the hillside that leads to the Hilton. Cross the boulevard Waterloo to the Chausée d'Ixelles. This street has many of the real-people stores of Belgium.

The way I do it is to walk up the backside of the Hilton, hang a right on boulevard Waterloo, shop, and then cross Waterloo to shop the malls. Afterward, I head back toward Porte de Namur (this is all of two blocks), and then hang a right onto Chaussée d'Ixelles. I recommend coming all the way over here only if you enjoy shopping like a local. If you want fancy and fresh, you want Louise, the other direction on Waterloo.

Avenue Louise

Fun? You want a weekend of fun and a little fancy shopping to light your fire? Step this way. The avenue Louise has a local reputation for being the fanciest place to shop. Although most of the big-name European designer shops are actually on the avenue Waterloo, it is Louise that is thought to be the best shopping street in town.

The best shopping is clustered right in the first block of avenue Louise at Waterloo and is often nestled into malls. Past place Stéphanie, avenue Louise is very difficult to shop because it widens out and runs on and on. You don't need that part; you can happily quit after you get to place Stéphanie.

BRUSSELS RESOURCES FROM A TO Z

Antiques

You came to Brussels for the antiques and they are everywhere—in flea markets, in galleries, and in free-standing stores. The greatest concentration of shops and galleries is around the place du Grand Sablon. See "Shopping Neighborhoods," above, and also "Flea Markets," below. It's no secret that dealers from Paris flock to Brussels to buy what they will resell in France for much more money.

Beer

There are almost 500 different kinds of beer sold in Brussels; it's readily available at all tourist traps, and even in handy carry-on packs at the airport. The least expensive place for the major brands is the grocery store **G.B.** If you want to get your feet wet, try the beer tasting held in the pub at the Royal Windsor Hotel.

Chocolate

When I began to research this section, I decided the only way to do it would be to visit every chocolatier in Brussels, buy a box of chocolate, and then do a taste tasting. I was planning on involving other people in the tasting as well, turning this into a mini-science project. On the second day of research, I became so sick of chocolate that I could not look at a bonbon for six months. Even now, I can bear only certain types of chocolate.

I suggest that you forego the notion of the chocolate tasting and stick to a few brands. Buy as much chocolate as you want—it certainly is inexpensive in Belgium—but forget about art and science. And don't wash it down with beer.

Like all products, each type of chocolate candy costs a different amount to make. Some cost more than others, depending on the ingredients and amount of work needed for the molding, and such. The reason chocolate shops have prepacked boxes of chocolate is that they can't make any money when you pick out the chocolates individually. In fact, they are losing money if you pick a whole box of one chocolate if that one style is an expensive one to make.

The moral to this story: Never accept a prepacked box of chocolates and always demand exactly which ones you want. Note that prices in duty-free shops are only a dollar or two less, and the chocolates sent to duty frees are in prepacked boxes, and are chosen for their shelf life. If you want the best chocolate, you want the freshest. Really good chocolate, especially made with fresh creams, lasts two weeks at the most.

When buying chocolates, look at the display of boxes in the store. This wedding cake–like tier of empty boxes shows you the exact size of each box by weight and by price. Thus, if you meet a language barrier, you can always point. Chocolate is always sold by the weight of the box, unless it comes prepackaged in a fancy container.

Prices for the same amount of chocolate vary so much that it is staggering. Furthermore, the prices vary on a global scale—the price in Belgium is less than in France and much, much less than in the U.S. In fact, I'd say the Belgian price is about one half the U.S. price. This does vary with the brand.

Your most valuable asset as a shopper is your sense of smell. The first step in deciding which brand of chocolate is right for you is to take a deep whiff of each chocolate shop you enter. If you don't smell chocolate, leave immediately. As you get used to the smell of chocolate, leave immediately if you don't smell good chocolate. You'd be surprised at just how quickly you'll learn to smell the difference.

Since I grew up in the South, I feel compelled to tell you that the word *praline* means "a piece of chocolate" in Belgium. It is not that gooey sugar confection with pecans in it that we thrive on in the South.

One final word: This section contains only the names of the most famous names and the best chocolatiers. A few of them mass-produce their chocolates, while others make theirs by hand. I have not included every souvenir shop that sells chocolate, and believe me, they all do.

Weight being constant, chocolates that are roughly the same quality cost the same, such as Neuhaus and Godiva. The least expensive quality chocolate in town is Leonidas. Basically, prices for quality chocolate hover around $20 a pound (500 grams). If the weight measurements don't mean much to you, figure that there are 16 pieces of chocolate in a 250-gram box and about 34 pieces in a 500-gram box of packed pralines. I won't begin to count the calories.

Neuhaus
1 rue de l'Etuve; Galerie de la Reine; Grand' Place; Chée de Waterloo.

Since Neuhaus is my favorite chocolatier, I start with it. Pronounce it "*Noy*-Haus." I say "charge it, please" and "thank you."

To me, Neuhaus is the best of the mass-market, high-falutin' chocolatiers. Not only am I addicted to the Astrid bonbon, but I like the fact that Neuhaus will sell you a tiny box with two chocolates in it— you pick them out—and wrap it beautifully. It costs about $1.25 and makes a fabulous gift.

Although Neuhaus is mass produced, it is of a very fine quality. It's sold in only a few select stores in the U.S. at outrageously high prices. In fact, it costs about $45 per pound in the U.S. In Brussels, it costs about $20 per pound.

Leonidas
46 blvd. Anspach; 49–51 blvd. Max; 17 rue des Fripiers; 5 Chausée d'Ixelles; 34 rue au Beurre.

I had heard of Leonidas before I arrived in Belgium; it is a very popular brand in France and has a tony image there as one of the fanciest mass-produced chocolatiers. Imagine my surprise when I discovered that Leonidas is the fast food of chocolatiers in Belgium! And get this, they don't even have shops, they have stalls. I thought I would faint when I discovered their down-market digs.

Their chocolate is another story completely; although this is not a fancy high-end chocolatier, they give excellent quality for the price and do not attempt to make things they cannot make well.

Leonidas is the cheapest among the contestants in the best-chocolate shop-in-the-world sweepstakes. If you aren't buying for yourself, do consider every gift you ever had to give. For about $6, you can look like a prince. Or princess.

Leonidas has branches all over Belgium, with a few in various international cities as well. Outside of Belgium, they pose as a fancy brand with prices to match. So buy in Brussels and buy big. Please note that they do not accept credit cards!

Since there are over a dozen in Brussels alone, I am just listing the addresses that are closest to the main tourist shopping areas. Once you stop by Leonidas and make your first purchase, the bag or paper wrap will list all the Belgian addresses, so you can stop by every shop.

GODIVA
22 Grand' Place; Brussels Hilton, 38 blvd. de Waterloo.

Chocolate lovers relish fighting over whether Godiva or Neuhaus is the best of the local choco-latiers. Certianly Godiva has an international luxury story that can't be beat.

Godiva is a mass-produced fancy chocolate brand; it came to the U.S. as a very high-end product, but since it was bought by Campbell's Soup, a little of the gilt has worn off. Godiva still manages to sell at very high prices in the U.S. and at moderately high prices in Brussels (and at the duty-free shop). They are most famous for their unique seasonal chocolates. Their double creams with two different fillings are the most sophisticated thing to come my way in years.

There is a small but very fancy shop right on the Grand' Place. There's another branch in the lobby of the Hilton. The Grand' Place store is open normal hours Monday through Saturday and Sunday from 10am to 4pm.

🛍 MARY
72 rue Royal.

Once you move beyond the mass-market chocolatiers, you are into those few firms that still hand-
make their pralines. Many therefore claim that Mary
is the fairest in the land, if only because the firm
was founded right after World War I and has a royal
warrant. Their praline named "Astrid" is also a
best-seller.

NIHOUL
298 ave. Louise.

It's pronounced "*Nee*-who-ll." Now that you can
pronounce it, you can be in with the upper-crust
set, which names this as one of the best chocolatiers
in Brussels. They have an adorable lunch and tea
room that is a must-stop if you are shopping on the
avenue Louise; they are as famous for their marzipan
as for their chocolate. Nihoul also makes pastry that
will leave you breathless.

🛍 WITTAMER
6 and 12–13 place du Grand Sablon.

Almost a local legend, Wittamer has a pastry shop,
a food shop, and a chocolate shop. They sell these
discs of chocolate with encrusted dried fruits and
nuts that are heaven; they cost about $10 for a gift-
size bag.

Like most kings of chocolate, Wittamer will
send chocolates overseas: A 750-gram box sent via
express mail to the U.S. costs 1960 BF. You may
order by fax (32/2-512-5209) and charge it to a
credit card.

PLANÈTE CHOCOLAT
57 rue du Midi.

This is a small, funky shop and factory; I pray that
it is still in business when you visit. The chocolate is

not extraordinary, but it's fun to watch it being made, and there's a tiny tea room upstairs where you can have a quiche and hot chocolate for lunch.

Children & Teens

All your kids want to do is hang around the *Manneken Pis* and buy *Pis* souvenirs. Here are a few other places to take them, or to purchase gifts for them.

GALERIE AGORA
3 rue de la Colline.

This is a mall that's set into a space the size of a city block, right off the Grand' Place. It's pretty hard to spot, because there's no sign. One of the entrances to the mall is directly across from the Tintin shop.

There are a few souvenir stands in the mall and a few snack shops, but mostly there are T-shirt dealers and guys selling cheap skirts from India. In short, this is a teen hangout. These are not items I came to Brussels to buy, but your teens may feel otherwise. From the density of the crowd, you get the feeling that every postpubescent to set foot in Belgium has a dire need to be here.

TINTIN SHOP
13 rue de la Colline.

This is, of course, where you can buy Tintin comic books. There are also souvenirs and logo products with panels from Tintin cartoons. Prices are pretty high. There is a similar shop in London, although Belgium is the country where Tintin was born.

ZARA
8–10 ave. Louise.

Zara is a Spanish chain that sells women's ready-to-wear that isn't very expensive, making it a favorite for teens and 'tweens. I'm crazy for this line and find it a happy mix of young and affordable, but not too young and not too cheap. There are stores in Paris, but this one is handy and great fun for all.

Department Stores

You did not come to Brussels to go to a department store, but **G.B.** is worth doing—most local department stores are not, unless you are in search of a French brand you can't get at home (such as Bourgois makeup). Downtown, there's a **Marks & Spencer** and an **Inno,** but these aren't the kinds of places I'd send you to if you're in Brussels only for the weekend. Inno Louise, on the avenue Louise, is an another story altogether.

🛍 Inno Louise
ave. Louise.

Although there are other branches of this famous French dime store in Brussels, I like this one best because it's the fanciest. There are four floors of fun with everything from clothing and an excellent perfume and beauty department to office supplies, linens, books, CDs, and one of the best lingerie departments in town. The store backs into the mall Galerie Louise.

Flea Markets

Let's face it, the reason you came to Brussels was to visit its flea markets. Sure, Paris has great flea markets—but they're expensive and overworked by pros. In Belgium, you get the goods for half the price. (Watch out for the French dealers.)

🛍 Marché Grand Sablon
Place du Grand Sablon.

To Americans, this is the most famous flea market in Belgium; I admit right up front that I am ambivalent about it as a shopping experience. While I always have a good time at this market, I also hate it. I hate it because it's fancy. I hate it because it's clean. I hate it because I don't think there are any bargains here, even though I have bought a few items here that I thought were quite fairly priced. In short, I hate it because it's perfect.

I could tell you about a spring Sunday in my life when the sky was blue and the sun was shining. I wandered the stalls and bought an antique chocolate mold for a fair-enough price ($40), nine yards of lace (that's how it was sold) for $22, and some little turn-of-the century pharmacy boxes ($6 each), and I even saw a person dressed in an Easter bunny suit handing out foil-wrapped chocolate eggs from one of the best chocolatiers in town. It was a magical hour. But it was unsatisfying because there's something so perfect about this market that I have no respect for myself for having a good time here. Anyone could have a good time here.

While this market does begin in the morning, I wouldn't rush to get here. Ignore what other guidebooks tell you. They are still setting up at 10am. In short, you have plenty of time to get to the "good" flea market first, so you can comparison-shop. The "good" market is the Vieux Market, which is held at the Place du Jeu de Balle (see below).

The market area is surrounded by upscale cafes where you can have brunch or dessert. It's an easy walk from the Grand' Place; take a taxi directly here if you are coming from Paris by train for the day.

In spring and summer, the Grand Sablon market is held on Saturday from 9am to 5pm, and Sunday from 9am to 2pm. In winter, it closes an hour earlier on both days. I wouldn't get there before 10am. If it is raining (it's always raining), don't think the market has been canceled. The stalls have awnings, which allow you to walk beneath them and still be sheltered from the elements.

🛍 Vieux Marché
Place du Jeu de Balle.

I refer to this as "the good" flea market. You may
hear it called the Jeu de Balle market or even the
Marolles market (for its neighborhood). It actually
has two parts to it; I mention this only because it
took me two years to discover the second part. Because this market is held every day, it varies tremendously with the day of the week and the season.
Weekends are best; there are very few tourists.

To me, this is the good market because it is filled
with junk. Scads of junk. You'll see gramophones
piled on broken chairs, parts of mannequins laid
out on blankets as if they've just barely survived the
last chainsaw massacre, dishes in boxes, plates in
bins, and paintings propped up against the few trees
that rim the park. Many dealers don't even have
tables; they have plots where they plop down a
blanket and display their wares. There are lots of
old used clothes that aren't glorious enough to be
called vintage. Sometimes, there are African arts and
crafts that look like they were brought back from
Africa by someone who came back with a few souvenirs too many.

Prices can be haggled over; deals can be made.

Once you've had just as much fun as you think
you can stand, walk toward the Grand Sablon market, where you'll find the tiny little alley called rue
des Renards (Vossenstraat). Here are more dealers
set up in the same lackadaisical manner. Be sure to
check out the antiques shops on this street—they're
open on Sunday!

🛍 Marché de Noël
Grand' Place.

This is one of Europe's grand Christmas markets. It
usually runs for several weekends in December. For
specific dates, call 212/219-2211.

Local Heroes

The following designer boutiques are another reason to come here. They are uniquely Belgian and are well worth checking out, if only to become an expert on Belgian style.

KAAT TILLEY
Galerie du Roi.

Fresh, original, cutting-edge, but wearable. The store is made up of two parts: One specializes in wedding gowns and the other displays the line of inventively cut and softly draped clothing. Everything is droopily chic, with beautiful fabrics and knits. The line has a faintly Asian Comme des Garçons kind of drape but is so creative and soft and pretty that anyone can wear it. You'll pay about $300 for a little something, but you'll never be sorry.

DELVAUX
Galerie de la Reine.

The most famous name in Belgian leather goods, Delvaux is drop-dead Paris chic. When I first visited the mother shop in Brussels, I was shocked to discover I couldn't find one handbag in the $300 price range. Not even $500 would buy the bag of my dreams. If you can afford it, there is no greater luxury.

Obviously, the house thinks they are the Belgian answer to Hermès. Certainly, neither the quality of their workmanship nor the beauty of their colors are in dispute. I guess that if you have a lot of money, want a very tony handbag, and want something from a line that few people have ever heard of, well, you have just found yourself a great resource.

CHARLOTTE DEL MARMOL
13 blvd. de Waterloo.

This is my favorite shop on the boulevard de Water-loo, mostly because it is not a branch of any big name, yet sells a variety of big names in its own quiet, chic way. The store mixes fashion with gift items and includes tabletop as well; there's a tea room upstairs. They sell Jil Sander, which should tell you a lot about the store and the kind of customers it attracts. While there's nothing particularly Belgian about the store, it has such elegance, it's worth a look-see.

NATAN
78 rue Namur; 158 ave. Louise.

Very simple, to-die-for clothes in neutral colors—not faddy or trendy, kind of a Calvin Klein look. When I make it, I will dress from here, tip-to-toe. I'll be in great company: The Queen of Belgium is already a customer.

LOUIS MIES
261 ave. Louise.

A local couturier who makes clothes for those rich and famous Belgians who are too proud to go to Paris, and insist that local talent is the best talent. Glamour personified.

HARRY DE VLAMINCK
57 blvd. de Waterloo.

A local resource for the well-dressed chic Belgian woman with a house in the country. The look is more French than British.

Makeup & Perfume

Unlike Paris, Brussels is not dotted with real or fake duty-free shops. However, with Belgium's more relaxed VAT laws, you may want to buy here.

Another incentive is the extensive selection of perfumes and makeup at the Brussels airport's duty free—it's one of the largest I've ever seen in my lifetime.

Inno Louise is a good source for makeup and perfume; so is the Galerie Louise, with its three separate *parfumeries*. The one I like best, for selection and attitude, is **Ici Paris**. This shop in the Galerie Louise gives a 20% discount (the VAT is 21%) and has a large selection of perfumes and beauty aids, as well as some big-name makeup.

Markets

Fresh produce is sold from various street markets dotted around town. You won't find the same one open daily; instead hours alternate among them, depending on the day of the week. Sunday happens to be a big day for fresh fruit and vegetable markets in various neighborhoods of Brussels; you owe it to yourself (and your camera) to go to at least one.

Midi Market
blvd. de l'Europe.

This, the most famous street market in Brussels, is held outside the Midi train station on Sunday. Watch your handbag. While there is some amount of dry goods, there are no antiques. The market is hopping by 8am (it opens at dawn) and lasts till 1pm.

Marché Boitsfort
Maison Communal, Boitsfort.

This market is slightly outside of central Brussels but is easily reached by taxi or public transportation. It's only about 20 minutes from downtown and worth the effort, especially on a beautiful Sunday morning. You'll go nuts from the beauty of the heaps of fresh fruits and vegetables.

MARCHÉ DU CHÂTELAIN
place du Châtelain, Lesbroussart.

This is a rare one—an afternoon market! Held on Wednesday only, it doesn't get going until 2pm and really only begins to sizzle after 5, when shoppers on their way home from work stop by. You may want to avoid the late-afternoon throng. The market is known for its specialty dealers; foodies from all over Europe flock here. It's well worth planning your day around.

FLOWER MARKET
Grand' Place.

This market is held every day except Monday on the Grand' Place, Brussels' central square. I wish I could tell you this was a fabulous market or that you shouldn't miss it. Every time I've seen it, I've looked, shrugged, and quickly moved on. Certainly summer is more glorious than winter, and I am usually in Brussels during the off-peak months, but as far as I'm concerned, this one barely rates a few frames of film. Since you will be at the Grand' Place a million times in your visit to Brussels, you can see for yourself. I also think the prices are high.

BIRD MARKET
Grand' Place.

I've never made it to the Bird Market because I've never been to Brussels in the summer. However, my editor, Erica, has a good friend, Sylvie, who grew up in Belgium, and Sylvie reports that if your taste leans toward the funky, this market is well worth a visit. Held on Sunday morning in the Grand' Place, this farmer's market cum flea market also contains a veritable menagerie of birds, chickens, and rabbits. If you are staying at the Royal Windsor, you are a block away, so it's no problem to take a quick peep. I mean, peek.

Musée Royal de l'Armée
Parc du Cinquantenaire 3.

Held once a month on the first Saturday from 9am until 4pm, this book and paper market brings in dealers from all over Europe with its low prices. Aside from rare books, there is ephemera.

Souvenirs

I don't need to tell you that the entire area surrouding the Grand' Place and all the way to the *Manneken Pis* is infested with tourist traps. I will tell you that my single favorite souvenir is the liquor that is packaged as pee from the *Manneken Pis*. Your teenage son will love the packaging (mine did).

Euroline
52 rue Marché aux Herbes; 55 blvd. A. Maxlaan.

Brussels seems more amused with its place as the capital of Europe than the rest of Europe, so there's a small chain of souvenir shops selling European Union souvenirs.

Gobelins Art
6 rue Charles Bulsstraat.

This is an extraordinarily fancy tourist trap, right off the Grand' Place, where they mostly sell reproductions of Gobelin-style tapestries, hence the name. If the store was disgusting, I wouldn't list it. While it is very touristy, there's a lot to look at and a scad of tourists buying like mad. The store has a medieval feel to it; it's easy to get carried away with yourself. Many gift items.

F. Rubbrecht
23 Grand' Place.

After you've seen as many lace shops in Belgium as I have, you, too, will run out of the country begging them to untie the knots. This shop is not only filled with lace everything, but once when I was there in the fall (during game season) they had much of the lace clothing displayed on dead, stuffed rabbits. Who could make this up? (Godiva, next door, was displaying chocolate game cartridges—so it must be a theme I'm not equipped to deal with.) All that aside, this shop has tons of lace. They make a rather nice lace flower brooch that borders between the wearable and the kitsch. I laughed at mine for a year (it was a gift), then started to wear it.

Supermarkets

While your perfect weekend on vacation may not include a trip to the grocery store, mine does. The grocery store is the perfect place to buy foodstuffs you can't possibly get at home or may not have time to shop for in Paris. I buy many French food products in Brussels, including my favorite mustard (Maille Provençale) and my tea (Red Fruits).

Beer purchased in a supermarket is half the cost of what is charged at a mini-mart or souvenir shop. I bought a bottle of Mandarine Napoléon, a local liqueur that happens to be one of the best buys in Belgium, for less in a Brussels supermarket than at the local duty-free shop.

Perhaps the best supermarket for a visitor is located downstairs in **G.B.**, which is pronounced *"Jay-Bay"* in French. There are bigger branch stores of G.B. in the suburbs, but the one downtown will do the trick for anyone looking for an offbeat adventure and some savings. G.B. is located about two blocks from the Grand' Place, on what I call the Chicken Street—rue du Marché aux Poulets. Simply follow rue du Marché aux Herbes, one of the city's main shopping streets; the street changes name, but you don't change streets. After you pass the Bourse and the big thoroughfare rue du Midi, in one more block the G.B. will be on your right. It's well marked.

Another favorite of mine is **Rob,** a gourmet food store that carries a collection of international foodstuffs as well as local gourmet goodies. It's on Chausée d'Ixelles (no. 9), right past the Porte de Namur, in a major shopping neighborhood.

DEPARTING BRUSSELS

If you are leaving from the Brussels airport, there are a few consumer tips to think about.

It has some of the best airport shopping in the world. The last time I passed through, I almost missed my flight I was having so much fun shopping! There's an enormous luxury goods duty free selling everything from perfume and men's clothing to **Ferragamo** shoes; there's **The General Store** for books, magazines, snacks, souvenirs, and postcards; there's a gourmet food store for chocolates and cheeses; and there's a liquor duty free. **Hermès** has its own shop! The airport concession is run by Sky Shops, which publishes a price list to the shops once a year.

YOUR COMPLETE WEEKEND TOUR

Friday

Depart Paris by train or rental car early Friday morning, arriving in Brussels in time for lunch. Check into your hotel. If you have not made dinner reservations from home, ask the concierge to make reservations now, especially for a Michelin-starred restaurant.

Walk to the Grand' Place to stretch your legs and get a quick fix on Brussels, then walk over two blocks to rue des Bouchers for lunch. It's time for the local meal: mussels and *frites*.

Spend the rest of the afternoon wandering the old city and downtown area, shopping the neighborhoods on both sides of the Grand' Place. Be sure to wander down the old alley-streets crammed with shops, but also walk toward the *Manneken Pis.* Buy chocolates as you walk, and don't forget to buy your cookies from Dandoy.

Have dinner at **Les 4 Saisons,** the Michelin one-star gourmet restaurant in the Royal Windsor Hotel. Not only will you enjoy the talents of the chef, André Smits, but you'll love the location. After dinner you are one block from the Grand' Place; stroll there to see the lights play on the ancient buildings. Then wander the alleys of the Ilot Sacré and end up back at the Grand' Place for one last look before bedtime. Magic.

Saturday

Although you are spending most of the day uptown, we begin in the Grand Sablon area by shopping the adorable boutiques on rue du Rollenbeck. If you have to go to the flea market, have a quick browse now, although you will be coming back tomorrow. Take advantage of all the stores in the side streets. Walk up the rue de Namur for the shops that are located on the backside of the Hilton.

Turn right at the top of rue de Namur onto the boulevard de Waterloo. Shop the boulevard Waterloo, taking as much time as you need in the big-name designer shops, and then cut into the Galerie Louise.

Shop your way through the Galerie Louise, a mall, and end up on the avenue Louise with its fancy shops. Keep shopping till you get to **Nihoul,** where you can plop down in their tea room for a salad or lunch and, of course, dessert from this famous chocolatier and pastry shop. If you don't want to go as far as Nihoul and prefer to stay in the convenient area right between boulevard Waterloo and place Stéphanie, try lunch at **Capicino,** an Italian bistro with salads, pizza, and pasta, right on avenue Louise.

Walk over to boulevard Waterloo, shopping as you go. If you can still stand to shop, walk two blocks along Waterloo until you get to Chausée d'Ixelles. Here, shop both sides of the street (don't miss **Rob**, the gourmet grocer) and then walk back down the hill for tea and pastry at **Wittamer** before you collapse.

For dinner, if you want to go casual and local, it's **Aux Armes de Bruxelles,** on the rue des Bouchers. Reserve. **Comme Chez Soi** does have an affordable menu for two that costs about 2000 BF per person ($70), without wine. If you're looking for a one-star restaurant that's convenient, fabulous, and romantic, book a table with a view overlooking the lights of the city at **Maison du Boeuf** in the Brussels Hilton. Despite the restaurant's name, I had one of the best cooked fish meals of my life here.

Sunday

Just because it's Sunday, don't sleep too late. First, go to the flea market at Jeu du Balle. Try to get there by 9am. Walk to place du Grand Sablon for the next flea market. Sablon closes at 2pm, so shop it well and then plan on a late lunch. You can go back to Jeu du Balle after lunch or simply enjoy your meal, have a final stroll, and head back to Paris. If you're flying home, book Delta's Sabena code-sharing flight that leaves at 7:30pm, so you get the whole day in town before you head home.

SIZE CONVERSION CHART

. . . .

Women's Clothing

American	8	10	12	14	16	18
Continental	38	40	42	44	46	48
British	10	12	14	16	18	20

Women's Shoes

American	5	6	7	8	9	10
Continental	36	37	38	39	40	41
British	4	5	6	7	8	9

Children's Clothing

American	3	4	5	6	6X
Continental	98	104	110	116	122
British	18	20	22	24	26

Children's Shoes

American	8	9	10	11	12	13	1	2	3
Continental	24	25	27	28	29	30	32	33	34
British	7	8	9	10	11	12	13	1	2

Men's Suits

American	34	36	38	40	42	44	48	48
Continental	44	46	48	50	52	54	56	58
British	34	36	38	40	42	44	46	48

Men's Shirts

American	$14\frac{1}{2}$	15	$15\frac{1}{2}$	16	$16\frac{1}{2}$	17	$17\frac{1}{2}$	18
Continental	37	38	39	41	42	43	44	45
British	$14\frac{1}{2}$	15	$15\frac{1}{2}$	16	$16\frac{1}{2}$	17	$17\frac{1}{2}$	18

Men's Shoes

American	7	8	9	10	11	12	13
Continental	$39\frac{1}{2}$	41	42	43	$44\frac{1}{2}$	46	47
British	6	7	8	9	10	11	12

INDEX

ABOUT THE AUTHOR

Suzy Gershman is an author and a journalist who has worked in the fiber and fashion industry since 1969 in both New York and Los Angeles, and has held editorial positions at *California Apparel News*, *Mademoiselle*, *Gentleman's Quarterly*, and *People* Magazine, where she was West Coast Style editor. She writes regularly for various magazines and her new essays on retailing are text for Harvard Business School. She frequently appears on network and local television; she is a contributing editor to *Travel Weekly*.

Mrs. Gershman lives in Connecticut with her husband, author Michael Gershman, and their son, Aaron. Michael Gershman also contributes to the *Born to Shop* pages.

Want to Go Shopping with Suzy Gershman?

What does Suzy Gershman do on vacation? She goes shopping, of course. But she takes people with her. If you've ever dreamed about shopping with the world's most famous shopper, this could be your chance.

Several times a year, **Born to Shop Tours** venture forth to Suzy's favorite destinations when she takes time to really show off her best finds. The pace is busy but relaxed compared to her regular schedule; several trips are booked through cruise lines to maximize the relaxation possibilities and to cut down on the stresses of transportation and dealing with luggage . . . but you do have to carry your own shopping bags.

Excursions often include lunch at just the right charming spot (perfect for resting tired feet), trips into back rooms and private warehouses not often seen by the public, or opportunities to buy at special discounted rates reserved just for Suzy's guests.

While the schedule varies from year to year (last year, she hosted a shop-a-thon on the QE2, there's almost always a trip to Hong Kong, a trip to New York, and a Mediterranean cruise or two. Space is limited to ensure the intimacy of the group and experience. To find out about current plans or to inquire about arranging your own tour, call Giants at 800/442-6871; ask for Bonnie.

Frommer's Born to Shop guides are available from your favorite bookstore or directly from Macmillan Publishing USA. For credit card orders, call 1-800-428-5331 (AMEX, MC and VISA).

Name _____

Address _____ Phone _____

City _____ State _____

Please send me the following **Frommer's Born to Shop** guides:

Quantity	Title	Price
_____	Born to Shop France	$14.95
_____	Born to Shop Great Britain	$14.95
_____	Born to Shop Hong Kong	$14.95
_____	Born to Shop London	$14.95
_____	Born to Shop Mexico	$14.95
_____	Born to Shop New York	$14.95
_____	Born to Shop Italy	$14.95
_____	Born to Shop New England	$14.95
_____	Born to Shop Paris	$14.95

Available in Fall 1997

_____	Born to Shop Caribbean Ports of Call	$14.95

Total for **Frommer's Born to Shop** Guides $ _____
Please include applicable sales tax

Add $3.00 for first book's S & H, $1.00 per additional book:
$ _____

Total payment: $ _____

Check or Money Order enclosed. Offer valid in the United States only. Please make payable to Macmillan Publishing USA.

Send orders to:
Macmillan Publishing USA
201 West 103rd Street
Attn: Order Department
BS96   Indianapolis, IN 46290